Birds of the
CANARY ISLANDS

HELM FIELD GUIDES

Birds of the CANARY ISLANDS

Eduardo Garcia-del-Rey

Illustrated by Chris Orgill and Tony Disley

CHRISTOPHER HELM
LONDON

Christopher Helm
An imprint of Bloomsbury Publishing Plc

50 Bedford Square	1385 Broadway
London	New York
WC1B 3DP	NY 10018
UK	USA

www.bloomsbury.com

BLOOMSBURY, CHRISTOPHER HELM and the Helm logo are trademarks
of Bloomsbury Publishing Plc

First published 2018

Text © Eduardo Garcia-del-Rey, 2018
Illustrations © Tony Disley and Chris Orgill, 2006

Eduardo Garcia-del-Rey has asserted his right under the Copyright, Designs and Patents Act, 1988,
to be identified as Author of this work.

All rights reserved. No part of this publication may be reproduced or transmitted in any form or by any means,
electronic or mechanical, including photocopying, recording, or any information storage or retrieval system,
without prior permission in writing from the publishers.

No responsibility for loss caused to any individual or organization acting on or refraining from action as a result
of the material in this publication can be accepted by Bloomsbury or the author.

British Library Cataloguing-in-Publication Data
A catalogue record for this book is available from the British Library.

Library of Congress Cataloguing-in-Publication data has been applied for.

ISBN: PB: 978-1-4729-4155-8
ePDF: 978-1-4729-4157-2
ePub: 978-1-4729-4156-5

2 4 6 8 10 9 7 5 3 1

Typesetting and page layout by Susan McIntyre
Printed and bound in China by C&C Offset Printing Co., Ltd.

To find out more about our authors and books visit www.bloomsbury.com. Here you will find extracts, author
interviews, details of forthcoming events and the option to sign up for our newsletters.

CONTENTS

	Plate	Page
PREFACE		7
ACKNOWLEDGEMENTS		8
INTRODUCTION		9
History of the birds of the Canary Islands		9
Geography		11
Climate		13
Habitats		13
HOW TO USE THIS BOOK		15
AVIFAUNA OF THE CANARY ISLANDS		16
Breeding species		16
Winter migrants		16
Seasonal visitors and true passage migrants		17
Vagrancy		17
BIRD CONSERVATION		18
WHERE TO WATCH BIRDS IN THE CANARY ISLANDS		19
SPECIES ACCOUNTS		28
Ducks and geese ANATIDAE	1–6	28–38
Partridges and quails PHASIANIDAE	7	40
Flamingos PHOENICOPTERIDAE	7	40
Divers GAVIIDAE	8	42
Grebes PODICIPEDIDAE	8	42
Austral Storm-petrels OCEANITIDAE	9	44
Northern Storm-petrels HYDROBATIDAE	9	44
Petrels and shearwaters PROCELLARIIDAE	10–11	46–48
Storks CICONIIDAE	12	50
Herons and bitterns ARDEIDAE	12–14	50–54
Ibises THRESKIORNITHIDAE	15	56
Frigatebirds FREGATIDAE	15	56
Gannets and boobies SULIDAE	16	58
Cormorants PHALACROCORACIDAE	16	58
Tropicbirds PHAETHONTIDAE	16	58
Osprey PANDIONIDAE	17	60
Kites, hawks and eagles ACCIPITRIDAE	17–21	60–68
Cranes GRUIDAE	22	70
Bustards OTIDIDAE	22	70
Sandgrouse PTEROCLIDAE	22	70
Rails and coots RALLIDAE	23–24	72–74
Stone-curlews BURHINIDAE	25	76
Oystercatchers HAEMATOPODIDAE	25	76
Stilts and avocets RECURVIROSTRIDAE	25	76
Plovers and lapwings CHARADRIIDAE	26–27	78–80
Sandpipers SCOLOPACIDAE	28–35	82–96
Coursers and pratincoles GLAREOLIDAE	36	98

	Plate	Page
Auks ALCIDAE	36	98
Gulls and terns LARIDAE	37–42	100–110
Skuas STERCORARIIDAE	43	112
Pigeons COLUMBIDAE	44–45	114–116
Cuckoos CUCULIDAE	46	118
Nightjars CAPRIMULGIDAE	46	118
Barn Owls TYTONIDAE	47	120
Owls STRIGIDAE	47	120
Swifts APODIDAE	48	122
Rollers CORACIIDAE	49	124
Kingfishers ALCEDINIDAE	49	124
Bee-eaters MEROPIDAE	49	124
Hoopoes UPUPIDAE	49	124
Woodpeckers PICIDAE	49	124
Falcons FALCONIDAE	50–51	126–128
Parrots PSITTACIDAE	52	130
Orioles ORIOLIDAE	52	130
Tits PARIDAE	52	130
Shrikes LANIIDAE	53	132
Crows CORVIDAE	53	132
Larks ALAUDIDAE	54	134
Swallows HIRUNDINIDAE	55	136
Old world leaf warblers PHYLLOSCOPIDAE	56	138
Reed warblers ACROCEPHALIDAE	57	140
Bush warblers LOCUSTELLIDAE	57	140
Sylvia warblers SYLVIIDAE	58–59	142–144
Goldcrests REGULIDAE	60	146
Starlings STURNIDAE	60	146
Thrushes TURDIDAE	60–61	146–148
Chats and flycatchers MUSCICAPIDAE	62–65	150–156
Waxbills ESTRILDIDAE	66	158
Sparrows PASSERIDAE	66	158
Wagtails and pipits MOTACILLIDAE	67–69	160–164
Finches FRINGILLIDAE	70–72	166–170
Longspurs CALCARIIDAE	73	172
New world blackbirds ICTERIDAE	73	172
Old world buntings EMBERIZIDAE	73	172
SYSTEMATIC LIST OF THE BIRDS OF THE CANARY ISLANDS		174
BIBLIOGRAPHY		187
INDEX		188

PREFACE

As most people know, the Canary Islands belong to a wider region, first described by David A. Bannerman as the Atlantic Islands and later known by many as Macaronesia (not to be confused with Macronesia in the Pacific).

Despite the fact that there are several field guides to this group of archipelagos, a thorough and detailed treatment of the Canary Islands in a single book is more than justified, not only due to the vast number of visitors to these islands who need an updated book, but because a field guide can make a big difference to the local knowledge of birds and to motivation for their conservation, a discipline rather forgotten by the Canarian authorities at both the island level (Cabildo Insular) and the archipelago level (Gobierno de Canarias) today.

In just the past 50 years, a number of bird species have been lost: Red Kite (all islands); Egyptian Vulture (El Hierro, La Gomera, Tenerife, Gran Canaria); Common Buzzard (Lanzarote); Kentish Plover (Tenerife); Lesser Short-toed Lark (Tenerife); Rock Sparrow (La Palma); and Trumpeter Finch (Tenerife). Some have also declined to alarming levels (for example, several farmland birds plus Barolo Shearwater) and the endangered birds, included in the list many years ago, have not improved their situation despite the efforts by the Gobierno de Canarias and Island Cabildo (for example Osprey, Gran Canaria Blue Chaffinch and Northern Raven). The only good news in all this conservation chaos is that the population of Egyptian Vultures on Fuerteventura has stabilised, this thanks to the efforts of Doñana Biological Station and Cabildo de Fuerteventura.

The main objective of this field guide is to present a rigorous and reliable snapshot of the current avifauna of the Canary Islands, for the local amateur and professional, and for the visitor keen to admire the natural wonders of this archipelago. This book also includes a section on where to look for the most emblematic and sought-after endemics and seabirds, as well as locations to try for migrants and/or the odd rarity/vagrant.

ACKNOWLEDGEMENTS

I have spent more than 25 years studying the birds of my home archipelago and it is, therefore, very difficult to rigorously acknowledge the great number of people (both local and foreign) who have contributed to improve my knowledge of the birds of the Canary Islands. Those not mentioned here, please forgive me!

First of all, I would like to thank the following professional and amateur biologists/ornithologists for helping me to learn about the breeding bird species of the Canary Islands: Christopher Perrins, Andrew Gosler, Ben Sheldon, Ian Owens, Nigel Collar, Will Cresswell, Mark Whittingham, Guy Anderson, John Quinn, Mike Wilson, Paul Donald, Phil Atkinson, Tristan Norton, Michael Wink, Christian Dietzen, Javier Gonzalez, Luis Gil, Nikos Nanos, Unai Lopez-de-Herredia, Charles T. Collins, Jan T. Lifjeld, Arild Johnsen, Terje Laskemoen, Oddmund Kleven, Jostein Gohli, Lars Erik Johannessen, Josep del Hoyo and Robert Lachlan. Within the Canary Islands I thank Prof. Jose Maria Fernandez-Palacios, Paco Feo, Dr Rüdiger Otto, Dr Juan Domingo Delgado, Pascual Gil Muñoz, Pascual Calabuig, Jose Manuel Moreno (Turquesa Ediciones), Keith Emmerson, Michael Barry Lancaster, Peter Crocker, Dan Lupton, Diego L. Sánchez, Victor Falcón and Antonio Acedo.

Secondly a special 'thank you' to all the observers who have contributed their records to advance the knowledge of the current status of the migrants and vagrants of this archipelago. Lastly I would like to acknowledge the members of my Facebook group for regularly posting interesting records with pictures. This has allowed me to update the status for some of the birds in this book.

INTRODUCTION

HISTORY OF THE BIRDS OF THE CANARY ISLANDS

Between the 14th and 17th centuries, the ornithological references by visiting naturalists to these islands should be treated with caution, as suggested for the first time by Bannerman (1963). This author considered the first real study of the natural history of the Canaries to be the *Histoire naturelle des iles Canaries*, Paris 1835–50. In September 1828, the British botanist Philip Barker Webb visited Tenerife and met the young French naturalist Sabin Berthelot, who had been on this island since 1820. Both spent two full years doing fieldwork before going to Paris in 1833 to prepare, in collaboration with Moquin-Tandon (responsible for the bird section) and other specialists, their monumental publication. Berthelot's Pipit (*Anthus berthelotii*) perpetuates the name of the young French ornithologist. This publication plus Ledru's *Voyage aux iles de Ténériffe…* in 1810 provided the baseline ornithological information on which all subsequent work on these islands has been built.

Webb and Berthelot were followed by a German naturalist, Dr Carl Bolle, who made two visits and published his results between 1854 and 1857 in *Journal für Ornithologie*. In 1871, Frederick Du Cane Godman, the president of the British Ornithologists' Union (BOU), visited La Palma, Tenerife and Gran Canaria and described one of the endemic pigeons: Bolle's Pigeon (*Columba bollii*) in honour of the German naturalist who first suggested that two different species were found in the laurel forest.

Between 1879 and 1882, Leandro Serra y Fernandez de Moratin, a Spaniard from Granada, published several ornithological articles in *Revista de Canarias*. In 1887 Savile Reid visited Tenerife, and Ramon Gomez, a local taxidermist, was living at Puerto de La Cruz during that time. However, in the autumn of that year the British naturalist Edmund Gustavus Bloomfield Meade-Waldo arrived on the island for a stay of three years and eight months, to provide a significant contribution to the knowledge of the Canarian avifauna, particularly to elucidate ranges and breeding biology. He discovered the Canary Islands Stonechat (*Saxicola dacotiae*), the Canary Islands forms of Blue Tit (then known as *Parus palmensis* and *Parus ombriosus*), and the Canary Islands Oystercatcher (*Haematopus meadewaldoi*) which was named later by D. A. Bannerman. His fine collection of eggs and skins is in the Natural History Museum, Tring.

The Reverend Henry Baker Tristram visited with E. G. B. Meade-Waldo and published some papers on birds from La Palma, Gran Canaria and La Gomera. He saw the last Bolle's Pigeon on Gran Canaria before the Doramas forest was completely destroyed. Around this time, in 1889, Dr Alexander Koenig, director of the museum at Bonn, discovered the Palman chaffinches and published a 230-page paper in

Laurel Pigeon, Los Tilos, La Palma (Eduardo Garcia-del-Rey)

Tenerife Blue Chaffinch, Las Lajas, Tenerife (Eduardo Garcia-del-Rey)

Journal für Ornithologie in 1890. In 1893 Mr Anatael Cabrera, living at La Laguna, published *Catalogo de las Aves del Archipielago Canario*, a list of birds, eggs and skins collected by him in a four-year period and kept as a private collection. During that time Dr Ernst Hartert described several subspecies: the chaffinch of El Hierro (ssp. *ombriosa*), the Blue Chaffinch from Gran Canaria (ssp. *polatzeki*), the Houbara Bustard from Fuerteventura (ssp. *fuertaventurae*), and the Western Barn Owl of the eastern Canaries (ssp. *gracilirostris*). He also clarified the taxonomic status of Laurel Pigeon (*Columba junoniae*) in this archipelago.

At the start of the 20th century, the activity by museum collectors increased exponentially, owing to the many new species and subspecies described on these islands. During this time, the Austrian Rudolf von Thanner took up residence at Vilaflor (c. 16 years) but returned after the 1914–1918 war. He was responsible for collecting many specimens for European museums but at the same time acquired a vast knowledge of the Canarian birdlife. During his time another Austrian settled in the eastern island, Captain Johann Polatzek, who discovered the Gran Canaria Blue Chaffinch. In 1908–1909 he published *Die Vögel der Canarien* in *Ornithologisches Jahrbuch*.

After the war, David Armitage Bannerman started collecting birds on these islands for the British Museum and began a series of expeditions in the Canaries for six consecutive years, returning again in 1920 to spend a long winter on Tenerife and to write his first book: *The Canary Islands. Their History, Natural History and Scenery* (1922). The important list of birds presented here was already published in *Ibis* and it was also later included and updated in the most important book of all ever published for this archipelago: *Birds of the Atlantic Islands. Vol. 1. A History of the Birds of the Canary Islands and of the Salvages* (1963). Between 1920 and 1947, very little was published on Canarian ornithology in Europe. It is worth mentioning the paper by F. H. Gurney in 1927 and the 12 species of birds found dead at the Eleonora's Falcon nests at Roque del Este by the Cambridge zoologist, Dr Hugh Cott.

In 1948 Dr David Lack, director of the Edward Grey Institute of Field Ornithology at Oxford, and his colleague Mr H. N. Southern, visited Tenerife and published their results the next year in *Ibis*. In that same year a Danish ornithologist, Dr Helge Volsøe, wrote voluminous papers on the origin and evolution of the Canarian avifauna after a short visit to the islands and Michael Cullen of the Department of Zoology (Oxford) studied the status and distribution of the avifauna of La Palma and La Gomera. Between 1956 and 1960 the work by R. D. Etchécopar and F. Hüe and the papers by A. M. Hemmingsen, T. Hooker (on Fuerteventuran bird status) and S. Knecht merit mentioning, and also the notes of J. H. McNeile of the Royal Scottish Museum of Edinburgh on the breeding biology of several species, later used by D. A. Bannerman.

Barolo Shearwater, South Tenerife pelagic, Tenerife (Eduardo Garcia-del-Rey)

An important discovery was made in the springs of 1960 and 1961 when birds bred very early according to Dr E. A. R. Ennion and D. Ennion. Other important contributions were the papers from J. Cuyas Robinson, R. Lovegrove, P. R. Grant, J. Heinze and N. Krott between 1960 and 1970.

Between 1975 and 2001, several books, field guides and an atlas were published, the most relevant being the following: *The Birds of the Canary Islands* by F. Perez (1970); *Atlas de las Aves Nidificantes en la Isla de Tenerife* by Martin (1987); *Guía de las Aves de las Islas Canarias* by Moreno (1988); *Los Silvidos en Gran Canaria* by Trujillo (1992); *Catalogo y Bibliografia de la Avifauna Canaria* by K. E. Emmerson (1994); *A Birdwatcher's Guide to the Canary Islands* by T. Clarke (1996); *Where to Watch Birds in Tenerife* by E. Garcia-del-Rey (2000); *Songs and Calls of the Birds of the Canary Islands* by Moreno (2000); *Checklist of the Birds of the Canary Islands* by E. Garcia-del-Rey (2001); and *Aves del Archipiélago Canario* by A. Martin (2001).

More recently, between 2001 and 2016 a vast number of scientific papers have been published (Web of Science) by several research groups (e.g. Macaronesian Institute of Field Ornithology), but also some relevant books: *Field Guide to the Birds of the Atlantic Islands* by T. Clarke (2006); *Atlas de las Aves Nidificantes en el Archipiélago Canario* by T. Lorenzo with data from 1997 to 2003 (2007); *Anuario Ornitológico de las Islas Canarias 2000–2006* by J. J. Ramos (2008), *Field Guide to the Birds of Macaronesia* (Azores, Madeira, Canary Islands, Cape Verde) by E. Garcia-del-Rey (2011); *Aves de Macaronesia* (Azores, Madeira, Canary Islands, Cape Verde) by E. Garcia-del-Rey (2011); *Rare Birds of the Canary Islands/Aves raras de las islas Canarias* by E. Garcia-del-Rey & F. J. Garcia (2013); a birdwatching magazine *Macaronesian Birds* edited by E. Garcia-del-Rey (2015); and the handbook *Birds of the Canary Islands* by E. Garcia-del-Rey (2015), plus the present work.

GEOGRAPHY

The Canary Islands belong to the Atlantic Islands of Macaronesia, a biogeographical region comprising five Atlantic Oceanic archipelagos: the Azores, Madeira, the Salvages, the Canary Islands and the Cape Verde Islands. Macaronesia is derived from the Greek *makarios* (fortunate) and *nessos* (islands) and was previously used by Ancient Greek geographers for the islands west of the Straits of Gibraltar. It was the British botanist Philip Barker Webb in 1845 who started designating this name to these five archipelagos, some of which shared similar flora and fauna. In addition, parts of Morocco have some phytogeographic affinity with Macaronesia (Sjörgen 2000). However, the precise limits of this region are still disputed because some authors, based on biotic affinities, consider it composed of the five archipelagos and a narrow strip of the African continental coast; the Atlantic Sahara between Agadir and Noadhibou, or even the Algarve region in continental Portugal. However, from an ornithological point of view I have defined the limits as shown in Figure 1.

The Canarian archipelago is located between 13° 23' and 18° 8'W and 27° 37' and 29° 24'N, and consists of a total of seven islands: La Palma, El Hierro, La Gomera, Tenerife, Gran Canaria, Fueteventura and Lanzarote. La Graciosa plus the islets of Roque del Este, Roque del Oeste, Montaña Clara and Alegranza constitute the Chinijo archipelago, off north-east Lanzarote. Other islands also have associated islets; for example Salmor islets (El Hierro), Anaga and Garachico islets (north Tenerife), and Lobos (north Fuerteventura).

This archipelago has a total area of 7,445 km² and is characterised by high mountainous islands in the west (highest peak at 2,423 m for La Palma and 3,718 m for Tenerife) and low islands in the east (Fuerteventura and Lanzarote are lower than 1,000 m above sea level). The shortest distance from the mainland is 96 km (Fuerteventura) and the average intra-archipelago isolation is 196 km. The origin of the Canaries is volcanic and therefore they have never been attached to the continent. The oldest island is Fuerteventura at 20 million years old, followed by Lanzarote (15.5 myo), and then Gran Canaria, Tenerife, La Gomera, La Palma and El Hierro (less than 1 myo).

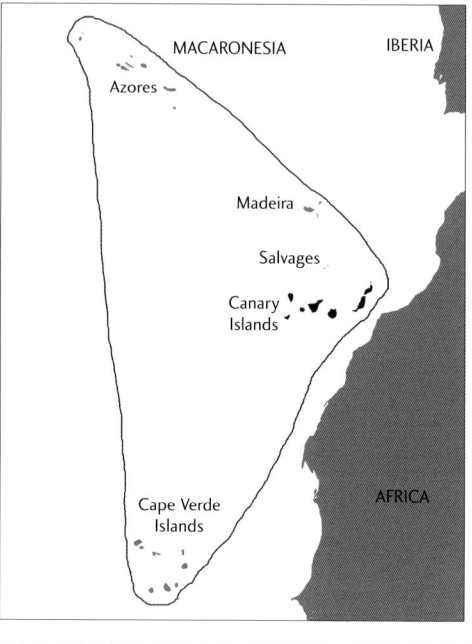

Fig. 1. The location of the five archipelagos of Macaronesia.

Fig. 2. The islands of the Canary Islands.

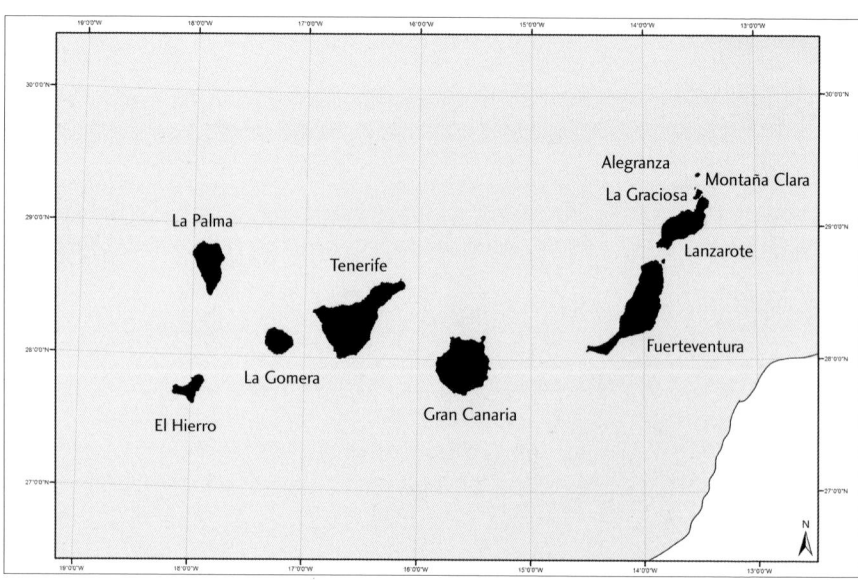

CLIMATE

The Canary Islands climate is characterised by mild temperatures and low rainfall, and consequently its islands show significant climatic differences (Table 1). The influence of the almost permanent anticyclone of the Azores allows the influence of the trade winds to create a 'sea cloud' between 800 and 1,500 m on the west and central Canaries. Easterly winds have their origin in the Sahara and bring hot air associated with dust, while on some occasions snow is formed above 1,500 m as the result of polar winter storms. The south-westerly storms tend to bring heavy torrential rain and strong winds.

Table 1. Climatic data for several Canary Islands localities with representation of coastal (proximal and distal), mid-altitude and summit meteorological stations.

Locality	Latitude (N)	Longitude (W)	Altitude (m)	Rainfall (mm)	Temp. (°C)
Arrecife, Lanzarote	28° 57'	13° 13'	10	139	20.2
Santa Cruz, La Palma	28° 44'	17° 46'	10	499	20.3
Pajonales, Gran Canaria	28° 00'	15° 39'	900	523	16.5
Izaña, Tenerife	28° 18'	16° 30'	2,367	514	9.7

Rainfall is very variable in the Canary Islands and starts in the autumn, peaking in the winter. La Palma is the wettest island with a mean annual rainfall of 731 mm, whereas the eastern islands of Fuerteventura and Lanzarote are very dry. The summer is normally very dry.

HABITATS

A total of six main native ecosystems has been described in the Canary Islands (Fernández-Palacios 2011). These are the coastal desert scrub, thermophilous woodland, laurel forest, pine forest and summit scrub that hold the steppe land birds, the farmland birds and the forest birds, and the rocky islets and coastline that provide breeding grounds for seabirds.

Fig. 3. The macrohabitats of the Canary Islands.

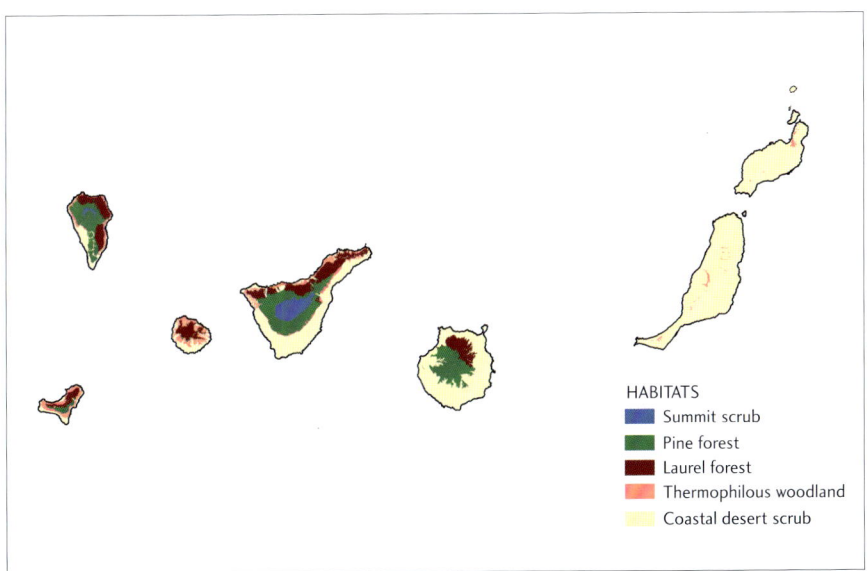

Coastal desert scrub This ecosystem is also known as the subdesert succulent coastal scrub and is characterised by the dominance of endemic spurge shrubs; *Euphorbia balsamifera*, *E. obtusifolia*, *E. lamarckii* (Fernández-Palacios 2011). According to this author this ecosystem is the African aspect of the Canary Islands. On this ecosystem the dominant group of birds are the steppe land birds (Houbara Bustard, Black-bellied Sandgrouse, Cream-coloured Courser, Eurasian Stone-curlew, Lesser Short-toed Lark, Trumpeter Finch). It is in this ecosystem where the farmland birds have become established (Common Quail, Common Linnet, Corn Bunting, Rock Sparrow) in both pasture and arable land. It is also within these limits where a good number of artificial ponds, dams and reservoirs are found, attracting migrants during migration periods and allowing the colonisation of this archipelago by the Ruddy Shelduck (Garcia-del-Rey & Rodriguez-Lorenzo 2010).

Thermophilous or thermophile woodland Several floristic elements are found in this habitat such as *Olea*, *Dracaena*, *Sideroxylon*, *Phoenix* (all tree species of Mediterranean origin), *Juniperus* and *Pistacia*. The endemic *Columba junoniae* (known as Laurel Pigeon or White-tailed Laurel Pigeon) is the sole representative species of the thermophilous woodland in the Canary Islands.

Laurel forest This ecosystem today is an impoverished version of the Palaeotropical Laurisilva that occurred in central and southern Europe, as well as North Africa, from the Pelaeocene up to the late Pliocene glaciations (Fernandez-Palacios et al. 2011). This habitat dominates the mid-altitudes of the Canary Islands. It can be generally described as a dense cloud forest with an important canopy (greater than 30 m). The dominant trees include genera such as *Picconia*, *Laurus*, *Ilex*, *Prunus*, *Myrica*, *Apollonia*, *Persea* and *Ocotea*. The endemic Bolle's Pigeon occupies this habitat type. It is also the main habitat of the African Blue Tit, although that species is also present in other ecosystems (Garcia-del-Rey 2004).

Pine forest This ecosystem is exclusive to the central and western Canary Islands (Gran Canaria, Tenerife, La Palma, El Hierro, absent from La Gomera) and is distributed at the same altitudes dominated by the palaeoendemic Canary Pine (*Pinus canariensis*). The endemic Tenerife Blue Chaffinch and the recently split Gran Canaria Blue Chaffinch (Lifjeld et al. 2016) are restricted to this ecosystem (Gran Canaria, Tenerife).

Summit scrub The summit scrub or Alpine scrub is found on the highest areas of two of the Canary Islands (La Palma and Tenerife) and the two main floristic elements are *Spartocytisus* and *Adenocarpus*. Several bird species of the lowlands also occur here, including Spectacled Warbler and Great Grey Shrike.

Rocky islets and coastline It is in these areas where the seabirds congregate in colonies or in pairs during the breeding period (for example Barolo Shearwater, Bulwer's Petrel, Madeiran Storm-petrel and White-faced Storm-petrel).

HOW TO USE THIS BOOK

INTRODUCTION
The introduction starts with a brief section on the history of the birds of the Canary Islands from early times to the present day. Some information on geography and climate is presented to help understand the next section covering the main habitats that occur on these islands. The 'Avifauna' section explains the different status of the birds, such as breeding species versus non-breeding, regular versus irregular winter migrants, seasonal visitors versus passage migrants, and ending with vagrancy. A section on bird conservation presents a snapshot of the last 50 years regarding monitoring, endangered species and, sadly, extinctions. However, it is the last section on where to watch birds on these islands that provides a practical site guide for the visiting birdwatcher. Divided by island, it covers the best birding spots to look for all the endemics, interesting seabirds and vagrants. Coordinates are given to reliably reach every site, and a list of potential species is presented for each locality.

PLATES
The plates are broadly arranged in taxonomic order following the *IOC World Bird List* (Gill & Donsker 2017). A few families or species appear out of sequence for presentational reasons. The figures on all the plates come from *Birds of the Atlantic Islands* (Clarke 2006). New figures have been painted for those species or subspecies that have been added to the Canarian list since 2006. For every species, the figures highlight important plumage characteristics with an emphasis on those plumages most likely to be encountered in the archipelago, but also include others that are less likely to occur. Whenever necessary, and for comparison, flight figures are incorporated onto the plates, and every figure is identified by sex and age. **Abbreviations used on plates:** ad = adult; juv = juvenile; imm = immature; sum = summer; win = winter; ssp. = subspecies.

SPECIES ACCOUNTS
The species accounts cover all those recorded in the archipelago with the exception of extreme vagrants; birds reliably seen only once between 1800 and 1 July 2017 have not been included in the species accounts, but they are all listed in the systematic list at the end of the book. Each species account is structured in a similar way. Taxonomy and nomenclature generally follows the *IOC World Bird List* (Gill & Donsker 2017), with some minor deviations to reflect the mainly European audience of this book. A total length (L) measurement is given for all species, and wingspan (WS) measured from wingtip to wingtip is given for those species for which it is most useful. The main text begins with a statement of status and habitat, followed by the most important section on identification (abbreviated as **ID**). The ID section usually starts by describing the most likely plumage to be encountered (e.g. summer or winter), followed by plumages less likely to be seen in the Canaries. Where sexes differ, the male is described first followed by the female. Finally, juvenile and immature plumages are described. Particular attention has been paid on comparing similar species. The ID section is followed by a **Voice** section and, when relevant, a taxonomic note is provided (abbreviated as **Tax.**). Some alternative names in common usage (abbreviated as Alt:) are given at the end in brackets.

SYSTEMATIC LIST
The systematic list at the end of the book is updated to 1 July 2017. This list generally follows the *IOC World Bird List* (Gill & Donsker 2017) with some minor deviations, and includes all birds reliably recorded in the Canarian archipelago. The list is divided by family, and for every species a status code is provided, followed by its occurrence on the eight principal inhabited islands (La Palma, El Hierro, La Gomera, Tenerife, Gran Canaria, Fuerteventura, Lanzarote and La Graciosa), as well as the uninhabited islets off NE Lanzarote known locally as the 'Chinijo archipelago' (Montaña Clara and Alegranza). The seabird hotspot located 45 miles NE of Lanzarote, known as Conception Bank, is also included in the list, as the second Western Palearctic record of Black-bellied Storm-petrel was recently recorded there.

AVIFAUNA OF THE CANARY ISLANDS

The most reliable and up-to-date Canarian avifaunal list comes from the checklist by Garcia-del-Rey (2017). This work suggests a total of 388 species divided as follows: 85 breeding species, 51 winter migrants, 70 seasonal visitors/true passage migrants and 182 vagrants.

BREEDING SPECIES

In the Canaries there is a total of 85 breeding bird species belonging to 38 families. Fringillidae is represented by the highest number of species (8) followed by Columbidae (7) and Sylviidae (5). The breeding species can be subdivided into resident breeders (RB, with 61 species), migrant breeders (MB, with 11 species, ten breeding in the summer and one in the winter), introduced species (I, with eight species) and occasional breeders (OB, with five species).

Resident breeders 61 species are present all year round and breed in the Canaries, representing 15.5% of the entire avifauna of this archipelago. All six endemics (Laurel Pigeon, Bolle's Pigeon, Canary Islands Stonechat, Canary Islands Chiffchaff, Tenerife Blue Chaffinch and Gran Canaria Blue Chaffinch) belong to this group, and other Macaronesian endemics are shared with other archipelagos (Plain Swift, Berthelot's Pipit, Atlantic Canary). A total of 40 endemic subspecies is found in this archipelago, including forms of Houbara Bustard, Eurasian Stone-curlew, Cream-coloured Courser, Great Spotted Woodpecker, European Robin, Goldcrest, African Blue Tit, Northern Raven, Common Chaffinch and Trumpeter Finch.

Migrant breeders 11 species (all non-passerines) are summer breeders in the Canaries. Most belong to Procellariidae (Cory's Shearwater, Manx Shearwater, Bulwer's Petrel) or Hydrobatidae (European Storm-petrel, White-faced Storm-petrel, Madeiran Storm-petrel). However, the latter is the only bird species breeding in the winter period on this archipelago. Other summer breeders include: Eleonora's Falcon (Falconidae), Common Tern (Sternidae), European Turtle Dove (Columbidae), Plain and Pallid Swifts (Apodidae). Part of the Common Quail (Phasianidae) population also arrives in spring to breed but this species is also a resident breeder.

Introduced species Eight bird species have been introduced into the Canaries. For hunting purposes Red-legged Partridge and Barbary Partridge (Phasianidae) have been introduced and thus maintain self-sustaining populations on these islands. The African Collared Dove (Columbidae) escaped from captivity and up to three species of Psittacidae have been introduced: Rose-ringed Parakeet, Monk Parakeet and Nanday Parakeet. House Sparrow (Passeridae) is currently considered as an introduced species onto Gran Canaria only, as well as Common Waxbill (Estrildidae). The family Threskiornithidae has a single representative, the Sacred Ibis, that has been breeding feral in the Canary Islands but today it is considered by many authorities as a former breeder.

Occasional breeders An occasional breeder is defined as a migratory species that has bred successfully at least once on any of the Canary Islands, but no more than ten times between 1900 and 2015. A total of five species is included in this group today and these are Marbled Duck (Anatidae), Red-billed Tropicbird (Phaethontidae), Little Bittern (Ardeidae), Roseate Tern (Sternidae) and Barn Swallow (Hirundinidae). Of these, the Little Bittern is the most likely to be removed from the list in the near future.

WINTER MIGRANTS

Species only present between autumn and spring can be divided into regular winter migrants (present every year since 1900, rWM) and irregular winter migrants (absent in some years, iWM). However, the Canaries are clearly influenced by their proximity to the African mainland and this is a key reason why they hold the highest number of wintering birds in Macaronesia, a total of 51 species belonging to 17 families of which most belong to Scolopacidae and Anatidae (13 and seven species respectively). This proximity is also responsible for migratory species reaching the Canaries accidentally and overwintering. For those species that rarely overwinter in the Canaries two categories have been created: 'accidental winter visitor' (1–10% of total observations) and 'occasional winter visitor' (11–25%). Only birds observed more than 25% of occasions have been considered regular or irregular winter visitors and given such status. Today, in the Canaries there are 18 irregular winter visitors and 33 regular winter visitors.

SEASONAL VISITORS AND TRUE PASSAGE MIGRANTS

According to Newton (2010) a passage migrant is a species of bird which appears each autumn and spring as it moves between the breeding area and the wintering area and back. This definition incorporates regularity in the movement and a well-defined migratory route. Although Bannerman (1963) applied the term for many Canarian migrants, today it can only be applied to birds that have been tracked through geolocator/GPS studies, such as Northern Gannet, Long-tailed Skua, Sabine's Gull and Arctic Tern – all considered recently as 'true passage migrants' by Garcia-del-Rey (2015).

Hence, birds erroneously considered in the past as 'passage migrants' in the Canaries are actually birds that have been blown off course or have shifted from their regular mainland (or coastal) migratory route. This explains why only single individuals or very small groups (1–3) are detected every season in the Canaries. If the islands were on a migratory route, hundreds or thousands of individuals should be detected and this is not the case. Today, in the Canary Islands, there are 67 'seasonal visitors' belonging to 29 families of which Sylviidae has the highest number of species (ten species) and four 'true passage migrants'.

VAGRANCY

Macaronesia is today not only considered as an important endemic bird area but also as a hotspot for vagrants. This region has significantly contributed to the Western Palearctic rare bird list, adding at least 14 first records (eight for the Azores, one for Madeira, one in the Canary Islands and four in the Cape Verde Islands). The Western Palearctic 'first' found in the Canaries was Dwarf Bittern, while the third Western Palearctic records of Tricolored Heron and Kelp Gull were also found here (Garcia-del-Rey & Garcia Vargas 2013). Currently, a total of 182 official vagrants have been noted by Sociedad Ornitologica Canaria (SOC).

BIRD CONSERVATION

Despite the fact that the Canary Islands belong to Spain and are part of the European Union, bird conservation is very far from optimal within the archipelago. To add to the extinctions noted in the Preface, some island populations have declined by 80% or more, mainly due to the contraction of their distribution (for example the farmland birds in Tenerife, particularly Rock Sparrow and Corn Bunting, and important seabirds such as Barolo Shearwater). At the time of writing there are only four species officially considered endangered by the Canarian Government (Egyptian Vulture, Osprey, Gran Canaria Blue Chaffinch and Northern Raven), but only two have an official 'recovery plan' approved and running. Actions undertaken thus far have not halted the declines and therefore the Canarian Government cannot yet remove any of the four from the list. One piece of good news is the stabilisation of Egyptian Vultures on Fuerteventura, thanks to the efforts of Doñana Biological Station and the Cabildo de Fuerteventura.

In the UK, populations of breeding birds are monitored annually (primarily by the British Trust for Ornithology). This allows early detection of population declines, and conservation measures can then be taken. In the Canary Islands, as there is not a single ornithologist in the Canarian government nor the seven island Cabildos, and there are no regular surveys, not even for the most iconic endemics such as Laurel Pigeon, Bolle's Pigeon, Canary Islands Stonechat and Tenerife Blue Chaffinch. To compound this lack of interest, some species belong to the Canarian government and others to the island Cabildo, creating confusion and thus conflicts, and as a consequence many Cabildos simply do not invest in bird conservation (for example, the Cabildo de Tenerife has not invested a single euro in bird conservation in the past 20 years).

With the current administrative conservation scheme it can easily be predicted that the steppe land birds will disappear from the western and central Canaries and will only be present in the eastern Canaries. The situation of the farmland birds is more serious as these have a strong association with human cultivation and many of these areas have been abandoned in the Canaries due to the expansion of the tourist industry in the 1970s and 1980s. Hence, the farmland birds will disappear from the bigger islands (such as Tenerife and Gran Canaria) and become localised and rare in the smaller islands (such as El Hierro), as no conservation actions are being undertaken by the Canarian government. Fortunately, the forests of the Canaries are protected by law, so if they remain untouched the associated species will survive in the years to come (for example Tenerife Blue Chaffinch). However, the Gran Canaria Blue Chaffinch will have to be managed in the source area (Inagua Reserve) and in the different sinks (suboptimal patches of pine forest such as La Cumbre) by constantly releasing a number of captive-bred individuals in these areas. Generally, some species will have to be maintained artificially by the Canarian government (for example supplementary feeding for the Northern Ravens on Tenerife and the Laurel Pigeons on Gran Canaria) if the objective of this administration is 'avian conservation'.

WHERE TO WATCH BIRDS IN THE CANARY ISLANDS

The locations for this section have been selected to maximise the opportunity to observe the target species (endemics and seabirds) and particularly for the visiting birder with a limited amount of time to go into the field. The western islands of La Palma, El Hierro and La Gomera are rarely visited by birders and therefore any migrant record is of interest to improve knowledge of the status of these birds (you can send these to garciadelreyeduardo@gmail.com). Tenerife holds all the endemics except for the recently split Gran Canaria Blue Chaffinch and the Canary Islands Stonechat, and they can all be seen on this island in a full morning of birding. Gran Canaria has many interesting sites and the Laurel Pigeon is being introduced here despite there being only 1% left of the original laurel forest and no thermophile woodland.

The eastern islands of Fuerteventura and Lanzarote are excellent for steppe birds such as the local subspecies of Houbara Bustard and the endemic Canary Islands Stonechat which is only found on Fuerteventura. During the right weather conditions, but mainly with strong easterly winds sometimes accompanied with thick Saharan dust, European migrants which lose their way from their main African migration route may reach the Canaries. Lanzarote and Fuerteventura, being closest to the mainland, receive higher numbers of such visitors than the central and western Canaries. The Canary Islands are also fantastic for encountering vagrants from both Africa and the Nearctic.

LA PALMA

There are very few resident birders on La Palma and therefore any records of migrants are worth reporting. A number of species have declined, such as Eurasian Stone-curlew and Corn Bunting, and some have even become extinct (such as Rock Sparrow). This island offers superb scenery and excellent thermophile and laurel forests, the habitat of the endemic Laurel and Bolle's Pigeons. The local subspecies of Common Chaffinch (ssp. *palmae*) and African Blue Tit (ssp. *palmensis*) can also be seen on La Palma along with the resident Red-billed Chough, not found on any of the other islands. For the rarity hunter, this island is strategically situated for Neartic vagrants and has produced the only record in the Canaries of Northern Waterthrush.

Los Tilos, La Palma (Robert Burton)

Airport pools (28°37'25.59"N 17°45'4.96"W) These intertidal saltwater pools are near the car park of the airport. To explore them in detail the best way is to access them via a dirt track located 250 metres from the N roundabout (28°37'43.15"N 17°45'15.75"W). The pools attract migrant waders in the winter and during migration periods. Nearctic waders such as American Golden Plover, White-rumped Sandpiper and the only recent record of Semipalmated Plover have been recorded here.

Lower Los Tilos (28°47'49.42"N 17°46'16.94"W) This gully holds an important population of Laurel Pigeon and from the viewpoint it is quite easy to see them and photograph their aerial circular displays.

Los Tilos (28°47'24.43"N 17°48'6.81"W) Officially known as the 'Los Tiles Biosphere Reserve', this pristine laurel forest is a must for any visitor to La Palma. The entrance to the gully (28°47'49.31"N 17°46'51.20"W) is signposted as 'Los Tilos'; follow the road until you reach the visitor centre and bar. Both pigeons can be seen here and all the other interesting forest birds such as African Blue Tit (ssp. *palmensis*) and Common Chaffinch (ssp. *palmae*). At night and during the summer, Manx Shearwaters can be heard when approaching their nests.

Barlovento reservoir (28°48'33.70"N 17°48'14.31"W) Locally known as 'Laguna de Barlovento', this freshwater area attracts the odd European duck in winter and rarities such as Ring-necked Duck have been reported. The surrounding areas are worth visiting for forest passerines.

La Cumbrecita (28°41'52.36"N 17°51'23.65"W) The road from the visitor centre of the Parque Nacional La Caldera de Taburiente reaches a parking place known as La Cumbrecita. It is here where Barbary Falcon can sometimes be seen patrolling for Rock Doves. The pine forest on either side of this road also holds Laurel Pigeon, the endemic subspecies of African Blue Tit and the endangered subspecies of Northern Raven (ssp. *canariensis*).

La Laguna reservoirs (28°38'27.74"N 17°54'47.04"W) Also known in the literature as 'Las Martelas', these reservoirs have attracted a good number of species, particularly the one located in the given coordinates, which has provided records of Common Pochard, Blue-winged Teal, Ring-necked Duck, Greater Flamingo, Jack Snipe, Long-billed Dowitcher, American Golden Plover, White-rumped Sandpiper, Pectoral Sandpiper, Lesser Yellowlegs, Gull-billed Tern, Little Swift and Water Pipit.

Fuencaliente saltpans (28°27'17.35"N 17°50'32.94"W) This area is right at the southern tip of the island and thus has attracted a number of migrants such as Common Shelduck, Greater Flamingo, the first record for the Canaries of Lesser Sand Plover, Semipalmated Sandpiper, White-rumped Sandpiper, Pectoral Sandpiper, Buff-breasted Sandpiper, Lesser Yellowlegs and Wilson's Phalarope.

EL HIERRO

Not a single birder lives on this island and therefore all the records to date are from visiting birders. Of the two endemic pigeons, Bolle's Pigeon is the more common and any record of the rare Laurel Pigeon is welcome. This island holds endemic subspecies of Common Chaffinch (ssp. *ombriosa*) and African Blue Tit (ssp. *ombriosus*). Of the steppe land birds, only Eurasian Stone-curlew can be found but the island holds a healthy population of Northern Raven, Rock Sparrow, Corn Bunting and Common Quail.

Terifabe dam (27°47'56.30"N 17°55'15.60"W) This freshwater dam has attracted migrants during the winter and migration periods. Follow the road to San Andres and exit on the following coordinates: 27°47'53.80"N 17°55'14.58"W. Follow the dirt track to the dam.

San Andres plains (27°45'48.81"N 17°58'49.49"W) This rural area holds cattle, and wheat is planted occasionally. It holds a healthy population of Rock Sparrow, Common Quail and Eurasian Stone-curlew. It is here where the only record of Sociable Lapwing for the Canaries was recorded and migrants are sometimes detected.

Llano de las Brujas Laurel forest (27°44'10.52"N 17°59'48.68"W) This area offers drinking places for humans and birds. All forest passerines can be observed here, including the endemic subspecies of African Blue Tit (ssp. *ombriosus*) and Common Chaffinch (ssp. *ombriosa*). The road from here to Frontera also offers great opportunities to explore this pristine forest.

Mencafete (27°43'58.42"N 18°4'28.87"W) This is the best place on this island to look for the endemic Bolle's Pigeon. Follow the road to Frontera until you reach the entrance of a dirt track at 27°44'21.15"N 18°2'52.93"W.

Frontera reservoir (27°45'27.23"N 18°0'56.12"W) This artificial freshwater reservoir is an important stopover for any birder visiting El Hierro. A good number of interesting birds have been found here, including Blue-winged Teal, Ring-necked Duck, Bonelli's Eagle, Semipalmated Sandpiper, White-rumped Sandpiper, Glossy Ibis and Jack Snipe.

La Restinga (27°38'24.28"N 17°58'48.96"W) This fishermen's town is famous for the fish restaurants and being at the southern tip of this island it offers the opportunity to find the odd rarity. Two firsts for the Canaries have been observed here; Double-crested Cormorant and Glaucous-winged Gull. Other interesting birds found on this area are Mediterranean Gull and Ring-billed Gull.

LA GOMERA

La Gomera is famous for its Garajonay National Park, with breathtaking laurel forest scenery that offers good birding opportunities for the two endemic pigeons and other forest birds. Seawatching is possible from the ferry that crosses from Los Cristianos (Tenerife) to San Sebastian, the capital of La Gomera. No local birders live on this island and therefore any record of migrants is welcomed. The Trumpeter Finch can also be observed in the south of this island, a species very localised and rare on Tenerife at the time of writing.

San Sebastian de La Gomera (28°5'20.61"N 17°6'38.58"W) The capital of La Gomera is worth exploring, particularly the beach, the gully that sometimes holds some water (28°5'22.02"N 17°6'42.68"W) and the park Torre del Conde. A number of interesting species have been observed here, including Ring-necked Duck, Temminck's Stint, White-rumped Sandpiper, Spotted Sandpiper, Mediterranean Gull, Laughing Gull, Common Gull and Bar-tailed Lark.

Chejelipes dam (28°6'55.39"N 17°10'2.56"W) On leaving the capital on the road to Hermigua and Vallehermos, there is a turning to Chejelipes (28°5'45.87"N 17°6'55.62"W). Follow this road until you reach the dam. The marshy area and the reservoir are worth checking; Common Moorhens breed here and Osprey is sometimes observed fishing.

La Carbonera (28°8'4.52"N 17°11'38.32"W) From the capital take the road to Hermigua until you pass a series of small tunnels about 400 metres before reaching the first building, where you can park. The forest area is good to see flying pigeons, and with some luck you may find one perched in the dead branches. All the forest passerines can be found here too.

El Cedro (Garajonay National Park) From the previous location continue on for 1 km and turn left to Monte El Cedro, stop carefully at vantage points (e.g. 28°6'44.24"N 17°13'4.83"W, 28°7'18.11"N 17°12'54.69"W, 28°7'30.21"N 17°12'31.53"W), watching out for traffic. The birding strategy here is to try to look at the biggest area of forest possible, to see the very fast Bolle's Pigeon and the slower Laurel Pigeon.

La Encantadora dam (28°10'0.68"N 17°15'44.09"W) Locally known as Presa de La Encantadora, this freshwater reservoir is worth checking for ducks and other associated species; Common Moorhen and Eurasian Coot breed here. Interesting species reported here include Ring-necked Duck and Common Pochard.

Valle Gran Rey pools (28°5'49.51"N 17°20'49.14"W) Locally known as Charco del Cieno, these intertidal pools attract waders in winter and during migratory periods. Both Pectoral Sandpiper and Spotted Sandpiper have been recorded and Barbary Falcon can be observed in the cliffs nearby.

Playa Santiago (28°1'38.38"N 17°12'33.15"W) The urbanised area below the airport is the most reliable site on this island to look for Trumpeter Finch. Other resident species recorded here include Eurasian Stone-curlew, Eurasian Hoopoe, European Goldfinch, Barbary Falcon, Northern Raven and Atlantic Canary.

Tecina Golf (28°1'56.03"N 17°11'13.07"W) Golf courses tend to attract migrants during migratory periods. The first record of Glossy Ibis was reported here.

Gomera Ferry (Los Cristianos to San Sebastian) This ferry crossing gives good opportunities for whales (Short-finned Pilot Whales) and seabird-watching (Cory's Shearwater). During the summer both Bulwer's Petrel (from April onwards) and the endangered Barolo Shearwater (mainly August) can be observed. European Storm-petrel arrives in May and departs in September whereas the Madeiran Storm-petrel is a winter breeder (September to March), but very difficult to see on this crossing, as is the rarer White-faced Storm-petrel that breeds in the eastern Canaries. Other seabirds recorded on this crossing include

Manx and Great Shearwaters, Great, Arctic and Long-tailed Skuas, Audouin's Gull, Sabine's Gull, Sooty Tern, Red-billed Tropicbird and Grey Phalarope.

TENERIFE

Tenerife is the biggest of all the Canary Islands and offers the opportunity to see all the endemics except Canary Islands Stonechat, only present on Fuerteventura, and the Gran Canaria Blue Chaffinch. There is a general belief (mainly among birdwatching tour operators) that the Laurel Pigeon is difficult to see on this island but this is not the case if any of the locations presented

Englishman's Peak, Tenerife (Eduardo Garcia-del-Rey)

here are visited. Unfortunately, some species have become extinct in recent years (such as Lesser Short-toed Lark) and some have declined severely (such as Eurasian Stone-curlew, Northern Raven and Rock Sparrow). The Trumpeter Finch has also been considered extinct since 2005, but a reintroduction project is being undertaken by the Sociedad Ornitologica Canaria.

Los Rodeos area (28°28'24.83"N 16°21'0.75"W) This is the only arable land in the Canaries and thus provides the opportunity to find all the farmland birds, such as Corn Bunting, Common Linnet, Atlantic Canary, European Greenfinch and Common Quail. This area is also fantastic to look for seasonal visitors (Western Marsh Harrier, Hen Harrier, Montagu's Harrier, Collared Pratincole, Eurasian Dotterel, Common Cuckoo, Greater Short-toed Lark, Barn Swallow, Common House Martin, Tawny Pipit, Willow Warbler, Red-throated Pipit), winter visitors (European Golden Plover, Northern Lapwing, Short-eared Owl, European Stonechat, Common Starling, Meadow Pipit) and vagrants (Pallid Harrier, Red-footed Falcon, Mistle Thrush, Ortolan Bunting).

La Laguna (28°29'42.36"N 16°18'46.43"W) This site is a reliable one to look for European Serin singing on the Australian Pine trees, as well as other finches and other resident birds.

Englishman's peak or Pico del Ingles (28°32'00"N 16°15'50"W) This viewpoint is worth a quick visit to try for the endemic pigeons, although they can also be seen anywhere in this Anaga Natural Park.

Valle Molina reservoir (28°29'42.36"N 16°18'46.43"W) This freshwater reservoir is interesting to look for ducks, gulls and waders. Unfortunately, it is closed to the public and thus the best approach is to take the northern road and search the reservoir with a telescope. Winter visitors include Grey Heron, Little Egret, Western Cattle Egret, Eurasian Spoonbill, Eurasian Wigeon, Eurasian Teal, Northern Pintail, Eurasian Coot, Northern Lapwing, Common Snipe, Common Greenshank, Green Sandpiper, Common Sandpiper, Black-headed Gull and White Wagtail, and on certain occasions Osprey can be seen. Rarities have also been found here, such as American Wigeon, Green-winged Teal, Blue-winged Teal, Ring-necked Duck, Pectoral Sandpiper, Spotted Sandpiper, Mediterranean Gull.

Tejina ponds (28°32'10.30"N 16°21'31.33"W) A total of six freshwater reservoirs (28°32'15.89"N 16°21'28.61"W, 28°32'19.21"N 16°21'26.33"W, 28°32'33.46"N 16°21'25.13"W, 28°32'39.97"N 16°21'14.24"W, 28°32'41.01"N 16°21'7.94"W, 28°32'38.75"N 16°21'14.11"W) provide interesting birding opportunities for a good number of seasonal and winter visitors, but also keep an eye out for vagrants. This is also the only breeding site for Little Bittern in the Canaries, and the second most important breeding area for

Black-crowned Night Heron on Tenerife. Also present are Little Bittern, Squacco Heron, Western Cattle Egret, Purple Heron, Great Egret, White Stork, Eurasian Spoonbill, Eurasian Wigeon, Eurasian Teal, Northern Shoveler, Tufted Duck, Western Marsh Harrier, Osprey, Spotted Crake, Little Crake, Baillon's Crake, Little Ringed Plover, Northern Lapwing, Curlew Sandpiper, Dunlin, Ruff, Common Snipe, Black-tailed Godwit, Wood Sandpiper, Common Sandpiper, Common Kingfisher, Common Cuckoo, Barn Swallow, Common House Martin, Common Redstart, European Stonechat, Northern

Tejina pond, Tenerife (Eduardo Garcia-del-Rey)

Wheatear, Sedge Warbler, Great Reed Warbler, Eurasian Reed Warbler, Willow Warbler and Woodchat Shrike. Rarities have also been reported, such as Ring-necked Duck, Blue-winged Teal, Greater Scaup, Eurasian Bittern, Allen's Gallinule, White-rumped Sandpiper, Semipalmated Sandpiper, Jack Snipe, Wilson's Snipe and Eurasian Crag Martin.

Punta del Hidalgo coastline (28°34'42.82"N 16°19'15.81"W) The coastal rocky shore provides an intertidal zone which is good for waders at low tide. Winter visitors include Little Egret, Whimbrel, Ruddy Turnstone, Grey Plover, Common Ringed Plover, Common Redshank and Common Sandpiper. Vagrant Ferruginous Duck and Purple Sandpiper have been recorded here too.

El Lance viewpoint (28°23'8.67"N 16°36'16.79"W) This small patch of thermophile woodland is a must for those who wish to see and photograph the Laurel Pigeon. From the viewpoint look down for flying pigeons that sometimes perch in the trees nearby. All the other forest passerines can be seen from here too.

Barranco Ruiz viewpoint (28°22'35.02"N 16°37'34.33"W) This steep gully offers great opportunities to observe the two endemic pigeons. A telescope is ideal for this site to spot and admire these birds.

Los Silos (28°22'2.59"N 16°49'14.34"W) A couple of irrigation tanks (for example at 28°22'2.59"N 16°49'14.34"W, 28°22'23.50"N 16°49'21.82"W) allow some birding for migrants and rarities as American Wigeon, Greater Scaup, Ring-necked Duck, Pied-billed Grebe, Great Egret, White-rumped Sandpiper, Pectoral Sandpiper and Lesser Yellowlegs.

El Fraile viewpoint (28°22'0.05"N 16°53'4.11"W) This is one of the best sites on Tenerife to try for Barbary Falcon, either perched on the walls above or patrolling for Rock Doves.

Teno Bajo (28°20'59.30"N 16°54'56.14"W) This area of semi-desert scrub and abandoned cultivated areas is worth searching for wintering migrants such as Eurasian Skylark but is also good for Rock Sparrow (when not breeding on Teno Alto) and Barbary Partridge. The endangered Northern Raven can also be seen. Seawatching from the lighthouse should produce Cory's Shearwater during the summer and migrant seabirds like Great Shearwater, Sooty Shearwater, Manx Shearwater and Arctic Tern from August to November. Rarities such as Little Gull have been reported.

Teno Alto (28°20'36.57"N 16°52'36.76"W) This rural area belongs to the Rural Park of Teno and is the last stronghold for Rock Sparrow in Tenerife. Breeding peaks in May when the grasshoppers become very abundant.

Erjos Monte del Agua (28°19'43.91"N 16°48'32.18"W) Upon reaching the town of Erjos and near the visitor centre, you'll find the entrance to a dirt track (28°19'32.53"N 16°48'25.63"W) to reach the entrance of the forest, which is fenced for cars. The strategy here is simple, just follow the main dirt track until you reach wooden viewpoints from where to look for flying pigeons. All the other forest birds can be observed here (Eurasian Sparrowhawk, African Blue Tit, European Robin, Goldcrest, Canary Islands Chiffchaff, Eurasian Blackcap, Common Blackbird, Common Chaffinch, Atlantic Canary).

Erjos ponds (28°19'9.88"N 16°48'31.91"W) These artificial freshwater ponds are worth checking if passing nearby. Take the dirt track (28°19'26.82"N 16°48'27.41"W) to reach the ponds. Green-winged Teal, Ring-necked Duck, American Bittern, Dwarf Bittern and Fieldfare have all been recorded as vagrants. Both Eurasian Coot and Common Moorhen breed here. Common Snipe occurs in the winter and migrants sometimes turn up during the right conditions.

Las Lajas (28°11'26.10"N 16°39'56.53"W) This picnic site is not far from the town of Vilaflor and is the most reliable site to look for the endemic Tenerife Blue Chaffinch, at any time during the year. Other pine-associated species such as Great Spotted Woodpecker can be seen here too.

Las Graveras (28°0'32.58"N 16°39'33.32"W) This area of intertidal pools is worth a quick visit for migrants, particularly waders and ducks.

Amarilla dam (28°2'44.40"N 16°37'8.48"W) This freshwater dam is located in the entrance of Amarilla Golf Course. A good number of migrants have been recorded here.

El Medano coastline (28°2'36.94"N 16°32'0.31"W) At low tide this area attracts waders, mainly in winter and during migration periods.

GRAN CANARIA

Despite the fact that Gran Canaria is a very big island, most of its forests are now fragmented (pine forest) or extremely localised and rare (laurel forest) compared to the original distribution. However, new taxonomic research is starting to adjust the endemic status of some of the common species of this island. Today, the Blue Chaffinch here is considered a distinct species and both the African Blue Tit and the Common Chaffinch will have their status adjusted in the near future. The island's form of European Robin is now classed as an endemic subspecies too. This island also has some interesting sites to look for migrants and vagrants.

Maspalomas (27°44'19.07"N 15°35'39.95"W) The oasis of Maspalomas is in the central area of a tidal lagoon called La Charca. This area attracts a good number of migrant species, and Common Moorhens breed here too. Two specialities occur around this location, Tree Sparrow and Common Waxbill. Interesting vagrants reported include Common Shelduck, Blue-winged Teal, Ring-necked Duck, Western Reef Heron, Greater Flamingo, Allen's Gallinule, Least Sandpiper, White-rumped Sandpiper, Pectoral Sandpiper, Lesser Yellowlegs, Laughing Gull, Audouin's Gull, Ring-billed Gull, Roseate Tern, Common Kingfisher, African Desert Warbler, Common Grasshopper Warbler, Mallard, Merlin, Black Tern, European Roller.

El Matorral reservoirs (27°49'27.21"N 15°27'16.70"W) A series of freshwater reservoirs offer great birding opportunities if passing by. As with Maspalomas lagoon, this is a hotspot for vagrants. Both Trumpeter Finch and Rock Sparrows can be found in the gullies nearby to the south of the reservoirs.

San Lorenzo reservoirs (28°4'38.65"N 15°28'45.83"W) These freshwater reservoirs are the breeding grounds of the recently established Black-crowned Night Heron. Migrants are also attracted during autumn and spring.

Golf (28°1'1.48"N 15°24'35.59"W) The reservoirs of this golf course attract breeding Ruddy Shelduck and other migratory species.

Llanos de la Pez (27°57'57.08"N 15°35'3.03"W) This is the most reliable site in the Gran Canaria pine forest to look, during the breeding period (May to July), for the recently split and endemic Gran Canaria

Blue Chaffinch. All forest species can be observed here including Great Spotted Woodpecker (ssp. *thanneri*), African Blue Tit (ssp. *hedwigae*), Common Chaffinch (ssp. undescribed) and European Robin (ssp. *marionae*).

FUERTEVENTURA

This rural island offers great opportunities to see all the steppe land birds found in the Canaries (such as Houbara Bustard, Cream-coloured Courser, Eurasian Stone-curlew, Black-bellied Sandgrouse, Lesser Short-toed Lark and Trumpeter Finch). During the local 'calima' weather conditions the

La Oliva, Fuerteventura (Eduardo Garcia-del-Rey)

island can be full of interesting migrants and the vagrant list is also impressive. The endemic subspecies of Egyptian Vulture still has its stronghold on this island, and Ruddy Shelduck, which colonised recently, is very common now in the brackish reservoirs. However, it is the Canary Islands Stonechat that is the jewel of this island and why most birders have to visit Fuerteventura.

Majanicho coastline (28°44'26.08"N 13°56'12.89"W) This lava coastline offers good birding during low tide, particularly for waders. Kentish Plover is resident here.

La Oliva (28°36'18.01"N 13°55'47.02"W) The cultivated areas near the school are very good to look for residents (Northern Raven, Corn Bunting, Common Linnet, Berthelot's Pipit, Great Grey Shrike, Lesser Short-toed Lark, Spectacled Warbler and Spanish Sparrow) and migrants during spring and autumn periods. The slopes of the mountains to the south are superb to look for the endemic Canary Islands Stonechat and other specialities such as Trumpeter Finch.

Tindaya plains (28°35'42.58"N 13°59'33.96"W) This is one of the best places on this island to look for the steppe land birds (Houbara Bustard, Cream-coloured Courser, Eurasian Stone-curlew, Black-bellied Sandgrouse, Lesser Short-toed Lark and Trumpeter Finch. The best strategy, which will also minimise stress to the birds, is to use the car as a hide and stop systematically, every 500 metres, to search with binoculars and telescope.

Parque Holandes (28°36'9.50"N 13°50'15.13"W) The area with water is worth a quick check for migrants.

Los Molinos dam (28°30'45.74"N 14°1'53.00"W) This brackish dam offers superb birding opportunities and is one of the few places in the Canaries where Black-winged Stilt, Eurasian Coot and Common Moorhen regularly breed. Flocks of Ruddy Shelducks can be seen here too, sometimes chased by Barbary Falcons. The slopes of the reservoir hold a few pairs of the endemic Canary Islands Stonechat, and Trumpeter Finch is a regular visitor to the goat farm at the entrance of the dirt track that leads to the dam (28°31'46.06"N 14°2'27.79"W). Rarities recorded here include Greylag Goose, Common Shelduck, American Wigeon, Blue-winged Teal, Greater Scaup, Ring-necked Duck, Black Stork, Lanner Falcon, Allen's Gallinule, White-rumped Sandpiper, Baird's Sandpiper, Pectoral Sandpiper, Buff-breasted Sandpiper, Little Swift and African Desert Warbler.

Castillo de Lara (28°24'46.54"N 14°3'2.56"W) This area of planted Canary Pine is the most reliable on this island to search for the African Blue Tit and the rarer Atlantic Canary. Other residents here include Barbary Partridge, Sardinian Warbler, Berthelot's Pipit and Northern Raven.

Vega de Rio Palmas/Las Peñitas dam (28°23'37.27"N 14°5'16.03"W) The gully from the entrance of the town to the reservoir is worth visiting for migrants and residents such as African Blue Tit, Sardinian Warbler and Trumpeter Finch. The dam is worth checking when holding water. Egyptian Vulture, Barbary Falcon and Northern Raven occur in the vicinity of the dam.

El Carmen saltpans (28°22'0.61"N 13°52'15.09"W) This area of saltpans is good for migrants in the winter and during migration periods.

Los Molinos dam, Fuerteventura (Eduardo Garcia-del-Rey)

Barranco de La Torre (28°22'4.49"N 13°53'34.11"W) This riparian gully with tamarisks is fantastic to look for migrants and particularly passerines during the migration periods on the nearby African continent, but also vagrants such as Western Olivaceous Warbler, Collared Flycatcher, Hawfinch and Ortolan Bunting.

Rosa de Catalina Garcia (28°18'0.88"N 14°1'31.92"W) This brackish lagoon is worth checking for migrants and vagrants such as Blue-winged Teal, Greater Scaup, Lesser Scaup, Ring-necked Duck, Little Grebe, Eurasian Bittern, Baillon's Crake, Little Crake, Allen's Gallinule, White-rumped Sandpiper, Pectoral Sandpiper, Buff-breasted Sandpiper, Lesser Yellowlegs, Water Pipit, Citrine Wagtail, Bluethroat, Common Reed Bunting and Fieldfare. Black-winged Stilt and Ruddy Shelduck are regular.

La Pared plains (28°10'51.67"N 14°12'46.66"W) This area holds healthy populations of steppe land birds such as Houbara Bustard, Black-bellied Sandgrouse, Cream-coloured Courser, Eurasian Stone-curlew and the introduced Barbary Partridge.

Costa Calma (28°10'1.78"N 14°13'21.38"W) The planted area of Australian Pine trees attracts migrants during the winter and during the mainland migratory periods, but also vagrants such as Chimney Swift, Yellow-browed Warbler and Brambling.

LANZAROTE

All the steppe land birds in the Canaries can be observed on Lanzarote except for Black-bellied Sandgrouse. This island offers the best opportunities to find migrants lost from their main migration route along the African coast. With luck one can find the Eleonora's Falcons that breed on the islets off north Lanzarote.

Orzola coastline (29°12'58.32"N 13°26'34.09"W) This lava coastline is worth a quick visit for waders. Along the cliffs of Orzola a pair of Red-billed Tropicbirds has been seen in recent years. The subspecies of African Blue Tit (*ultramarinus*) occurs in town.

Guinate viewpoint (29°11'4.66"N 13°30'4.15"W) This is a good place to look for Barbary Falcons that nest on the cliffs. Sometimes Eleonora's Falcons that breed in Montaña Clara and Alegranza can be observed patrolling in this area.

Bosquecillo (29°7'52.35"N 13°31'2.16"W) Both the African Blue Tit (ssp. *ultramarinus*) and Atlantic Canary are regular in this small forest patch, which is also ideal to look for migrants during migration.

Mala dam (29°6'33.35"N 13°28'43.71"W) This reservoir attracts migrants in winter and during migration.

Los Cocoteros saltpans (29°3'26.32"N 13°27'54.70"W) This area has been a hotspot for migrants, despite recent degradation, including Common Shelduck, Temminck's Stint, White-rumped Sandpiper, Pectoral Sandpiper, Lesser Yellowlegs and Grey Phalarope.

Costa Teguise golf (29°0'7.87"N 13°31'4.51"W) As with other golf courses in the Canaries, this site attracts migrants and is a reliable spot to observe Barbary Partridge. Also recorded here are Eurasian Scops Owl, European Roller, Rufous-tailed Scrub Robin, Mistle Thrush, Great Reed Warbler, Western Olivaceous Warbler, Collared Flycatcher, Brambling, Hawfinch and Little Bunting.

Tias golf (28°56'6.54"N 13°39'19.41"W) This golf course has an impressive bird list of both migrants and vagrants. Ruddy Shelduck breeds on the reservoir. Vagrants and other interesting migrants reported here include Greater Scaup, Glossy Ibis, Jack Snipe, Black Tern, Baillon's Crake, Purple Swamphen, Allen's Gallinule, American Golden Plover, Temminck's Stint, Pectoral Sandpiper, Buff-breasted Sandpiper, Long-billed Dowitcher, Common Cuckoo, European Roller, Water Pipit, Citrine Wagtail, Western Orphean Warbler, Lesser Whitethroat, Common Grasshopper Warbler, Common Reed Bunting, Ortolan Bunting and Bobolink.

Famara plains (29°4'22.15"N 13°36'11.68"W) This plain holds the highest density of Houbara Bustards in the Canaries. It is also a classic spot on this island to look for the other steppe land birds (Cream-coloured Courser, Eurasian Stone-curlew and Trumpeter Finch). Vagrants are also possible here (for example Black-eared Wheatear).

La Santa (29°6'38.59"N 13°39'45.25"W) The rocky coastline is worth exploring for waders and possible rarities. American Golden Plover, Purple Sandpiper, Semipalmated Sandpiper, Temminck's Stint, Mediterranean Gull, Rock Pipit and Western Orphean Warbler have all been observed here.

Janubio (28°56'9.58"N 13°49'31.95"W) This saltwater estuary and associated saltpans attract interesting birds and are the breeding grounds of Black-winged Stilt. Other birds reported include Mallard, Common Shelduck, Blue-winged Teal, Greater Scaup, Lesser Scaup, Little Grebe, Northern Fulmar, Greater Flamingo, Corn Crake, White-rumped Sandpiper, Pectoral Sandpiper, Marsh Sandpiper, Spotted Sandpiper, Grey Phalarope, Wilson's Phalarope, Mediterranean Gull, Slender-billed Gull, Blue Rock Thrush, Common Grasshopper Warbler and Ortolan Bunting.

Arrecife (28°57'23.69"N 13°32'53.19"W) The coastline attracts waders and a good number of rarities and interesting seasonal visitors have been reported, such as Sooty Shearwater, Red-billed Tropicbird, Sacred Ibis, Greater Flamingo, White-rumped Sandpiper, Terek Sandpiper, Grey Phalarope, Little Gull, Mediterranean Gull, Slender-billed Gull, Audouin's Gull, Common Gull, Ring-billed Gull, Glaucous Gull, Roseate Tern, Little Tern, Gull-billed Tern, Common Guillemot, Little Swift, Eurasian Crag Martin, Citrine Wagtail, Fieldfare and Eurasian Siskin.

PLATE 1: DUCKS AND GEESE I

Brent Goose *Branta bernicla*   L 55–66 cm, WS 115–125 cm

Vagrant. Winters on tidal mudflats and coastal grassy fields. **ID** Adult has black head, neck and breast, darkish grey breast and mantle, plain grey-brown upperparts and white vent. Overall a small, very dark goose when compared to Barnacle. The white neck patch is diagnostic for all races, but is sometimes difficult to see at long range. In flight shows white uppertail-coverts and pale flanks contrasting with very dark underwing. Juvenile has upperwing-coverts tipped with white, which creates white bars on mantle. Pale-bellied race *hrota* is illustrated. Nominate race has a darker belly. **Voice** A rolling, guttural *raunk, raunk rhut*, not easy to hear in Canary Islands. [Alt: Brant Goose]

Greylag Goose *Anser anser*   L 75–90 cm, WS 150–180 cm

Vagrant. Freshwater ponds, reservoirs and wetlands. **ID** A large and bulky goose with uniform greyish-brown plumage. Unlike other dark grey geese, the head does not contrast with the rest of the body. Legs dull pinkish. Bill pinkish-orange or pink (great variation depending on subspecies). Confusion likely with juvenile Greater White-fronted, but that has orange legs and darker head and neck than Greylag. In flight differs from all other grey geese in distinctive light grey forewing and pale grey underwing-coverts. **Voice** A deep *aahng-ahng-ung* in flight.

Greater White-fronted Goose *Anser albifrons*   L 65–78 cm, WS 135–165 cm

Vagrant. In natural range breeds on tundra. **ID** Adult can be differentiated from other grey geese by the white patch present around the base of the bill (reaching the crown) and the bold, black belly markings. Juvenile lacks the white blaze around the base of the bill and has a pinkish bill with a dark nail; lacks the irregular black belly patches. The adult in flight appears less well-marked than other similar species. **Voice** In flight a *kyu-yu* or *kyu-yu-yu*.

Common Scoter *Melanitta nigra*   L 44–54 cm, WS 70–84 cm

Vagrant. In marine coastal waters and estuaries in winter. **ID** Adult male is entirely black and has a knob at the base of the bill, yellow-orange culmen and pointed tail. In flight paler primaries give it a two-tone wing pattern. Adult female is browner with paler cheeks. In flight paler primaries separate adult female Common Scoter from adult female Surf Scoter (not recorded in Canary Islands). Juvenile resembles adult female, but has whitish belly. Confusion likely with Nearctic Black Scoter, a potential vagrant to Canary Islands, which has a bright swollen yellow-orange area on the bill and males lack the black knob at the base of the bill. Female Black difficult to separate from Common Scoter in the field. **Voice** Silent when not on breeding grounds.

PLATE 2: DUCKS AND GEESE II

Common Shelduck *Tadorna tadorna* L 58–67 cm, WS 110–135 cm

Vagrant. Prefers saltwater lagoons and reservoirs, but also saltpans. **ID** A large black-and-white duck with a dark green head, pinkish legs, a conspicuous red bill and a rusty breast-band. Bill deep red, in male with knob at base during breeding season. In flight the white upper and underwing similar to Ruddy Shelduck. Juvenile has brownish crown and hindneck, pinkish bill and legs, and no rusty breast-band (in flight has a white trailing edge to wings). **Voice** Female a whinnying *gagagagagaga...* and also a disyllabic *a-ank*. Male a whistle *sliss-sliss-sliss* and also a disyllabic *piu-pu*.

Ruddy Shelduck *Tadorna ferruginea* L 61–67 cm, WS 120–145 cm

Resident breeder (T, GC, F, L). Prefers artificial and brackish reservoirs and gullies with running water and tamarisk vegetation. **ID** A brown-orange duck with creamy-white head and dark legs and bill. The male has a narrow, black neck-collar in the breeding season. Both male and female have conspicuous white face masks. In flight the pure white upper and underwing is diagnostic. Flight feathers black with greenish gloss on secondaries. Juvenile resembles female, but has grey wash on white of forewing and diffuse rufous tips on scapulars. **Voice** A honking *aaakh* in flight.

Marbled Duck *Marmaronetta angustirostris* L 39–42 cm, WS 63–70 cm

Occasional breeder (GC, F), rarely reported on other islands (T, L). Prefers brackish artificial reservoirs with dense tamarisk vegetation for breeding, but also found in freshwater areas. **ID** The shaggy crest, most prominent on males, is diagnostic. A small pale sandy-brown duck with white spotting over whole plumage (mainly visible on the darker upperparts), dusky eye-patch and dark legs and bill. No speculum is visible in flight but this is the palest part of the wing. Similar to female Northern Pintail (Plate 6), which lacks dark eye-patch. Juvenile very similar to adult but spots duller and more diffuse. Confusion also possible with Garganey, which has a white trailing edge to secondaries and is darker overall. **Voice** A nasal *jeeeep* is sometimes produced by the male during display. Female a disyllabic *pleep-pleep*. [Alt: Marbled Teal]

Common Pochard *Aythya ferina* L 42–49 cm, WS 72–82 cm

Irregular winter migrant (all islands except H). Mainly on freshwater but also on brackish reservoirs in eastern Canary Islands. **ID** A medium-sized, diving duck with a sloping forehead and a relatively long bill. Summer male has reddish-chestnut head, red eye, black breast and ventral region, pale grey flanks and upperparts, dark legs and a pale grey band on dark bill. Adult male eclipse is similar to summer male, but duller overall. Adult female has diffuse head markings and a dull greyish subterminal band on the bill, present only during the winter, dark brown chest and tail, and greyish flanks and mantle tinged with brown. Juvenile browner than adult female, with yellowish eye and no line behind eye. In flight all plumages show a grey band on the upperwing, as in Nearctic vagrant Ring-necked Duck (Plate 3). **Voice** When flushed utters a *krrah*, not often heard in the Canary Islands.

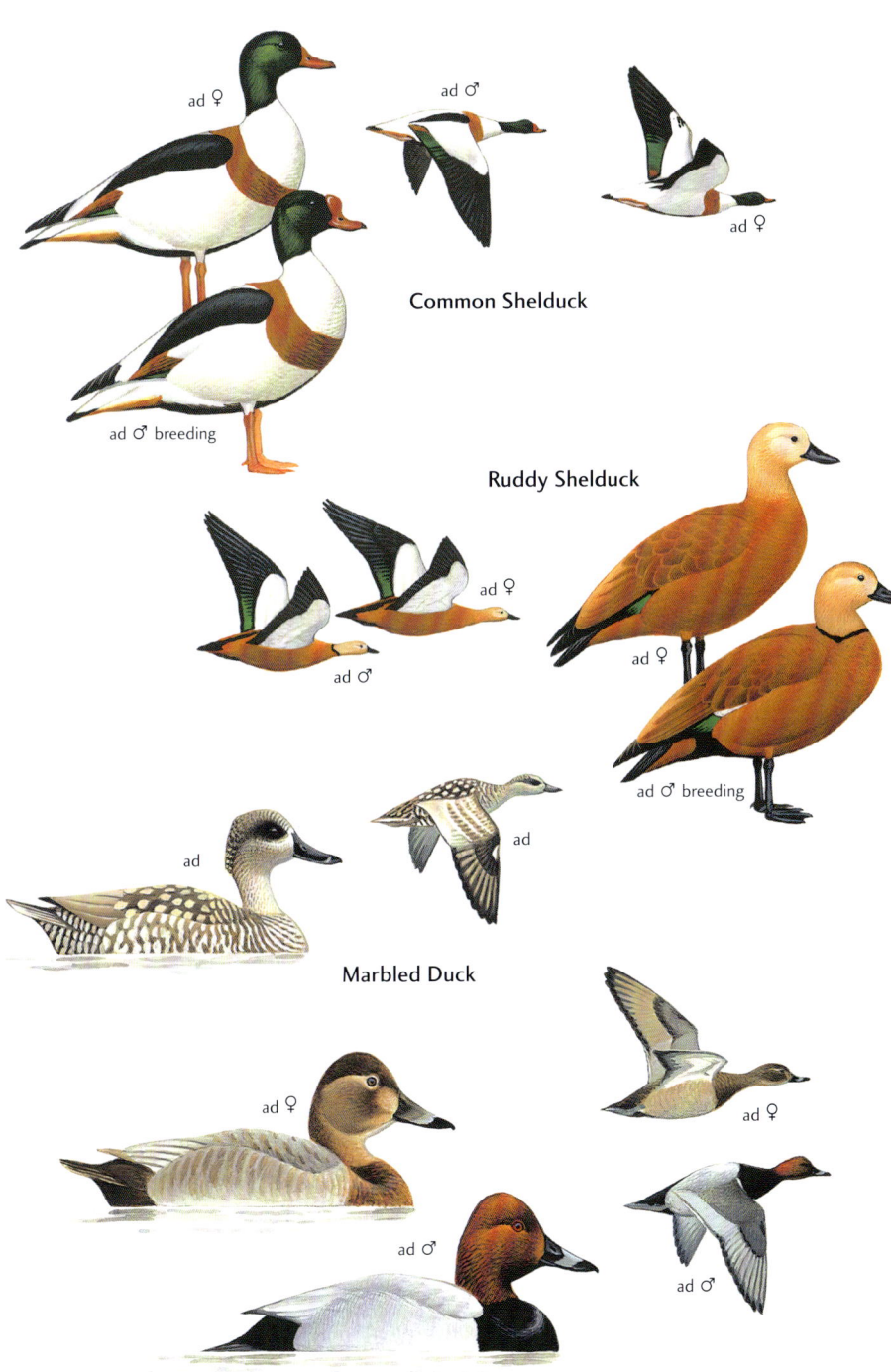

PLATE 3: DUCKS AND GEESE III

Ring-necked Duck *Aythya collaris*   L 37–46 cm, WS 61–75 cm

Vagrant. Freshwater artificial reservoirs, also on brackish reservoirs. **ID** Summer male as Tufted Duck, but with no tuft, light grey flanks (not white), a white 'spur' at wing-bend, and conspicuous white band near the tip of the bill. Eclipse male has dark head, breast and mantle, yellow eye, brownish flanks and lacks white bill band, although may sometimes show some white around the base of the bill. Adult female recalls female Common Pochard (Plate 2), but has a darker back, pale loral patch, peaked hind-crown, white band on the bill, pale eye-ring and a pale line behind the eye. In flight grey wing-bar on secondaries and primaries is diagnostic for both sexes. Juvenile like adult female, but with faint subterminal bill band (almost all-dark bill). In flight it can be separated from other *Aythya* ducks by greyish upperwing-bar. **Voice** Mostly silent while in the Canary Islands.

Tufted Duck *Aythya fuligula*   L 40–47 cm, WS 65–72 cm

Regular winter migrant (all islands except L). Found in both fresh and brackish reservoirs. **ID** Summer male has long drooping crest on rear of crown, black head, breast and upperparts, white flanks, yellow eye and black ventral region. Adult male eclipse has a small tuft and has browner flanks. Adult female is dark brown overall with lighter flanks, yellow eye and in some cases with white on face like vagrant Greater Scaup and Lesser Scaup, but tuft or hint of tuft are important clues. Juvenile duller brown than adult female and with just a hint of tuft, eye brown. In flight both male and female have similar upperwing pattern to Greater Scaup, but male has black back, not whitish, and female lacks the subtle greyish vermiculation on mantle. **Voice** Male gives a *wheep-wee-whew* and female a *err, err, err…*, rarely heard in the Canary Islands.

Greater Scaup *Aythya marila*   L 42–51 cm, WS 71–80 cm

Vagrant. Freshwater reservoirs but also brackish ponds. **ID** Summer male has rounded black head with green gloss, black breast and ventral region, white flanks, greyish vermiculated back, and grey bill with small black nail. Eclipse male similar to breeding male, but with a brownish head, flanks and back. Adult female brownish overall with greyish vermiculation on flanks and back, broad white band around the base of the bill; how this band extends over the culmen is an important clue for separating this species from female Tufted. A pale cheek patch is sometimes observed during the spring and summer months. Juvenile resembles adult female, but with less white above the bill and a browner body. In flight white wing-bar extending to primaries separates Greater from Lesser Scaup. **Voice** Silent in the Canary Islands.

Lesser Scaup *Aythya affinis*   L 38–46 cm, WS 66–74 cm

Vagrant. Freshwater ponds and artificial reservoirs but also on brackish dams. **ID** Summer male has darker vermiculation on back and less rounded head than Greater Scaup, with purple rather than green gloss. The white wing-bar is restricted to the secondaries in Lesser, best seen in flight or when flapping wings. Eclipse male is similar to adult female, but normally darker on the head and breast and some show a hint of grey vermiculation on mantle. Adult female as female Greater Scaup, but the white on face is less extensive and white wing-bar is restricted to secondaries, which separates this duck from all plumages of Tufted Duck. Juvenile similar to adult female, but with brownish not yellowish eye. **Voice** Mostly silent in the Canary Islands.

PLATE 4: DUCKS AND GEESE IV

Ferruginous Duck *Aythya nyroca* L 38–42 cm, WS 63–67 cm
Vagrant. Freshwater reservoirs. **ID** A dark duck with a long bill, peaked crown and a high forehead. Summer male has dark chestnut on head, breast and flanks, with darker upperparts and a conspicuous white eye and white undertail-coverts. Adult female duller and browner, similar to eclipse male, but with dark eye (not white). Juvenile resembles adult female, but sides of head and foreneck are lighter. Similar to female Tufted Duck (Plate 3), but lacks any hint of tuft at rear of head. In flight very conspicuous all-white primaries and secondaries recall female Greater Scaup or Tufted Duck. **Voice** Male gives a short *chuck* during display or a *wheeoo*, female utters a snoring *er, err, err....*

Wood Duck *Aix sponsa* L 43–51 cm, WS 70–76 cm
Vagrant. Lakes, freshwater ponds and lakes with dense wooded vegetation. **ID** Male has orange-white bill, red eye and long crest. Generally, shows iridescent dark plumage (greenish gloss), buff on flanks, and rusty breast. Also has complex white facial and throat markings and a white vertical breast stripe. Confusion possible with escaped Mandarin Duck, which has a double white, vertical breast-stripe and distinctive orange 'sails' on wings. Female, eclipse male and juvenile drab brown, with a broad and slightly uneven white eye-stripe, brownish legs and thin spots on flanks. In flight narrow white trailing edge to secondaries on both upperwing and underwing is diagnostic. **Voice** When flushed an *oo-eek* by the female and a high *jeeeeeee* by the male.

Northern Shoveler *Anas clypeata* L 44–52 cm, WS 73–82 cm
Regular winter migrant (all islands except Go). Prefers freshwater but also brackish areas. **ID** Shovel-shaped bill diagnostic. Summer male with green head, yellow eye, chestnut flanks, white breast and black-and-white ventral region. Pale blue upperwing, white bar on greater coverts and green speculum in flight. Eclipse male as adult female, but more rufous on flanks, head darker and in flight pale blue upper forewing visible. Adult female similar to female Mallard (Plate 5), but huge bill diagnostic at close range and in flight has green speculum with no white trailing edge, as well as grey forewing and dark belly. Juvenile darker overall than adult female, particularly on the crown and hindneck. **Voice** Female has a *gak-gak-gak-gak-gak*, not often heard in Canary Islands.

Blue-winged Teal *Anas discors* L 37–41 cm, WS 60–64 cm
Vagrant. Found in both freshwater and brackish reservoirs. **ID** Summer male with a white, crescent moon-shaped facial patch near the bill, greyish head, brownish speckling on breast and flanks, black-and-white ventral region, and yellowish legs. In flight shows bright blue upper forewing, broad white band along the greater coverts, and dark greenish speculum without pale trailing edge. Adult female and juvenile similar to Garganey, but yellowish legs and no white trailing edge to wings diagnostic. **Voice** A thin whistle *tsee-tsee* is sometimes uttered by the male, not often heard in Canary Islands.

PLATE 5: DUCKS AND GEESE V

Gadwall *Anas strepera*   L 46–56 cm, WS 84–95 cm
Irregular winter migrant (all islands except H and Go). Freshwater reservoirs but also on brackish areas. **ID** Adult male and female easily separated from all other ducks by the small white speculum on inner secondaries, which often shows when bird is on the water. Adult male generally grey and finely vermiculated, grey-black bill, yellow legs. In flight black and chestnut on upperwing and white speculum are noticeable. Adult female, eclipse male and juvenile similar to Mallard, but dark bill has orange sides, clean whitish belly. **Voice** Female has a quacking and repeated *gag-ag-ag-ag-ag*, similar to Mallard.

Eurasian Wigeon *Anas penelope*   L 45–51 cm, WS 71–85 cm
Regular winter migrant (all islands). Prefers inland freshwater and brackish artificial reservoirs. **ID** In all plumages has bluish bill with black nail. Summer male has chestnut head and neck with a creamy-buff forehead that extends along the centre of the crown, black-and-white ventral region, pinkish breast and blue-grey on flanks and mantle. Green speculum and large white patch on upper forewing are distinctive in flight. Eclipse male is reddish-chestnut with white belly and white upper-forewing patch. Adult female and juvenile variable, but overall plumage coloration ranges from uniform rufous-brown to greyish-brown with a whitish belly. Best separated from American Wigeon by greyish axillaries, visible in flight. **Voice** Male a whistling *wheeooo* and female a *krrr* or *karr*.

American Wigeon *Anas americana*   L 48–56 cm, WS 75–86 cm
Vagrant. Freshwater/artificial reservoirs. **ID** Summer male has whitish forehead and central crown-stripe, broad dark green stripe over the eye extending to the nape, and is pinkish-brown overall with black ventral region. Upper forewing similar to Eurasian Wigeon in flight. Adult female, eclipse male and juvenile have grey head, neck and upperparts that contrast with the rufous flanks and breast. White axillaries diagnostic in all plumages (greyish in Eurasian Wigeon). **Voice** Disyllabic *wheeoo-wo*.

Mallard *Anas platyrhynchos*   L 50–60 cm, WS 81–95 cm
Vagrant but feral birds also present. **ID** Summer male with green head, thin white neck collar, yellow bill, chestnut breast, grey flanks and mantle, black-and-white ventral region, central tail-feathers curled upwards, orange legs. Adult female confusable with Gadwall, but purple-blue speculum with broad white borders, uneven orange at sides of bill, and whitish sides to tail are diagnostic. Eclipse male with uniform yellow bill. Juvenile similar to adult female. Purple-blue speculum with broad white borders in both sexes obvious in flight. **Voice** Anxiously repeated notes *quak-quak-quak-qua....*

Gadwall

Eurasian Wigeon

American Wigeon

Mallard

PLATE 6: DUCKS AND GEESE VI

Northern Pintail *Anas acuta* L 55–60 cm, WS 80–95 cm
Regular winter migrant (all islands except Go). On both fresh and brackish artificial reservoirs. **ID** Summer male with blackish head, grey flanks, white breast and belly, black-and-white ventral region, darkish-grey legs and long central tail feathers. Green speculum bordered white behind and creamy in front is diagnostic in flight. Adult female with grey bill, speculum dark brown and tail long and pointed, but no eye-stripe. Juvenile as adult female, but is more scalloped overall and speculum is dull brown, although greenish in males. Eclipse male as adult female, but retains some features of adult male such as the two-tone greyish bill, longer and greyer scapulars and upperwing pattern. **Voice** Male a soft *prep-preep* similar to Eurasian Teal.

Eurasian Teal *Anas crecca* L 34–38 cm, WS 58–64 cm
Regular winter migrant (all islands). Freshwater and brackish artificial reservoirs. **ID** Summer male has grey body with a horizontal white stripe, chestnut head with greenish sides that appear bordered by whitish-yellowish line, a black-bordered yellow ventral region, and a white-bordered green speculum (diagnostic in flight). Eclipse male and juvenile very similar to adult female. Adult female with brown streaked body, but has a white-bordered green speculum, some orange at the base of the bill, a conspicuous white stripe at the base of the tail, plainer face pattern, and a brownish throat. **Voice** A nasal *quak* by the female, often heard when flushed. [Alt: Common Teal]

Green-winged Teal *Anas carolinensis* L 36–37 cm, WS 58–59 cm
Vagrant. Prefers freshwater ponds but also artificial brackish reservoirs. **ID** Summer male has a diagnostic vertical white line on side of breast and no or narrower buff lines bordering the green on the head than Eurasian Teal. Adult female shows more cinnamon-buff on the leading edge of the speculum, but this is variable and sometimes difficult to assess. **Voice** Similar to Eurasian Teal. **Tax.** Sometimes treated as conspecific with Eurasian Teal.

Garganey *Anas querquedula* L 37–41 cm, WS 59–67 cm
Seasonal visitor (all islands except Go). Freshwater reservoirs but also brackish dams in eastern Canary Islands. **ID** Summer male has brownish-purple head with a conspicuous white crescent over the eye extending to the nape, brownish breast, pale grey flanks, black-and-white scapulars and dark legs. In flight pale grey upperwing contrasts with the brownish speculum, which has broad white margins. Eclipse male like adult female, but retains pale blue-grey on forewing. Adult female with no orange at the base of the bill, a neatly striped facial pattern with a pale loral patch near the base of the bill, no pale patch at base of tail feathers, and whitish throat. White border to brownish speculum broader on the trailing edge, diagnostic in flight. Juvenile has narrower white trailing edge to secondaries than adult female. **Voice** A *quak* in flight, resembling Eurasian Teal.

Northern Pintail

Eurasian Teal

Green-winged Teal

Garganey

PLATE 7: PARTRIDGES, QUAIL AND FLAMINGOS

Barbary Partridge *Alectoris barbara*   L 32–34 cm, WS 46–49 cm
Introduced (all islands except GC). Occurs from lower semi-desert scrub of *Euphorbia* to higher Alpine zone, but prefers cultivated areas. **ID** Adult has diagnostic light grey bib bordered by a reddish-brown, white-spotted collar. Dark brown median crown-stripe. Similar to Red-legged Partridge in slate-grey breast, rufous belly and undertail-coverts, red bill and legs, and heavy streaks on flanks. In flight shows reddish outer tail-feathers as in Red-legged, but shoulders are pale blue-grey (not brownish-black). **Voice** A repeated *ka-ke-lick, ka-ke-lick…*, often heard at long distance. The male has a rising territorial whistling call *thooeeeH*, often given from top of a rock. A rapid and loud *tre tre tre tre cheecheche tre tre tre tre…* when flushed. **Tax.** Ssp. *koenigi* in the region.

Red-legged Partridge *Alectoris rufa*   L 32–35 cm, WS 47–50 cm
Introduced (GC). Favours semi-desert scrub, cultivated areas in lowland and grassy hillsides. **ID** Similar to Barbary Partridge, but has a white throat (not light grey) bordered with black, and heavy black streaks on the upper breast (reddish-brown collar with white spots on Barbary). Slate grey on lower breast, rufous belly and undertail-coverts, red legs and bill, heavy streaks on the flanks and brownish mantle, but no dark median crown-stripe as Barbary. In flight shows reddish-brown outer tail-feathers. **Voice** Males advertise presence by harsh repeated *goCHAK-CHAK-CHAK goCHAK goCHAK-CHAK…*. **Tax.** Ssp. *intercedens* on Gran Canaria.

Common Quail *Coturnix coturnix*   L 16–18 cm, WS 32–35 cm
Resident breeder and migrant breeder in the summer (all islands), mainly in cereal crops, but also mixed crops with potatoes and in grasslands. **ID** Both sexes are brownish overall with buff underside, with a creamy supercilium extending towards nape, narrow white streaks on mantle and heavy whitish stripes on flanks. Male has a black anchor-shape on throat, often surrounded by rufous; female has a pale throat. Juvenile recalls adult female, but has spotted not streaked chest and flanks, and facial pattern is less marked. In flight, the rapid wing-beats, produced by long wings and direct low flight, are diagnostic. Confusion only likely with chicks of the *Alectoris* species, which have blunt-tipped wings and much slower flight. **Voice** A trisyllabic *wet-my-lips* by male, also a low *maaiwhit*. Female a cricket-like *cree-cree, cree-cree, cree-cree…* rarely heard. **Tax.** Ssp. *confisa* in the past but today the nominate subspecies is broadly accepted.

Lesser Flamingo *Phoeniconaias minor*   L 80–105 cm, WS 95–120 cm
Vagrant, but since birds are kept in collections some records may be of escapes. Prefers freshwater reservoirs when available. **ID** In flight similar to Greater Flamingo, but deep pinkish-plumaged individuals easy to spot. In structure also similar to Greater but smaller with shorter legs. Bill shape and colour diagnostic, abrupt bend and deep red bill (not pinkish as in Greater) with black tip, also red eye surrounded by bare skin. Deeper pink plumage, but this is variable and therefore not diagnostic as paler-plumaged individuals can be found. Juvenile very similar to juvenile Greater. Juvenile Lesser shows darker purplish-brown bill, compared to the pale greyish of Greater with contrasting dark tip. This, along with darker plumage and structural differences, are the best ways to separating them. **Voice** A high-pitched *kwirrik* similar to White-fronted Goose may be given in flight.

Greater Flamingo *Phoenicopterus roseus*   L 120–145 cm, WS 140–170 cm
Vagrant. Associated with saltpans, freshwater and brackish reservoirs. **ID** Easy to identify but confusion likely with Lesser (which see). Adult is white with a pink tinge overall, pinkish bill with dark tip, reddish legs and wing-coverts, and black flight feathers. Juvenile is similar to adult, but smaller (recalling Lesser) and overall appearance is grey-brown with white belly and ventral region, greyish bill and dark legs. In flight neck and legs are held fully extended and red on wing-coverts is conspicuous even at long range. **Voice** In flight gives a repetitive *kuk-kuk, ke-kuk, kuk-kuk…*, and a typical Greylag Goose-like honking *ka-ha*.

Barbary Partridge — ad

Red-legged Partridge — ad

Common Quail — ad ♂, ad ♀

Lesser Flamingo — ad, juv

Greater Flamingo — juv, ad

PLATE 8: DIVERS AND GREBES

Great Northern Diver *Gavia immer* L 69–91 cm, WS 127–147 cm

Vagrant. Coastal waters during the winter in Canary Islands. **ID** Adult in summer unmistakable, with black head and neck, a white collar consisting of vertical white lines (also smaller patch near the throat), white chest, evenly spaced white patches on mantle, straight dark bill, peaked forehead and red eye. Adult in winter holds its grey-white bill horizontally, shows a different neck pattern to winter Black-throated Diver (dark half-collar with white indentation above is diagnostic) and has a conspicuous white eye-ring. Juvenile recalls adult in winter but creamy fringes of feathers create a scaly aspect to the mantle. In flight, all plumages show very large feet compared to other divers. **Voice** Unlikely to be heard in the Canary Islands. [Alt: Common Loon]

Black-throated Diver *Gavia arctica* L 58–73 cm, WS 110–130 cm

Vagrant. Prefers coastal waters while in the archipelago. **ID** Adult in summer plumage has grey crown and hindneck, black neck patch and throat, white patches on mantle and a straight dark bill. Non-breeding adult has half neck white, a steep forehead, white flank patch at the rear, a prominent chest, blackish mantle and pale grey bill with dark tip. Juvenile as adult in winter, but browner with neat scales on the mantle. At long range the absence of a dark half-collar and a white indentation above identifies Black-throated from Great Northern Diver. **Voice** Generally silent on wintering grounds or while dispersing. [Alt: Black-throated Loon]

Pied-billed Grebe *Podilymbus podiceps* L 31–38 cm, WS 56–64 cm

Vagrant. Prefers freshwater reservoirs. **ID** Confusion possible with Little Grebe. During the winter, the plumage most likely to be found, the adult loses the band on the bill and the black throat but bill still thick and heavy compared to other similar-sized grebes. Summer adult dark brownish-grey overall with a conspicuous black vertical band on the greyish bill, black throat, white eye-ring and white ventral region (darkish while moulting from winter to summer plumage). In flight no obvious white patches are visible as in most other grebes, Little Grebe excluded, but a thin whitish trailing edge sometimes visible on secondaries. Juvenile lacks black band on bill and the whitish eye-ring. **Voice** Silent when in the region.

Black-necked Grebe *Podiceps nigricollis* L 28–34 cm, WS 56–60 cm

Regular winter migrant (all islands except Go). In the Canary Islands favours coastal lagoons (e.g. Janubio) and inland freshwater artificial reservoirs. **ID** Summer adult has black head with peaked crown, black throat, chest and upperparts, chestnut flanks, a conspicuous golden fan of feathers on the cheeks and a red eye. Winter adult has steep forehead, peaked crown and darkish cheeks – black extending well below the eye. Juvenile similar to juvenile Little Grebe, but separated by red eye and the lack of black stripes on the face. In flight in all plumages Black-necked only shows white patches on the secondaries and some inner primaries. **Voice** Mostly silent in the Canary Islands.

Little Grebe *Tachybaptus ruficollis* L 23–29 cm, WS 40–45 cm

Vagrant. In the archipelago prefers coastal lagoons and brackish inland reservoirs. **ID** Summer adult has chestnut cheeks and foreneck, black crown and nape, conspicuous yellow gape, straight, black bill and black upperparts. Winter adult is generally brown-buff (not grey-white as in *Podiceps* grebes), contrasting with darker crown and upperparts; bill becomes pale during the non-breeding period. Confusion likely with Nearctic vagrant Pied-billed Grebe, but bill thinner. Juvenile as winter adult, but with different face pattern created by two dark horizontal lines – one below the eye and another at the bill base. In flight no white on the wings is visible, as in Pied-billed Grebe. **Voice** Silent when not breeding.

Great Northern Diver

ad breeding

ad non-breeding

Black-throated Diver

ad breeding

ad non-breeding

Pied-billed Grebe

ad breeding

ad non-breeding

Black-necked Grebe

ad breeding

ad non-breeding

Little Grebe

ad breeding

ad non-breeding

PLATE 9: STORM-PETRELS

Wilson's Storm-petrel *Oceanites oceanicus*   L 16–18 cm, WS 38–42 cm

Vagrant. Breeds in the Southern Hemisphere, migrating to and from the north Atlantic in May/June and then October/November. **ID** Similar to European and Madeiran in shape and amount of white on rump, but often white extends far down on sides and encircles the tail. The square tail is similar to European, but Wilson's lacks a white line on the underwing, and toes project beyond the tail, diagnostic to separate Wilson's from similar species. Pale carpal bar on upperwing similar to Madeiran, but shape of wings shows no angle on leading edge, permitting long glides on flat wings. Often follows boats. **Voice** Feeding birds at sea often give a soft chattering call, but mainly silent.

White-faced Storm-petrel *Pelagodroma marina*   L 19–21 cm, WS 41–44 cm

Migrant breeder in summer (mc, a), from March to August. Breeds colonially in burrows excavated in the sand and disperses to pelagic waters outside the breeding season. **ID** Unmistakable but at long range and in rough seas the grey-brown upperparts may recall a winter-plumaged Grey Phalarope, but note diagnostic paddle-shaped (not pointed) wings and very long legs. Flight action differs from Grey Phalarope, sailing low and regularly kicking off the surface in a bouncing manner. Sometimes associated with cetaceans, but does not tend to follow boats. At close range the face mask and the yellow webs are visible. **Voice** In breeding burrow utters a mournful and monotonous *coo*, repeated every three or six seconds and lasting for a couple of minutes. Silent at sea. **Tax.** The ssp. *hypoleuca* breeds in Canary Islands.

Black-bellied Storm-petrel *Fregetta tropica*   L 19–21 cm, WS 43–63 cm

Vagrant. Only recorded near the Conception Bank, off north-east Lanzarote. Pelagic away from the breeding grounds. **ID** In size is similar to the more common Madeiran, but toes project slightly beyond tail tip. A black storm petrel with white flanks and underwing contrasting with the black line on the belly. White undertail-coverts. **Voice** Silent at sea.

European Storm-petrel *Hydrobates pelagicus*   L 15–16 cm, WS 37–41 cm

Migrant breeder in summer (H, Go, T, F, g, mc, a), from June to October. Breeds in crevices in piles of boulders on offshore islets or along inaccessible coastlines. Mainly pelagic when not breeding. **ID** It can be separated from all other black storm-petrels in the region by the broad whitish band on the centre of the underwing and a more active flight with frequent twists, turns, glides and bat-like fluttering near the surface. When feeding holds wings in V-shape and tends to patter on surface, although this is sometimes hard to see in rough conditions. Often follows small fishing boats, but not large ferries. At first sight at sea, it may recall a House Martin. **Voice** Gives a harsh *aurrr-r-r-r-r-r-r-r-r* ending with a hiccup-type *chikka*, in the burrow. During courtship flight utters a sharp *terr-chick*, accentuated on the second syllable.

Madeiran Storm-petrel *Oceanodroma castro*   L 19–21 cm, WS 44–46 cm

Migrant breeder in winter (H, T, L, mc, a), from October to February. Visits offshore islets and inaccessible rocky coasts, and nests in crevices in piles of boulders or in burrows made in sandy and soft substrates. Pelagic away from breeding grounds and often seen alone or in very small parties. **ID** A black storm petrel with a white rump, similar to Leach's, but less so to smaller European or Wilson's, whose feet project beyond tail when in the air. It can be separated from Leach's by the less conspicuous carpal bar, a wider rump that in most individuals extends to sides, less forked tail, and black face (not greyish). In flight Leach's has more pronounced angle at carpal joint than Madeiran (with similar wing span), whereas Wilson's has a shorter and straighter wing overall. In flight takes diagnostically few deep wing-beats interspersed with long shearwater-like glides, and tends to zigzag low on water. **Voice** Silent away from breeding grounds. Most typical call in burrow is a six-syllable *kair chuc-a-chuc-chuc-chuc*. [Alt: Band-rumped Storm-petrel]

Swinhoe's Storm-petrel *Oceanodroma monorhis*   L 18–21 cm, WS 45–48 cm

Vagrant. Pelagic when not breeding. **ID** An all dark storm-petrel from east Asia, similar to Leach's in size, structure, plumage and flight action. It can be separated from all storm-petrels in Canary Islands by the lack of a white rump patch and the presence of white on the shafts of the outer primary feathers, though the latter is difficult to see even at close range. Confusion is also likely with larger Bulwer's Petrel (Plate 11). Does not follow boats. **Voice** Silent away from the breeding colonies and when at sea.

Leach's Storm-petrel *Oceanodroma leucorhoa*   L 18–21 cm, WS 43–48 cm

Seasonal visitor (all islands except H). Breeds in the north Atlantic, but moves to south Atlantic in winter. Pelagic when not breeding. **ID** A black storm-petrel larger than European, but most similar in size to Madeiran. It can be separated by its longer forked tail, a V-shaped white rump divided in the middle and not reaching far down each side (not visible at long range). In flight may recall a tern and the carpal bar is sometimes more conspicuous than the white rump, the opposite to most Madeirans. Face is sometimes greyish (not black). In strong winds a few tern-like powerful wing-beats are interspersed by shearwater-like gliding (most typical flight action in Madeiran). Occasionally follows boats. **Voice** Silent away from breeding colonies and at sea.

Wilson's Storm-petrel
ad

White-faced Storm-petrel
ad
hypoleuca

Black-bellied Storm-petrel
ad

European Storm-petrel
ad

Madeiran Storm-petrel
ad

Swinhoe's Storm-petrel
ad

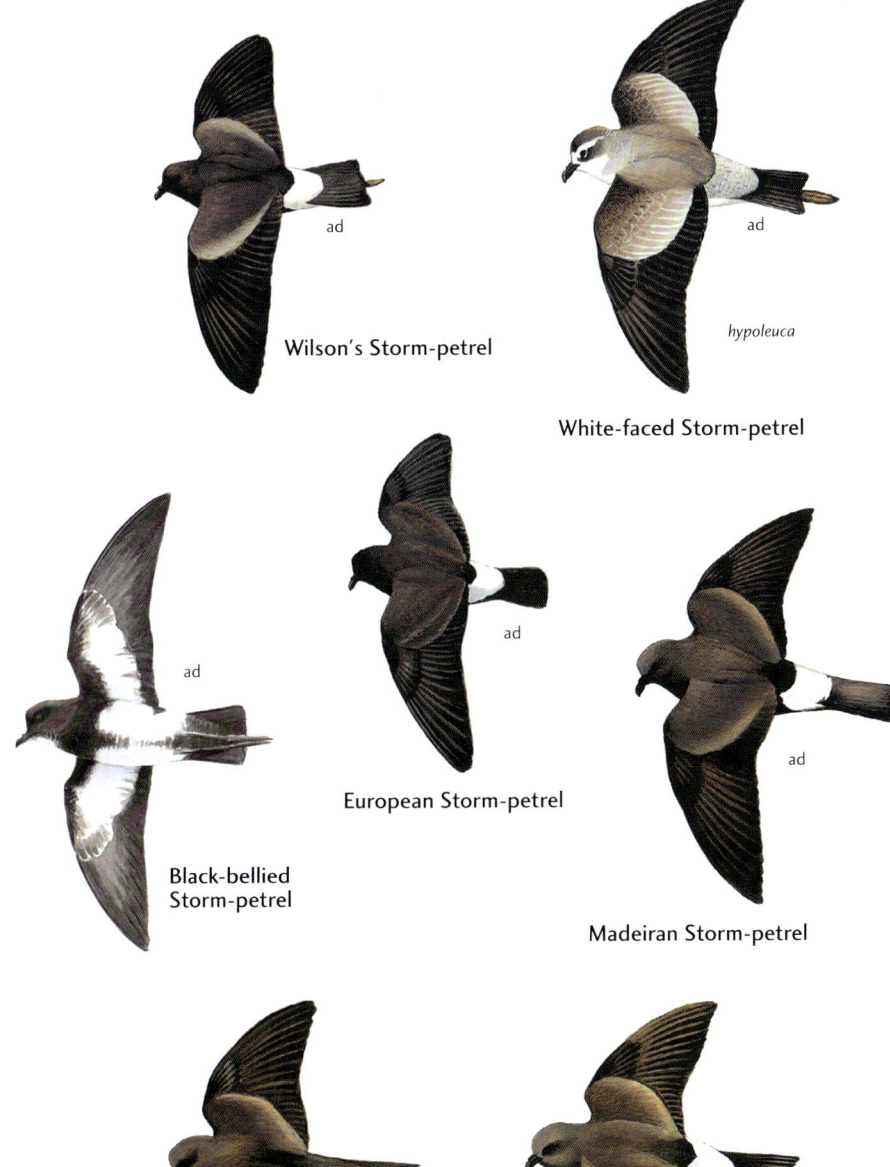

Leach's Storm-petrel
ad

PLATE 10: PETRELS AND SHEARWATERS I

Northern Fulmar *Fulmarus glacialis*   L 45–50 cm, WS 102–112 cm

Vagrant. Pelagic away from the breeding colonies, but can occur in inshore and offshore waters. **ID** Similar to slightly larger Yellow-legged Gull, but no dark wingtips with white mirrors, lack of white trailing edge, stout grey-yellow bill, pale primary patches on the upperwing, thicker neck and a shearwater-like flight pattern. Several morphs can be found which are not clearly differentiated. Most common plumage in Canary Islands is light grey above and white below with a white head and a black spot next to eye. An almost all-dark morph exists, with black lores, vertical band on the bill and conspicuous white panels on the upperwings. This dark morph can be confused with Cory's Shearwater, which is structurally different, browner and flies with less stiff wing-beats. **Voice** Silent when not breeding and hence difficult to hear in Canary Islands.

Desertas Petrel *Pterodroma deserta* (not illustrated)   L 36–37 cm, WS 86–94 cm

Vagrant, identified only as one of *Pterodroma feae/deserta/madeira*. Visits breeding colonies only at night and pelagic at sea during the rest of the year. **ID** At very long range could be mistaken for a Cory's or Great Shearwater but normally flying much higher than the shearwaters. A cryptic species, very similar in shape, structure and plumage to Fea's Petrel (which see) and very difficult to separate at sea from this and from Zino's Petrel. Differs from Fea's and Zino's Petrels genetically and by having a significantly longer and deeper bill, also a longer tarsus. Desertas Petrel starts visiting its breeding sites off Madeira from mid-May onwards while Zino's returns slightly earlier, from mid-April onwards. **Voice** Silent at sea but near the colonies gives a relatively long mournful sound not unlike Zino's. **Tax.** Recently split from Fea's Petrel. *P. deserta*, *P. feae* and *P. madeira* form a monophyletic clade with the closely related Bermuda Petrel *P. cahow* and Black-capped Petrel *P. hasitata*. [Alt: Bugio Petrel]

Zino's Petrel *Pterodroma madeira*   L 32–34 cm, WS 80–86 cm

Vagrant, identified only as one of *Pterodroma feae/deserta/madeira*. Pelagic at sea away from the breeding season and visits breeding colonies only at night. **ID** Almost identical in plumage to Desertas and Fea's Petrels, but the smallest of all (in the hand). At sea the thinner bill and shorter wingspan of Zino's is very difficult to evaluate objectively. **Voice** Mainly silent at sea, but near the colonies gives a whimpering cry and a Tawny Owl-like *uuuu…u-u-u-u*, less mournful than Desertas Petrel. [Alt: Madeira Petrel]

Fea's Petrel *Pterodroma feae*   L 36–37 cm, WS 86–94 cm

Vagrant, identified only as one of *Pterodroma feae/deserta/madeira*. Pelagic when not breeding. **ID** In flight, almost all-dark underwing contrasting with white underside, and high, arcing flight manner, are diagnostic features of this genus. Across the upperparts an M-shape is sometimes visible. The tail is long, all whitish-grey and pointed; has stout, black bill and dark spot below the eye. Very similar to Desertas and Zino's Petrels, but intermediate bill differences can aid separation (though most useful in the hand). Away from Cape Verde Islands between May to November. **Voice** Silent at sea but near colonies moaning calls are similar to Zino's Petrel, but on average slightly lower pitched (the high-pitched whimpering calls of Zino's are seldom heard). Most typical sound is a relatively long mournful call similar to Tawny Owl. [Alt: Cape Verde Petrel]

Cory's Shearwater *Calonectris borealis*   L 50–56 cm, WS 118–126 cm

Migrant breeder in summer (all islands) from February to November. Nests in burrows on cliffs near the coast and in holes of inland gullies at mid-elevation. Pelagic during the non-breeding period, when it migrates toward Brazilian waters. **ID** Overall is brownish on top and white below, with dirty-grey head, neck and sides of breast. In flight wings are held slightly forward and flexed; normal flight action consists of a few strong wing-beats followed by a long glide near the water's surface. Very often follows boats and may congregate in big flocks (rafts) near the coast. Similar to Great Shearwater (Plate 11) and smaller than Cape Verde Shearwater (Plate 11), but lack of white on nape (collar) and yellowish bill with dark tip are diagnostic, even at very long range. Confusion also likely with vagrant Scopoli's Shearwater, which has white on underwing extending to tip of wing. **Voice** At night and near its breeding burrows has a repetitive *keeowwrrah*. Silent at sea. **Tax.** Recently split from Scopoli's Shearwater, based on significant genetic, morphological and ecological differences.

Scopoli's Shearwater *Calonectris diomedea* (not illustrated)   L 45–52 cm, WS 112–122 cm

Vagrant. Pelagic away from breeding grounds, mixing with Cory's Shearwater in winter at the Benguela and Agulhas currents, the Brazilian current and the Canary current. **ID** Almost identical to Cory's Shearwater but on average slightly smaller with a less heavy bill, but these features very difficult to assess at sea. With the correct light conditions the most useful field mark is the amount of white on the outer tip of the wings (less extensive on Cory's), most easily assessed when photographed. **Voice** Unlikely to be heard in the Canary Islands. **Tax.** Considered to be a separate species from the closely related Cory's, based on genetics, morphology and ecological differences.

Northern Fulmar

Zino's Petrel

ad
ad
ad

Fea's Petrel

ad
ad

Cory's Shearwater

ad
ad

PLATE 11: PETRELS AND SHEARWATERS II

Cape Verde Shearwater *Calonectris edwardsii*   L 40–41 cm, WS 90–110 cm
Vagrant. Pelagic when not breeding, dispersing to waters near the south coast of Brazil and Uruguay. In the Canary Islands all birds ringed in May–June and never recorded reliably at sea. **ID** Very similar to Cory's but bill all dark, slightly smaller with more plumage contrast overall, darker head and upperparts. Confusion likely with bigger Great Shearwater, but lacks that species' distinctive white collar on nape. Flight action similar to Cory's and often follows boats; also forms rafts at sea near breeding colonies. Overall blackish on upperside, with whitish underside and a subterminal band on the tail. **Voice** Silent when not breeding. **Tax.** Now considered a distinct species from Cory's.

Great Shearwater *Ardenna gravis*   L 43–51 cm, WS 105–122 cm
Seasonal visitor (all Canarian seas), from August to October, when returning to the South Atlantic to breed. Pelagic away from the breeding colonies. **ID** Differs from Cory's in white collar on the nape, creating a conspicuous cap that is visible at very long range, thin, dark bill, whiter subterminal band on tail, dirty-looking belly and vent, and dark markings on axillaries. In flight has stiffer and more rapid wing-beats than Cory's, similar to Manx Shearwater, and often follows boats. Juvenile resembles adult. As with other tubenoses, sexes are alike. **Voice** Mainly silent at sea.

Sooty Shearwater *Ardenna grisea*   L 40–50 cm, WS 95–110 cm
Vagrant, mainly from August to October when it moves south to its breeding grounds in the southern hemisphere. Pelagic when migrating. **ID** A medium-sized all-dark shearwater (including bill and legs), which can be confused with Balearic Shearwater, which, though, is slightly smaller, often with a whitish centre to belly (not visible at long range or on darker individuals), shorter wings and may appear fatter on the belly and less slim and athletic in the air. In flight has long and narrow wings and the shearwater-like long glides are followed by a few quick stiff-winged flaps. With good light conditions shows brownish plumage overall with silvery-grey underwings, but in bad light looks all black, including the underwing. **Voice** Silent when not in breeding grounds.

Manx Shearwater *Puffinus puffinus*   L 30–35 cm, WS 71–83 cm
Migrant breeder in summer (P, possibly extinct on T), from February to September. Breeds in burrows in laurel forest. **ID** A medium-sized shearwater with black upperparts (no white subterminal band on the tail), white underside including the underwing, dark bill and dark area of head extends below the eye. Does not normally follow boats. Confusion likely only with Barolo Shearwater and vagrant Boyd's Shearwater, which have an auk-like direct flight with stiff-winged wing-beats. **Voice** When approaching the breeding colonies and at night utters a loud *chi-ki-ga-how*. Silent at sea when foraging.

Barolo Shearwater *Puffinus baroli*   L 25–30 cm, WS 58–67 cm
Resident breeder (Go, T, L, g, mc, a), but declining. Breeds in crevices on coastal cliffs and disperses probably within Macaronesia. **ID** Its black-and-white appearance can cause confusion with Manx, but shorter and rounder wings produce a diagnostic flight action consisting of a series of rapid wing-beats in a straight line (auk-like), followed by a very short, low glide from side to side, even in strong winds. Does not follow boats. The vagrant Boyd's Shearwater from the Cape Verde Islands has black reaching below the eye (as in Manx) and dark undertail-coverts. **Voice** At night when approaching the cliffs it utters a high-pitched *he-he-he-he-he-heooow*, the introductory notes varying from five to eight. Silent at sea when foraging or resting within rafts of other shearwaters. **Tax.** Formerly treated as a subspecies of Little Shearwater *P. assimilis* or Audubon's Shearwater *P. lherminieri*. [Alt: Macaronesian Shearwater]

Bulwer's Petrel *Bulweria bulwerii*   L 25–29 cm, WS 67–73 cm
Migrant breeder in summer (all islands except F), from April to November. Pelagic; visits colonies only at night. **ID** Unmistakable. A medium-sized, all-dark petrel, with narrow wings, longish tail and creamy carpal bar (only visible in good light). In flight tends to zigzag dynamically and erratically when gliding low over water. Does not follow boats and normally observed singly, never in flocks. Confusion likely with Sooty and Balearic Shearwaters but no silvery-white on underwings. **Voice** Silent away from the breeding colonies where a repetitive dog-like bark may be heard: *gow, gow, gow, gow....*

Cape Verde Shearwater

Great Shearwater

Sooty Shearwater

Barolo Shearwater

Manx Shearwater

Bulwer's Petrel

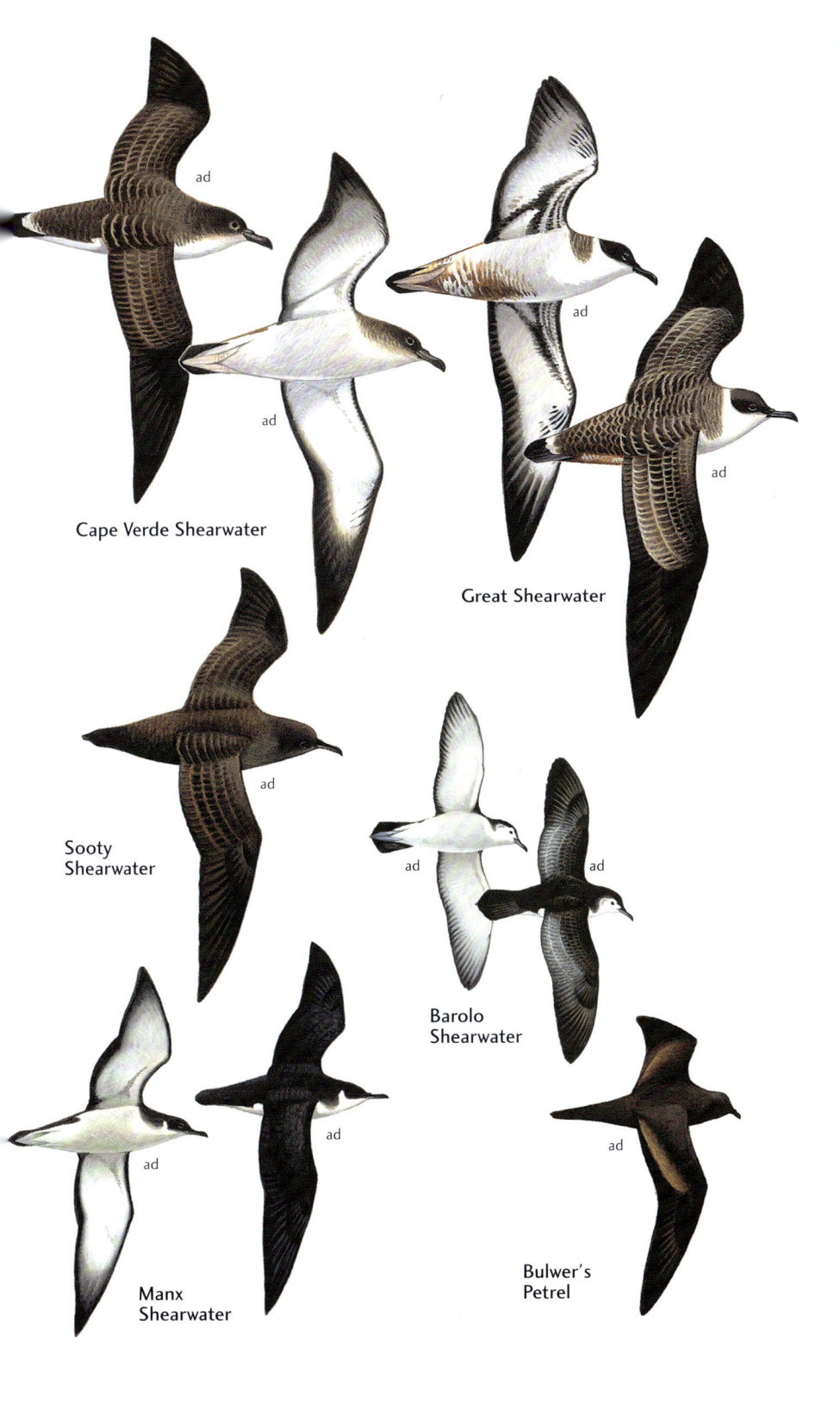

PLATE 12: STORKS AND BITTERNS

White Stork *Ciconia ciconia*　　　　　　　　　　　　　　　L 95–110 cm, WS 180–218 cm

Seasonal visitor (all islands). Favours semi-desert coastal scrub and rubbish dumps for foraging but also intertidal coastal lagoons and freshwater reservoirs. **ID** In flight neck held straight and legs projecting; white underwing-coverts contrasting with black primaries and secondaries (diagnostic). Adult has white head, neck, mantle, wing-coverts and underside, red bill, red-pinkish legs, and short dark line across the eye (visible at closer range). Juvenile similar to adult in overall plumage and leg coloration, but bill is reddish with a dark tip, best observed at close range. **Voice** Silent away from the breeding areas.

Black Stork *Ciconia nigra*　　　　　　　　　　　　　　　L 90–105 cm, WS 173–205 cm

Vagrant. In the Canary Islands associated with freshwater artificial reservoirs. **ID** In certain strong light the upperparts can look as white as White Stork. Juvenile is similar to adult, but bill, legs and bare skin around the eye are grey-green (not red), upperparts are dull greenish-black. Adult has violet green metallic gloss on head, neck, chest and upperparts contrasting with red bill and legs, white belly and ventral region; reddish area of bare skin around the eye. In flight underwing-coverts almost all black, but a white triangle appearing near axillaries. **Voice** Unlikely to be heard in the region.

Eurasian Bittern *Botaurus stellaris*　　　　　　　　　　　　L 69–81 cm, WS 100–130 cm

Vagrant. Prefers freshwater ponds with dense fringing vegetation of reeds. **ID** In flight the upperwing is uniformly dark and the primaries and secondaries are heavily barred. Shorter legs and thicker bill than Grey Heron and normally assumes a typical posture when camouflaged in reedbeds, with the bill pointing to the sky. Buff-brown overall with a black crown. Distinguished from the vagrant American Bittern by the absence of a pale eyebrow. The adult also has a black moustachial stripe, which is brownish in juveniles, as is the crown. **Voice** Unlikely to be heard away from breeding areas, but a harsh *krau* in flight is sometimes heard.

Little Bittern *Ixobrychus minutus*　　　　　　　　　　　　L 33–38 cm, WS 49–58 cm

Occasional breeder (T) and seasonal visitor (all islands). Breeds in small freshwater irrigation ponds with dense fringing vegetation. Prefers freshwater but also in brackish reservoirs when visiting. **ID** Adult male has black crown and upperparts contrasting with orange belly, greyish face and conspicuous buff-white wing patches, yellow bill and greenish legs. Adult female is browner and streakier overall, with dark brown crown and dark streaked upperparts, brownish face and neck, buff-brown wing patches, yellow bill and greenish legs; the thin streaks on the foreneck extend toward the flanks. In flight male can be separated from female or juvenile by the buff-white wing patch (not buff-brown). Juvenile similar to adult female, but more heavily streaked on sides of neck, upperparts and wing patches, and has yellow bill and greenish legs. The male of the vagrant ssp. *payesii* has chestnut on the neck. **Voice** A continuous series of low *hogh* notes repeated every two seconds, often heard at dusk. **Tax.** Nominate ssp. *minutus* breeds in the region.

Dwarf Bittern *Ixobrychus sturmii*　　　　　　　　　　　　L 30–31 cm, WS 50–52 cm

Vagrant. Favours small freshwater ponds and reservoirs with dense fringing vegetation. **ID** Superficially similar to Little but mainly dark bluish on head, hindneck, mantle and wings. Foreneck has dark streaks that extend to the flanks and belly, while ventral region is deep reddish. The bill is dark, contrasting with the blue facial skin, only visible at close range. The legs and feet are deep yellow. Sexes are similar; juvenile differs from adult in having duller and browner mantle and wing-coverts, and more rufous on the underside, extending from the chest to the ventral region. **Voice** Gives a soft *croak* when flushed.

White Stork ad

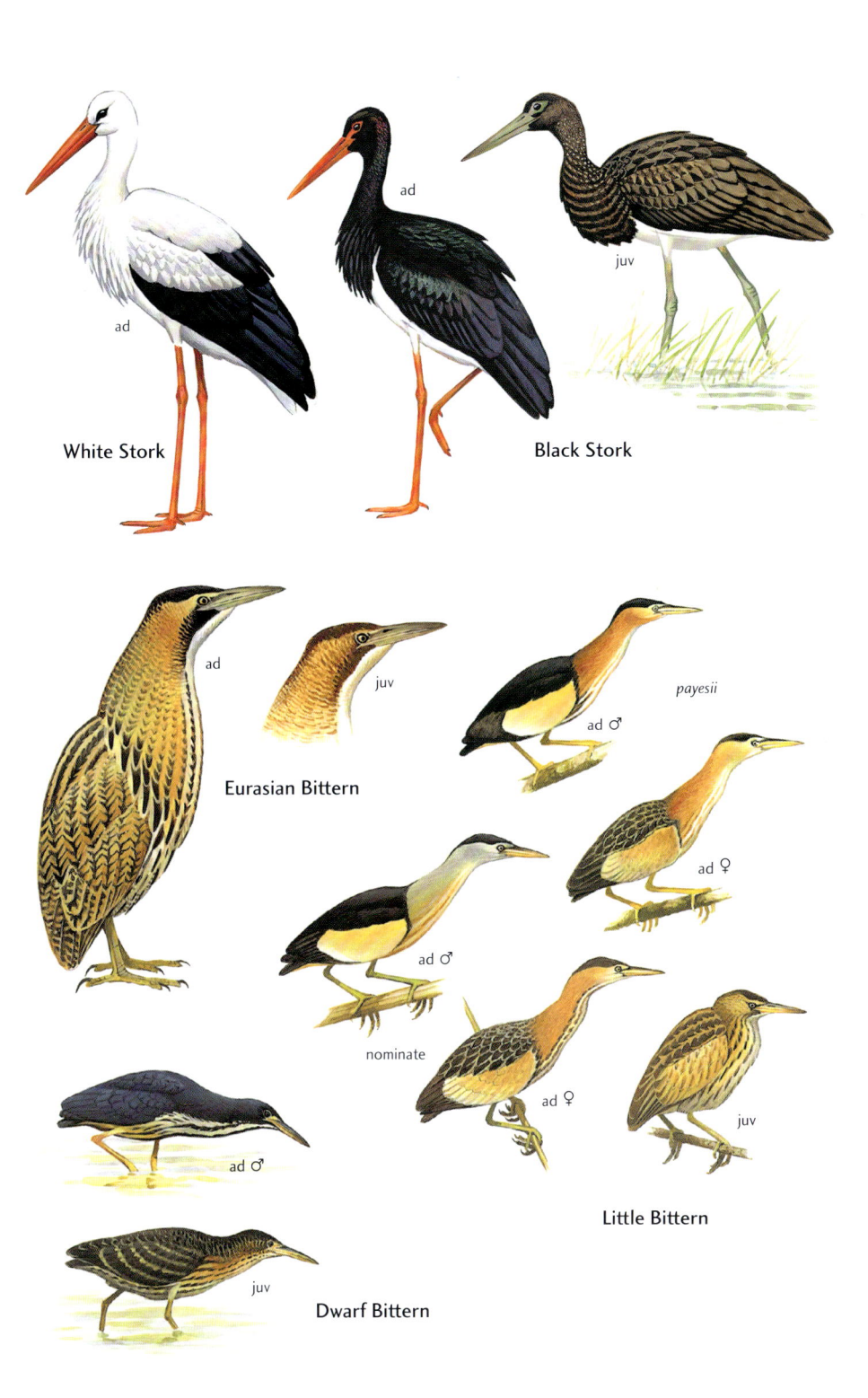

Black Stork ad

juv

Eurasian Bittern ad

juv

Little Bittern
payesii ad ♂
ad ♀
nominate ad ♂
ad ♀
juv

Dwarf Bittern
ad ♂
juv

PLATE 13: HERONS I

Black-crowned Night Heron *Nycticorax nycticorax*   L 58–65 cm, WS 90–100 cm
Resident breeder (T, GC) and seasonal visitor (all islands). Breeds in very small colonies close to freshwater ponds and artificial reservoirs. Non-breeding birds visit both freshwater and brackish areas. **ID** Sexes similar. In flight the light grey wings contrast with the black back, although sometimes difficult to see at long range, and the bill often points down. Adult has black crown and upperparts contrasting with lighter grey of rest of body, yellow legs (reddish during breeding), dark bill, red eye and white plumes that are often visible during the breeding season. Juvenile and first-winter are mainly brownish with streaks on the chest and are heavily pale-spotted on upperparts. Confusion possible with immature and adult winter Squacco Heron, which lacks pale spots on upper body. Second-winter individuals are similar to adult, but have grey-brown on crown and upperparts and some diffuse streaks on chest are still visible. **Voice** A frog-like *quark* sometimes heard in flight. **Tax.** Nominate race breeds in the archipelago.

Squacco Heron *Ardeola ralloides*   L 40–49 cm, WS 71–86 cm
Seasonal visitor (all islands except H). Favours freshwater ponds and reservoirs with lush fringing vegetation when available. **ID** Adult in winter, and immature plumage, differs from adult summer plumage in having heavily streaked head and neck, darker upperparts, no elongated nape feathers and yellowish legs. Summer adult shows light brown upperparts and chest contrasting with white underside and wings, elongated nape feathers, bill with bluish base and dark tip, reddish legs and yellow eyes. In flight and at long range the brownish upperparts are sometimes difficult to see and birds tend to look all white. **Voice** May give a frog-like *kaahk*.

Western Cattle Egret *Bubulcus ibis*   L 45–52 cm, WS 82–95 cm
Resident breeder (L) and regular winter migrant (all islands). Nests colonially on trees and overwinters near chicken farms, freshwater reservoirs and golf courses. **ID** Less elegant than other white egrets, with a round head, short retracted neck and a short bill. Adult non-breeding all white with a yellow bill and greyish legs. Adult in summer has orange crown, chest and rump, reddish bill and orange legs contrasting with white body. In flight flocks do not maintain formation, and fast wing-beats are diagnostic. **Voice** A hoarse buzz may be heard at breeding colony and a soft flight-call *kre* is often heard. **Tax.** Eastern Asian form now separated as Eastern Cattle Egret *B. coromandus*.

Western Reef Heron *Egretta gularis*   L 55–68 cm, WS 88–112 cm
Vagrant. Prefers freshwater ponds and artificial reservoirs, inland and near the coast. **ID** Two colour morphs. The dark morph (most likely) has a white throat and a yellowish bill contrasting with the dark grey body and dark legs, but also has yellowish toes. The white morph is very similar to Little Egret, but can be separated by sabre-shaped bill, which is longer and slightly downcurved. Bill colour variable, most often partly yellowish with dark culmen. Legs similar to Little, but not clean black, and has duller yellow toes. Immatures often have traces of dark along the head, neck and upperparts. **Voice** Silent when not breeding. [Alt: Western Reef Egret]

Black-crowned Night Heron

ad

juv

Squacco Heron

ad breeding

juv

Western Cattle Egret

ad breeding

ad non-breeding

Western Reef Heron

ad dark morph

ad white morph

PLATE 14: HERONS II

Little Egret *Egretta garzetta* L 55–65 cm, WS 88–106 cm
Regular winter migrant (all islands) and occasional breeder (T, L). Prefers the rocky lava shoreline but also freshwater reservoirs. Breeds in small colonies in trees. **ID** An elegant white egret with long legs and neck, easily identified by straight and all-dark bill, and dark legs with yellow feet. Confusion likely with similar white morph Western Reef Heron (which see). Beware winter dark morphs that can be confused with dark morph Western Reef Heron. The blue-grey lores are diagnostic outside the breeding season, but become reddish when breeding; two elongated nape feathers also present during this period. In flight the legs project well beyond the tail; less so than in Great Egret and more so than in Western Cattle Egret, and show conspicuous yellow toes. **Voice** At breeding colonies gives a monosyllabic *aaah*, also a disyllabic *da-wah* and a characteristic gargle *gulla-gulla-gulla....* Silent during the non-breeding period. **Tax.** Nominate race in the Canary Islands.

Great Egret *Ardea alba* L 85–100 cm, WS 145–170 cm
Vagrant. Prefers freshwater ponds and irrigation reservoirs. **ID** Outside the breeding season the bill is bright yellow-orange, contrasting with all-white body and dark legs with pale creamy tibia. Similar in size to Grey Heron. Summer adult all white with an almost all-dark bill, with just a hint of yellow at the base, greenish lores, reddish tibia and dark legs and toes. Confusion likely with smaller Little Egret or white morph Western Reef Heron. Can be separated from Little by slower flight action with long dark legs and feet projecting well beyond the tail, yellow bill (non-breeding) and lack of nape feathers in summer. Differs from white morph Western Reef in dagger-shaped bill (not sabre-shaped) and larger body. **Voice** When flushed may give a rolling *krr-rr-rr-rra*.

Purple Heron *Ardea purpurea* L 70–90 cm, WS 110–145 cm
Seasonal visitor (all islands). Prefers freshwater and brackish reservoirs. **ID** Has long narrow bill, reddish-brown on sides of neck with thin vertical black stripes on sides, black stripes on the face, reddish thighs and bluish-purple upperparts. Confusion possible with Grey Heron and vagrant Great Blue Heron. Juvenile recalls adult, but is duller rufous-brown overall, dark stripes on face are less well-marked and has black lines down the neck and creamy fringes to wing-coverts. **Voice** A soft *kreek*, similar to Grey Heron in flight. **Tax.** Nominate race in the Canary Islands.

Grey Heron *Ardea cinerea* L 84–102 cm, WS 155–175 cm
Regular winter migrant, seasonal visitor and resident but with no breeding confirmed (all islands). Prefers freshwater reservoirs near the coast but also forages on arable land. **ID** Summer adult shows white crown and forehead, two dark nape plumes that are often hard to see, pale greyish-white neck sides with a dark streaked line down the centre, dark grey upperparts, black-and-white shoulders and yellow-orange bill. Second-winter is intermediate between adult and juvenile in colour patterns with strong dagger-shaped bill (greyish-yellow) when separating it from Purple Heron. Juvenile or first-winter has dark crown and forehead, darker greyish sides to neck similar to upperparts. In flight neck keel rounded. Retracted neck separates it from vagrant Common Crane. Confusion possible with vagrant Great Blue Heron, which shows rufous thighs and black/rufous shoulders in all plumages. **Voice** In flight a frog-like alarm *kah-ahrk*. **Tax.** Nominate race in the archipelago.

ad breeding

juv

Little Egret

Great Egret

ad non-breeding

ad

juv

Purple Heron

ad

Grey Heron

juv

PLATE 15: IBISES AND FRIGATEBIRD

Glossy Ibis *Plegadis falcinellus* L 55–65 cm, WS 88–105 cm
Seasonal visitor (all islands). Prefers freshwater reservoirs but also visits golf courses. **ID** Summer adult has purple-brown plumage, green gloss on wing-coverts and flight feathers, and blue lores with white edges, most easily seen at close range. Outside the breeding season the overall coloration becomes duller brown and is speckled with white on the head and neck; the lores become all dark at this time. Long dark legs, long decurved bill. Juvenile and first-winter recall adult winter, but paler brown overall. In flight legs project beyond the tail. **Voice** May give a *grru* call in flight.

African Sacred Ibis *Threskiornis aethiopicus* L 65–75 cm, WS 112–124 cm
Former breeder (F), from birds escaped from captivity, but today does not maintain a self-sustained population. Also recorded on other islands (T, GC, L) where true vagrancy unlikely. Associated with built-up areas, foraging in gardens and nesting in palm trees. **ID** Sexes alike. Adult has black head, neck, legs, rump, tail and decurved black bill, which contrast with white upperparts and underside. In flight shows black tips to wing feathers and legs projecting only slightly beyond tail. Juvenile similar to adult, but head and neck black and white, and lacks the dark tail-plumes of adult. **Voice** Sometimes gives a frog-like *croak* in flight.

Eurasian Spoonbill *Platalea leucorodia* L 80–90 cm, WS 115–130 cm
Regular winter migrant and seasonal visitor (all islands). Prefers freshwater reservoirs when available. **ID** A large white waterbird which can be confused with large egrets such as the Great Egret, if the spoon-shaped bill is hidden while resting. Summer adult shows elongated nape feathers that form a short crest, and has a patch of tawny-yellowish coloration on breast, black bill with yellow tip and yellow throat. During the non-breeding season the crest and tawny-yellow patch disappear – this plumage is more likely to be seen in the region. Black tips to outer primaries and lighter legs and bill are diagnostic to identify juvenile and first-winter individuals. In flight the neck is extended (retracted in egrets), and the wing-beats are fast and mixed with short glides. **Voice** Unlikely to be heard in the region.

Magnificent Frigatebird *Fregata magnificens* L 95–110 cm, WS 215–245 cm
Vagrant, but no records in the Canary Islands have been identified to species level. Forages over both inshore and pelagic waters. **ID** A large aerial seabird, unmistakable in flight with all-black plumage, very long pointed wings, forked tail and long bill, with a pronounced hook at the tip. Male is all black with an inconspicuous orange-red gular pouch, which can be inflated and transformed into a spectacular scarlet balloon while displaying from the ground. Female brownish-black with a conspicuous white collar, extending on underside onto flanks and chest (visible at long range). Also pale grey band across lesser coverts. Juvenile as adult female, but head white. Tends to follow boats and while foraging will often parasitise other seabirds. **Voice** Male gives a quick rattling and drumming by clicking its bill while displaying in breeding colony; unlikely to be heard in the Canary Islands.

Glossy Ibis

Eurasian Spoonbill

African Sacred Ibis

Magnificent Frigatebird

PLATE 16: GANNET, BOOBIES, CORMORANT AND TROPICBIRD

Northern Gannet *Morus bassanus*   L 85–97 cm, WS 170–192 cm
Seasonal visitor and passage migrant (all islands). Highly pelagic and mobile away from breeding colonies in the North Atlantic. **ID** Adult is mainly white with yellowish forehead, crown and hindneck, black legs and feet, silvery bill and bluish eye. Adult in winter shows less yellowish on head. In flight and when plunge-diving shows conspicuous black wingtips. Juvenile is entirely grey-brown with whitish subterminal band on tail. Second-winter birds have white underside and subterminal band on tail, also darker upperparts interspersed with white spots. Third-winter birds have head and underside as adult, but upperparts mainly black with white patches and black wingtips. Fourth-winter as adult, but with some small dark patches on secondaries. **Voice** Unlikely to be heard in the Canary Islands.

Red-footed Booby *Sula sula*   L 66–77 cm, WS 124–142 cm
Vagrant. Highly pelagic away from its breeding colonies on islands in the Atlantic, Pacific and Indian Oceans. **ID** Two morphs. Adult brown morph similar to Brown Booby, but dark underwing and in some individuals (white-tailed brown morph) with white on rump, tail and ventral region. Adult white morph recalls subadult Northern Gannet in the last stages of moult, when most of the dark feathers on mantle, rump and secondary coverts are missing, but Red-footed's slightly smaller red feet diagnostic at closer range. Juvenile similar to juvenile Brown Booby and juvenile Northern Gannet, but separated from the former by all-dark underwing and from the latter by agile and elegant flight action, an important feature in all plumages because feet start yellowish and turn reddish later. **Voice** Silent at sea.

Brown Booby *Sula leucogaster*   L 65–75 cm, WS 135–150 cm
Vagrant. Prefers shallow seas for foraging and coastal cliffs for nesting. **ID** Adult is dark brown on head, chest and upperparts, white on the underwing and underparts, with yellow legs and feet, and pale bill and facial skin. The bill base is bluish during the breeding season. Juvenile has dirty brown underparts. At long range both adult and juvenile can be confused in flight with juvenile and second-winter Northern Gannet, but lack extensive white patches on the body and upperparts, white sub-terminal band on the tail, white spots on the upperparts and pale chin and throat of immature and juvenile Northern Gannet. Flight action is similar to Northern Gannet, but due to smaller and slimmer size the wing-beats are faster. Dives vertically like Northern Gannet and also at shallow angles. **Voice** Silent at sea when foraging for food.

Great Cormorant *Phalacrocorax carbo*   L 77–94 cm, WS 121–149 cm
Irregular winter migrant (all islands). Prefers rocky coasts, but also artificial freshwater reservoirs. **ID** Summer adult is black overall with bluish and greenish gloss, wings slightly bronzed; the yellow patch at the base of the lower mandible is surrounded by white on throat and cheeks. Winter plumage, more likely to be seen on Canary Islands, is less glossy overall, and greyish, not white, on cheeks and throat. Juvenile and first-year birds are browner; the former often showing white belly, light greyish bill and dark legs and feet. Confusion likely with vagrant Double-crested Cormorant. **Voice** Unlikely to be heard in the region.

Red-billed Tropicbird *Phaethon aethereus*   L 90–105 cm (including tail streamers of 45–50 cm) WS 100–110 cm
Occasional breeder (H, F, L) and reported near all the islands. Nests mainly on offshore islets and rocky coasts on islands, in piles of boulders and crevices on inaccessible sea cliffs. **ID** Flies well above surface with a pigeon-like flight when foraging for flying-fish and cephalopods, which are captured by plunge-diving. Does not follow boats, but will briefly inspect fishing boats. Adult all white, with black barring on the mantle, black wingtips, black eye-stripe, red bill and long white tail-streamers. Juvenile could be mistaken for Caspian Tern as no long tail streamers are present, but the absence of black on the underside of primaries, the lack of a forked tail, its orange bill and its typical flight action are diagnostic. **Voice** Most typical call is a shrill whistle given at sea or near the breeding colony, also from the nest-site. **Tax.** The ssp. *mesonauta* breeds in the region.

Red-footed Booby

ad pale morph

ad brown morph

juv

ad

juv

Northern Gannet

Brown Booby

ad

juv

ad

Great Cormorant

ad non-breeding

juv

Red-billed Tropicbird

ad

juv

PLATE 17: OSPREY AND KITES

Osprey *Pandion haliaetus*   L 52–60 cm, WS 152–167 cm

Resident breeder (H, Go, T, L, mc, a) and recorded elsewhere (P, GC, F, g), but on the endangered list. Prefers calm inshore waters near cliffs for nesting, frequents freshwater man-made reservoirs. **ID** Confusion likely with pale morph Booted Eagle (Plate 21) and Egyptian Vulture (Plate 18), but silhouette with narrow wings, white crown and black eye-stripe extending towards the shoulder diagnostic. Sexes similar and adult in flight shows four fingers on wingtips, brown upperparts, black carpal and underwing-bar, dark terminal tail-band, brown chest collar (broader on females). Tends to hover and then dive for fish. Juvenile recalls adult, but its wing-coverts still have buff fringes, and eyes orange, not yellow. **Voice** A characteristic *kew-kew-kew-kew…* mainly given in flight, also a contact call *pyep* and a mournful *pe-eep, pe-eep, pe-eep.* **Tax.** Nominate subspecies *haliaetus* in the region. [Alt: Western Osprey]

Black Kite *Milvus migrans*   L 48–58 cm, WS 130–155 cm

Seasonal visitor (all islands) with 1–2 unsuccessful breeding attempts (GC). Prefers open areas with or without forests, also in grassland, semi-desert and near towns and villages. **ID** Has a different flight silhouette to Common Buzzard, with distinctive grey-brown forked tail. Frequently twists tail from side to side and fans it out so the fork changes in shape and sometimes even disappears; this twisting is diagnostic in kites. Adult is mainly brown with a pale panel across the inner wing, more conspicuous on juveniles. Confusion likely with Red Kite which has a rufous and more deeply forked tail and dark morph Booted Eagle, which has a square tail, pale uppertail-coverts and a pale patch at the base of forewing. Juvenile in flight shows white-tipped greater and primary coverts, but this is visible only at close range. **Voice** In flight gives a whining *pee-errrr,* similar to Red Kite.

Red Kite *Milvus milvus*   L 60–66 cm, WS 155–180 cm

Extinct as breeding bird (H, Go, T, GC); today occurs as a vagrant. Prefers foraging in open areas such as grasslands. **ID** More elegant and larger than Common Buzzard. Adult is mainly rufous with fine dark streaks on neck and underside, pale greyish head, yellow eye, cere and legs. The pale rufous upperside to the deeply forked tail diagnostic, although beware vagrant Long-legged Buzzard. Differs from Black Kite in more deeply forked tail and more conspicuous light windows on the underwing. Juvenile recalls adult, but is paler overall (yellowish tinge) and the upper greater coverts are tipped white, although this is difficult to see at long range. **Voice** A mewing *peee-ooo.*

Osprey

Black Kite

Red Kite

PLATE 18: VULTURES AND HAWKS

Egyptian Vulture *Neophron percnopterus* L 55–65 cm, WS 155–170 cm

Resident breeder (F, L, a), but extinct from other islands (H, Go, T, GC). Nests around small caves and crags on rocky cliffs of deep gullies. **ID** Sexes similar. In flight all ages show characteristic silhouette with broad, well-fingered wings, wedge-shaped tail and small head with thin hooked bill. Adult has a yellow cere and bare head, thin bill, black primaries and secondaries contrasting with white body, wing-coverts and tail. The crown, median coverts, breast and tail are rufous-tinged, giving adults a dirty look. Subadult recalls both juvenile and adult and is usually intermediate in plumage pattern and coloration. Juvenile varies in overall plumage coloration, but is mainly dark brown with ochre-buff on mantle and tips of wing-coverts. Confusion possible with Osprey (Plate 17). **Voice** At the nest gives grunts and groans, silent when foraging. **Tax.** The endemic Canary Islands ssp. *majorensis* is bigger and with more rufous-tinged plumage than the nominate.

Northern Goshawk *Accipiter gentilis* L ♂ 49–56 cm, ♀ 58–64 cm, WS ♂ 93–105 cm, ♀ 108–127 cm

Vagrant. In natural range prefers coniferous forests and extensive woodlands. **ID** Sexually dimorphic in size but not in plumage. A medium-large raptor. Both sexes have a white supercilium, orange eye, yellow cere and feet, dark grey crown, slate-grey upperparts and fine grey bars on the underside, and three to four bands on the tail. The wingspan of an adult female is similar to that of Common Buzzard. Adult male can be confused with female Eurasian Sparrowhawk, but has shorter neck, thinner tail-base and less pointed wings. Juvenile is buff-brown and heavily streaked on the underside, brown on the upperparts and has yellow iris. In flight, gliding at treetop-level is diagnostic. **Voice** Unlikely to be heard in the region.

Eurasian Sparrowhawk *Accipiter nisus* L ♂ 29–34 cm, ♀ 35–41 cm, WS ♂ 58–65 cm, ♀ 67–80 cm

Resident breeder (P, H, Go, T, GC) and irregular winter migrant (F, L, a). Prefers laurel forest, but also present in pine forests and in small clumps of non-natural woodland near cultivated areas, rarely in city gardens. **ID** Sexually dimorphic. Male has similar grey upperparts as female, but differs in rufous cheeks and breast. Female greyish overall and slightly larger, with dark grey upperparts and fine grey bars on chest and breast; tail pattern similar to male. Confusion of the female likely with vagrant male Northern Goshawk, which has longer neck, broader tail-base and pointed wings. Juvenile (of both sexes) is browner on the upperparts and heavily barred brown on underside. In flight the silhouette of the broad wings separate it from similarly sized Common Kestrel. **Voice** Female, during nesting, gives a disyllabic food-call *pii-ih* and a rapid *ke-ke-ke-ke-ke*. **Tax.** The Macaronesian endemic subspecies *granti* differs from nominate in darker upperparts and thicker bars on the underside.

Egyptian Vulture

Northern Goshawk

Eurasian Sparrowhawk

PLATE 19: HARRIERS

Western Marsh Harrier *Circus aeruginosus* L 43–55 cm, WS 115–140 cm
Seasonal visitor (all islands except P). Favours cultivated cereal fields when available and abandoned pastures for hunting. **ID** Adult male has pale yellowish-white head and chest, chestnut belly and ventral region, dark brown wing-coverts extending as far as inner secondary coverts (except for thin white patch on forewing), bluish-grey tail, and wings with black tips as in other harrier species. Adult female is mainly dark brown with conspicuous creamy-buff crown, throat and forewing, and red-brown tail. Juvenile recalls adult female, but darker overall and pale areas of adult female are yellowish in juveniles. Second-summer male also recalls adult female or juvenile, but retains black wing-tips clearly visible on underwing. Some rare morphs are all dark. As in congeners, in flight diagnostic soaring with wings held in a shallow 'V' position; often lands on ground. Confusion likely with the other three harrier species (which see). **Voice** Unlikely to be heard in the region.

Hen Harrier *Circus cyaneus* L 45–55 cm, WS 97–118 cm
Seasonal visitor (all islands). Favours stubble fields of cereal crops and other cultivated areas. **ID** All ages can be separated from Montagu's by the five primaries ('fingers') that show in flight (four in Montagu's). Adult male is blue-grey on the head, mantle, wings and chest, with white underside, and in flight shows a diagnostic dark trailing edge to the underwing, black wing-tips and white rump. Has a characteristic low soaring flight with wings held in a shallow 'V' position. Adult female is mainly brown above and boldly streaked dark brown on white breast, with white rump and yellowish patch on upperwing-coverts. Juvenile recalls adult female, but has pale tips to greater coverts above and bold dark brown streaks on rusty-yellow breast. **Voice** Unlikely to be heard in the region.

Pallid Harrier *Circus macrourus* L 40–50 cm, WS 97–118 cm
Vagrant. Prefers open cultivated areas and dry grasslands for foraging while migrating. **ID** In flight all ages soar with wings held in a shallow 'V' position. Adult male similar to adult male Montagu's and Hen, but paler plumage overall, especially on the underside, less black on wingtips; also lacks the black bands on secondaries of Montagu's and the dark trailing edge on the wing of Hen. Adult female more difficult to separate from adult female Montagu's or Hen, but inner secondaries and secondary coverts duskier giving the impression of very dark axillaries; it also has a more prominent white collar on neck. Juvenile similar to juvenile Montagu's with chestnut underside, but neck collar conspicuous and has paler patches under the wing created by white-tipped primaries. **Voice** Unlikely to be heard in the region.

Montagu's Harrier *Circus pygargus* L 39–50 cm, WS 96–116 cm
Seasonal visitor (all islands except H and Go). Favours arable land with cereal crops for foraging during migration, but also abandoned fields and semi-desert scrub. **ID** Adult male similar to Hen but in flight two black lines across the secondaries on the underwing and one on the upperwing diagnostic. Four visible primaries/fingers, more black on wingtips, tricoloured upperwings with black tips, dark grey on wing-coverts and the rest light grey, and rusty streaks on breast. Adult female extremely similar to adult female Hen, but with thinner and narrow wings, slightly different silhouette, a diagnostic black line across the secondaries on upperside of wing and a broad pale band between the dark trailing edge and the black line across the secondaries on underside. Juvenile as juvenile vagrant Pallid in chestnut underside, but no diagnostic white neck collar visible at long range. **Voice** Unlikely to be heard in the region.

Western Marsh Harrier

Hen Harrier

Pallid Harrier

Montagu's Harrier

PLATE 20: HONEY BUZZARD AND BUZZARDS

European Honey Buzzard *Pernis apivorus*　　　　　　　　　　　　　　　L 52–59 cm, WS 113–135 cm

Vagrant. Favours forests with clearings for hunting. **ID** Adult male has diagnostic barring on underwing and undertail, the latter only visible at close range. Similar to Common Buzzard, but with longer and narrower wings, projecting 'cuckoo-like' head and neck, and longer tail with slightly convex sides and rounded corners. Pale, rufous, dark and intermediate morphs possible. Note the distance between the broad black bar on the trailing edge of the wings and the inner one or two black bars. The same pattern of well-spaced barring is present on tail, with a black terminal band and then two thinner bars. Adult female has more bars on the underwing and undertail than male. Juvenile shows more evenly barred underside to flight feathers and under the tail, and also darker underside to secondaries. **Voice** Unlikely to be heard in the region.

Common Buzzard *Buteo buteo*　　　　　　　　　　　　　　　　　　　　L 46–58 cm, WS 110–132 cm

Resident breeder (all islands, extinct L). Prefers pine and laurel forest for nesting, but also found in semi-desert scrub, both on coast and inland mainly in eastern Canary Islands. **ID** Sexes similar; occurs in several morphs ranging from light to dark. All adults show pale band on chest extending to underwing-coverts, broad black terminal band on tail and trailing edge to the wing, and black fingers. Juvenile lacks the black terminal band in all different morphs; the juvenile light morph may be confused with adult light morph Booted Eagle, which lacks the black carpal patch on the neatly black-and-white underwing. Confusion also possible with vagrant Long-legged and European Honey Buzzard (which see). **Voice** A high-pitched scream in flight *cleeaaaarrr*. **Tax.** Based on plumage and size differences, ssp. *insularum* is found in Canary Islands.

Long-legged Buzzard *Buteo rufinus*　　　　　　　　　　　　　　　　　　L 50–55 cm, WS 115–125 cm

Vagrant, but records under review. In natural range favours semi-desert habitats from plains to mountains. **ID** Several morphs. All have dark carpal patch on upper and underwing. Dark morph adult is dark brown overall with a black terminal tail-band, like Common Buzzard, but lacking the pale breast and underwing-bar. Intermediate morph adult is reddish-brown overall with a rufous tail and a darkish belly. Juvenile shows some rufous tinge to the crown, chest, underwing-coverts and tail, which contrast with the very dark belly and dark carpal patches. The North African resident ssp. *cirtensis* is slightly smaller than the nominate and has a rufous belly (dark morph rare). The juvenile of this ssp. differs from juvenile nominate in its blue not yellow cere and feet. **Voice** Mainly silent but sometimes a repetitive *aaah*.

European Honey Buzzard

Common Buzzard

Long-legged Buzzard

PLATE 21: EAGLES

Short-toed Snake Eagle *Circaetus gallicus*   L 62–69 cm, WS 162–178 cm

Vagrant. In natural range prefers open woodland, hills and mountains. **ID** In flight tends to hover and frequently dangles its legs, and also has a characteristic silhouette while gliding with carpal joints held well forward. Similar to Osprey or pale morph Common Buzzard, but tail has three or four evenly spaced dark bars (visible from above and below) and the lack of prominent dark carpal patches on the underwing is diagnostic at all ages. When perched, adult appears owl-like with short neck and large head, dark brown head, chest and upperparts, coarse barring on the breast; at close range the lack of feathers on legs is visible. Ageing is difficult due to variability in plumage patterning, but some juveniles have all-pale throat and are lighter overall. **Voice** Unlikely to be heard in the region. [Alt: Short-toed Eagle]

Booted Eagle *Hieraaetus pennatus*   L 42–51 cm, WS 110–135 cm

Seasonal visitor (all islands). Prefers hills or mountainous areas when visiting Canary Islands. **ID** Several morphs but pale morph most likely. Pale morph is dark on the upperwings with creamy brown carpal wing patches and can only be confused in the region with adult Egyptian Vulture, since both have pale underside and underwing-coverts contrasting with black flight feathers. Booted, however, has three whitish inner primaries (present in both morphs) and a different silhouette due to sharp corners to tail (not wedge-shaped). Confusion of pale morph also possible with Osprey (Plate 17). Dark morph can be confused with Black Kite (Plate 17), but small white patches near the neck visible at close range and tail not forked when folded. Juvenile pale and dark morphs resemble adult, but generally are more rufous on head and underside. **Voice** Unlikely to be heard in the region.

Bonelli's Eagle *Aquila fasciata*   L 55–65 cm, WS 145–165 cm

Vagrant. In natural range favours mountainous areas and forests. **ID** Sexes similar. Black carpal and underwing-bar and broad black terminal band on tail are diagnostic. Adults have a whitish patch on the mantle, but not on juveniles, which also lack the black terminal band on their finely barred tails. Juvenile is mainly rufous-buff on throat (finely streaked), breast and underwing-coverts, which contrast with black wing-tips in flight. Some pale juveniles have all white underwing-coverts. Glides with straight rear edge of wing and carpals slightly projected. Confusion possible with smaller Booted Eagle. **Voice** Unlikely to be heard in the region.

Short-toed Snake Eagle

Booted Eagle

Bonelli's Eagle

PLATE 22: CRANE, BUSTARD AND SANDGROUSE

Common Crane *Grus grus*   L 96–119 cm, WS 180–222 cm
Vagrant. In natural range favours lakes for nesting, and flat cultivated areas during the non-breeding period. **ID** Summer adult has black head and foreneck, white hindneck and bare-red patch on crown, grey with brownish on upperparts and centres to coverts, dark-tipped tertials protrude to form a bushy 'tail'. In flight black and grey wing feathers contrast with pale grey coverts, neck extended as in the *Ciconia* storks but unlike herons. Juvenile has brown head and neck, contrasting with grey body plumage. **Voice** In flight a trumpeting contact call *crrooah* can be heard from male, female answering with a lower pitched *kraw*.

Houbara Bustard *Chlamydotis undulata*   L 55–65 cm, WS 135–170 cm
Resident breeder (F, L, g). Prefers low semi-arid grasslands and scrublands away from human settlements. **ID** Sexes differ slightly. Adult male has a diagnostic black line along the side of the neck, white crown, dirty white foreneck and underside, pale sandy-brown upperparts, and black centres to feathers that show as thick bars on the upper body. Adult female is slightly smaller and has less clean-cut black line on neck. Juvenile has no black line on side of neck. In flight a white patch is visible near the wingtips, contrasting with black primary coverts and flight feathers. Male display includes raising neck and crown feathers while retracting head on to back, and running in circles or in straight line. **Voice** Mostly silent in the field but adult may give a coughing *tucg*. **Tax.** On slight morphological differences (darker above and smaller in size) the endemic ssp. *fuertaventurae* has been proposed, but recent genetic analyses suggest poor differentiation from nominate.

Black-bellied Sandgrouse *Pterocles orientalis*   L 30–35 cm, WS 70–73 cm
Resident breeder on a single island (F) but reported from others too (L, g). Prefers flat sandy areas with very little vegetation. **ID** Sexes differ. Adult male has pale grey head, neck and upper breast (finely fringed black), orange throat patch with black centre, cream band on lower breast and black belly, upperparts are mainly spotted golden. Adult female is pale brown overall with cream breast-band and black belly, upperparts finely vermiculated, and creamy throat with small black centre. Similar in size to the common Barbary Partridge. In flight black belly is diagnostic in both sexes. **Voice** A horse-like or snoring call *churrll-urrll* given in the air aids detection, even at great distances. **Tax.** Nominate ssp. *orientalis* occurs in the Canary Islands.

Common Crane
ad
ad sum
juv

Houbara Bustard
ad
ad
fuertaventurae

Black-bellied Sandgrouse
ad ♂
ad ♂
ad ♂
ad ♀

PLATE 23: CRAKES

Corn Crake *Crex crex* L 22–25 cm, WS 46–53 cm

Vagrant. Associated with open grasslands and cultivated areas while in the archipelago. **ID** Sexes differ. In flight all plumages show diagnostic reddish-brown wings and legs projecting beyond the tail, dangling when flushed, although it prefers to creep away rather than take flight. Adult male is brownish on the crown and upperparts with dark centres to feathers making the bird look heavily spotted above; grey supercilium and breast sides, white and reddish bars on flanks, red-brown wing feathers, short yellowish bill and pinkish legs. Adult female recalls adult male, but lacks the grey on supercilium and breast. Juvenile like adult female, but less conspicuously barred on flanks. **Voice** Singing male gives a sharp *crex-crex* repeated every second.

African Crake *Crex egregia* L 20–23 cm, WS 40–42 cm

Vagrant. Prefers grasslands at edges of freshwater reservoirs. **ID** Sexes similar. Adult is olive-brown on the crown, nape and upperparts, with the pale grey on the face extending towards the breast, and has black-and-white barred belly, pinkish-brown legs, red eye and white throat. Juvenile resembles adult in structure, but differs in duller underside and is darker overall with dark bill and greyish eye. Confusion likely with slightly larger vagrant Water Rail but short bill with dark tip and reddish base diagnostic. All the smaller crakes differ in bill and leg colour. **Voice** In flight when migrating both sexes utter a *kiu* but most typical call of male is a series of rapid *krrrr* notes.

Spotted Crake *Porzana porzana* L 19–22 cm, WS 37–42 cm

Seasonal visitor (all islands). Favours freshwater reservoirs with dense reedbeds. **ID** Sexes similar. Adult is brown on the crown, nape and upperparts with black centres to feathers, bluish-grey face extending to the chest, brown and white bars on the flanks and belly, dark eye, lores and chin, short yellow-grey bill with reddish base, greenish legs, white transverse bars on tertials, usually buff on undertail-coverts and diagnostic white spots over whole plumage sometimes even on vent. In flight adult Spotted shows a whitish leading edge to the wing, most likely to be seen from below. Juvenile and first-winter similar to adult, but lack the dark lores and chin and the bluish-grey on face and chest; throat whitish. Confusion likely with Little or Baillon's Crake (which see). **Voice** May utter a sharp alarm call *krek*, a high-pitched *whuitt* repeated every second, usually at night, and croaking *qwe-qwe-qwe*.

Little Crake *Porzana parva* L 17–19 cm, WS 34–39 cm

Vagrant. Favours freshwater reservoirs with lush aquatic vegetation. **ID** Sexes differ. Adult male has brown crown and nape, but pale brown upperparts with faint black-and-white markings, blue-grey face, foreneck and underside, greenish legs, red eye and yellowish bill with reddish base black, white stripes are limited to undertail-coverts, but not above the tibia. Could be confused with male Baillon's, which shows greenish bill and pinkish legs. Adult female has pale bluish supercilium, white throat and upper chest, creamy buff underside, pale edges to tertials and long primary projection. Juvenile has only a hint of red on bill base and no pale bluish supercilium, whitish throat and upper chest and similar long primary projection. Beware of similar bill colour in slightly bigger Spotted Crake. **Voice** Male gives a frog-like *quek… quek…quek, quek, quek, kua-kua-kua*.

Baillon's Crake *Porzana pusilla* L 17–19 cm, WS 33–37 cm

Vagrant. Favours freshwater ponds with low herbaceous and aquatic vegetation on the edges. **ID** Sexes alike. Adult is dark brown on crown, hindneck and upperparts, mantle with thick white stripes, greenish bill, red eye and pinkish legs. Confusion possible with Little Crake but shorter primary projection, black-and-white bars extend in front of tibia, and no red at bill base diagnostic. Juvenile similar to juvenile or first-winter Spotted or juvenile Little, but separated from Spotted by black-and-white bars (not buff) on undertail-coverts and from Little by shorter primary projection, more barring on chest and no hint of red at bill base. In flight shows characteristic dangling legs like other crakes, and occasionally can be surprisingly tame and easy to approach while foraging. **Voice** A frog-like *trrrrr-trrrr* every one or two seconds.

Corn Crake

African Crake

ad (Corn Crake)
juv (African Crake)
ad (African Crake)

Spotted Crake

ad (Spotted Crake)
imm (Spotted Crake)

Little Crake

ad ♂
ad ♀
juv

Baillon's Crake

ad
juv

PLATE 24: COOT AND GALLINULES

Eurasian Coot *Fulica atra* — L 36–38 cm, WS 70–80 cm
Resident breeder (Go, T, GC, F) and regular winter visitor (all islands except H). Prefers freshwater reservoirs when available, but also associated with brackish water. **ID** Sexes alike. All black with white frontal plate and bill and red eye. First-winter similar to adult but white frontal plate smaller and thinner. In flight has a white trailing edge to wing. Likely to be confused with resident Common Moorhen (which see). Juvenile is grey-brown with some white on face, foreneck and breast, and lacks white undertail-coverts and white patchy line along the flanks that are present in juvenile Common Moorhen. The chicks are similar to Common Moorhen chicks, but have yellow down on neck. **Voice** A typical, repetitive *kwok*. **Tax.** Nominate ssp. *atra* occurs in the region. [Alt: Common Coot]

Common Moorhen *Gallinula chloropus* — L 27–31 cm, WS 50–55 cm
Resident breeder (all islands except H and L). Freshwater ponds and reservoirs with aquatic vegetation. **ID** Sexes similar. Adult has red bill with yellow tip, dark brown on mantle and wings, and uppertail-coverts contrast with overall slate-grey plumage, greenish legs, white outer undertail-coverts and a broken white line along the flanks. First-winter similar to adult, but with whitish throat. Juvenile is brown in general, no red frontal plate, has white throat, darkish bill, white outer undertail-coverts and white patchy line along the flanks. Tends to flick its tail when walking, and jerks head constantly when swimming. Downy chicks are black with red bill and can easily be confused with those of Eurasian Coot. In flight legs project beyond the tail. **Voice** An explosive *kporrrl* or a rapid *kreck-kreck-kreck*. **Tax.** Nominate ssp. *chloropus* occurs in the region.

Allen's Gallinule *Porphyrio alleni* — L 22–24 cm, WS 48–52 cm
Vagrant. Prefers freshwater ponds with dense aquatic vegetation, also brackish water areas. **ID** Sexes similar. Adult has dark violet-blue plumage, greenish upperparts and wing feathers, red bill and legs, blue frontal plate, and black centre to white undertail. Juvenile unmistakable with brownish plumage and diagnostically black-centred feathers on upperparts and wing-coverts, as well as pale buff undertail-coverts, blue-green tinge to wing feathers, and dark bill and legs. Adult can be confused with Purple Gallinule but bill tip and legs yellow and no black on undertail-feathers. **Voice** May give an alarm call *click* when flushed.

Purple Gallinule *Porphyrio martinica* — L 30–36 cm, WS 50–55 cm
Vagrant. Associated with freshwater reservoirs. **ID** Sexes similar. Adult is violet-blue overall and green above, with yellow legs, white vent and red bill with yellow tip. More elegant than Common Moorhen with longer neck and legs. Confusion likely with adult Allen's Gallinule from Africa (which see). Juvenile is brown, like juvenile Common Moorhen or Allen's Gallinule, but separated from both by the blue-green of wing-coverts and feathers. **Voice** Most typical calls are a cackling *kak-kak-kak* when alarmed and a sharp *kyik*. [Alt: American Purple Gallinule]

Eurasian Coot

Common Moorhen

Allen's Gallinule

Purple Gallinule

PLATE 25: STONE-CURLEW, OYSTERCATCHER, STILT AND AVOCET

Eurasian Stone-curlew *Burhinus oedicnemus*   L 38–45 cm, WS 76–88 cm

Resident breeder (all islands). On western and central islands favours sparse semi-desert scrub and in the eastern islands associated with agricultural areas, steppe with low shrub cover, and sandy areas with grasses and small shrubs. **ID** Sexes similar. Adult has a diagnostic white wing-bar bordered black above and below, yellow eye, shortish legs, black-tipped bill, brown overall with finely black-streaked crown, hindneck and throat, but with thicker dark streaks on upperparts. At closer range shows white supercilium, throat and lores, giving a unique facial pattern. Juvenile is similar to adult, but white wing-bar and supercilium are less conspicuous. In flight shows two large white patches on wing when flushed and the black primaries are diagnostic. Mainly active at dusk and night but daytime activity and calling also occurs during breeding season. **Voice** Most typical call is a loud *cur-lee* sometimes repeated 4–6 times. **Tax.** Two ssp, *distinctus* (P, H, Go, T, GC) and *insularum* (F, L, g, a), the former is slightly darker than nominate, while the latter is paler on the upperparts.

Eurasian Oystercatcher *Haematopus ostralegus*   L 39–44 cm, WS 72–83 cm

Seasonal visitor and irregular winter migrant (all islands). Prefers freshwater reservoirs, but also rocky shorelines. **ID** Sexes similar. Winter adult similar to summer but has white semi-collar on throat, extending towards ear-coverts. Summer adult has black head, upper chest and upperparts, red bill, eye and eye-ring, and pinkish legs. Juvenile like summer adult, but with greyish legs, brownish upperparts and blackish bill tip. Strong and compact in structure with characteristic black-and-white plumage in all seasons and a long straight bill. In flight underwing all white, but upperwing black with stripe on primaries and secondaries, and white tail has black terminal band. **Voice** Flight call is a shrill *peep*.

Black-winged Stilt *Himantopus himantopus*   L 33–36 cm, WS 67–77 cm

Resident breeder (F, L), but also occasional breeder (T, GC). Favours saltpans for breeding, visits freshwater reservoirs when not nesting. **ID** Sexes differ slightly. Adult male has variable amount of black on head and hindneck, green-glossed black upperparts, and white throat and underside. Adult female has only a little black on head and neck, and has brownish upperparts. Juvenile has browner upperparts with pale fringes to upperpart feathers, giving a scaly pattern above, a brownish tinge to crown and hindneck, and duller red legs. In flight extremely long reddish legs visible at long range, dark wings show a conspicuous white trailing edge. Mantle with large white wedge, upper tail feathers also white. **Voice** A *kek* contact call and a repetitive high pitched *kuik-kuik-kuik-kuik-kuik...* while nesting. **Tax.** The nominate ssp. *himantopus* occurs in the Canary Islands.

Pied Avocet *Recurvirostra avosetta*   L 42–46 cm, WS 67–77 cm

Seasonal visitor (all islands except Go). Prefers coastal tidal saltwater pools and saltpans, but also freshwater reservoirs. **ID** Unmistakable. In flight black wing-tips, carpal bar and crown contrast with entirely white body, and legs project well beyond the tail. Adult male has black-and-white on wings, blue-grey legs and diagnostic black upturned bill, dark forehead, crown and hindneck contrasting with white underside. Adult female like male, but has a shorter and more sharply curved bill (although this is difficult to assess with single birds), also brownish head markings. Juvenile similar to adult, but with brownish tinge on cap and upperparts, duller legs. **Voice** A loud *kluep, kluep, kluep...* may be given, but mainly silent when not breeding.

Eurasian Stone-curlew
ad *insularum*
ad *distinctus*

Eurasian Oystercatcher
ad breeding

Black-winged Stilt
ad ♂
1st-win

Pied Avocet
ad

PLATE 26: PLOVERS AND LAPWING

Eurasian Dotterel *Charadrius morinellus*   L 20–24 cm, WS 57–64 cm

Irregular winter migrant (all islands except H). Favours both open sandy and stony semi-desert with sparse shrub vegetation. **ID** Summer adult is grey with white supercilium, white throat, black-and-white breast-band, rusty chestnut breast, white ventral region, yellowish legs, black belly and bill, and reddish tinge to flight feathers and coverts. Female brighter than male. Sexes similar in winter. Winter adult has white supercilium (orange-buff behind the eye), is otherwise generally slate-grey with yellowish tinge to flanks, has inconspicuous pale breast-band, greenish legs, rufous fringes to wing-coverts and black bill. In flight all plumages show white shaft on external primaries and lack of wing-bar. Juvenile or first-winter similar to adult in winter, but upperpart feathers have neat black centres with creamy fringes. Can be quite tame and approachable. **Voice** Typical call is a soft Dunlin-like *keeer* when flushed and a repeated *pwit-pwit-pwit*….

American Golden Plover *Pluvialis dominica*   L 24–27 cm, WS 66–72 cm

Vagrant. Prefers freshwater ponds, reservoirs and sewage ponds, but also along rocky coastline and on golf courses. **ID** Summer adult has black face, throat and underside including undertail-coverts, coarsely golden-patterned upperparts, white supercilium extending along the sides of neck to upper chest, and black legs and bill. Juvenile is greyish with prominent pale supercilium and conspicuous dark ear-spot. Dark grey axillaries/underwing diagnostic at all ages to separate from other *Pluvialis* species, but this best told by photographing the individual in flight. **Voice** A disyllabic *klee-i* or *kleep* and a Northern Lapwing-like *klu-eet*.

European Golden Plover *Pluvialis apricaria*   L 26–29 cm, WS 67–76 cm

Irregular winter migrant (all islands except H and Go). Favours arable fields in winter but also semi-desert coastal scrub. **ID** Sexes similar in winter. Adult in winter lacks black-and-white patterning on head and underside and is mainly golden, with faint supercilium, and white axillaries and underwing-coverts in flight. Summer adult recalls summer adult Grey Plover, but slightly smaller, white supercilium extending down neck-sides and along flanks to ventral region. Golden upperparts and all-white axillaries and underwing-coverts. Juvenile resembles adult in winter, but more finely grey-barred on belly and flanks; adult has whiter belly. In the Canary Islands often associates with Northern Lapwing. **Voice** Most typical call is a disyllabic *too-ee* or *tloo*.

Grey Plover *Pluvialis squatarola*   L 27–30 cm, WS 71–83 cm

Regular winter migrant and seasonal visitor (all islands). Prefers rocky shorelines and rarely found in freshwater reservoirs. **ID** Winter adult is mainly grey with whitish underside, and has a faint white supercilium, whitish-fringed wing-coverts and white underside; black on axillaries diagnostic and best seen in flight. Juvenile similar to adult in winter, but with a yellowish-buff mantle and fringes to wing-coverts, showing a neat spotted pattern. Summer adult, also possible in the region, shows black-and-white pattern on head, upperparts and underside. In flight all plumages show black axillaries contrasting with white underwing-coverts, white rump and thick white wing-bar, all diagnostic features that separate this species from any other *Pluvialis* species recorded in the Canary Islands. **Voice** A melancholy trisyllabic whistle *tlee-oo-ee*, similar to European Golden Plover. [Alt: Black-bellied Plover]

Northern Lapwing *Vanellus vanellus*   L 28–31 cm, WS 62–72 cm

Irregular winter migrant (all islands). Favours arable land for wintering, but sometimes also in semi-desert scrub near the coast or near freshwater reservoirs both inland and coastal. **ID** Winter adult has white chin and creamy fringes to upperpart feathers. Juvenile resembles adult in winter, but has shorter crest and upperpart feathers are finely scalloped, with creamy fringes and black spotting. In flight wing has very broad hand that gives a characteristic flight action with slow wing-beats; white underwing-coverts contrast with black secondaries and primaries (tipped white), and black terminal tail-band contrasts with white rump. Summer male has long crest, black bill, black patch on chest, black chin and throat, black-and-white head pattern, white underside, orange patch on undertail-coverts and ventral region, reddish legs and green-purple iridescence on dark upperparts. Summer female similar to adult male, but has black on foreneck less extensively speckled with white, and a shorter crest. **Voice** Most likely to be heard is a flight call *pee-wit* when alarmed.

Eurasian Dotterel

ad breeding
ad non-breeding
juv

American Golden Plover

ad breeding
ad non-breeding
juv

European Golden Plover

ad breeding
ad non-breeding
juv

Grey Plover

ad breeding
ad non-breeding
juv

Northern Lapwing

ad breeding
ad non-breeding
juv

PLATE 27: SMALL PLOVERS

Little Ringed Plover *Charadrius dubius* — L 15–18 cm, WS 32–35 cm
Resident breeder (T, GC, F) and seasonal visitor (all islands, not Go). During breeding favours freshwater reservoirs with sandy edges, but also near golf courses with ponds, and gullies with running water. **ID** Sexes slightly different. Summer adult has conspicuous yellow eye-ring, dark bill and pinkish legs, all diagnostic criteria for separating from Common Ringed (which see). Adult female differs from male in brownish cheeks, but this is difficult to discern at long range and in strong light. In winter both sexes become brownish on the crown, cheeks and collar, although buff supercilium and yellow eye-ring are still diagnostic. In flight all plumages can easily be separated from Common Ringed by the absence of white wing-bar on secondaries and primaries. Juvenile recalls winter but has narrow eye-ring and scaly pattern on upperparts created by the pale fringes to body and covert feathers. **Voice** A piping monosyllabic *pew* and a repetitive *kree-ah…* during display. **Tax.** The ssp. *curonicus* occurs in the archipelago.

Common Ringed Plover *Charadrius hiaticula* — L 17–19 cm, WS 35–41 cm
Regular winter migrant and seasonal visitor (all islands). In winter prefers rocky coastline and saltpans, but occasionally also on freshwater reservoirs. **ID** Sexes slightly different in summer. Summer male has diagnostic orange bill with black tip, bright orange legs, a white spot behind the eye, no yellow eye-ring and a conspicuous white wing-bar in flight. Summer female recalls adult male, but black head markings and collar tinged brownish. Winter adult has dark bill (as Little Ringed) and legs duller orange (pinkish-grey in Little), but can be reliably separated by conspicuous white supercilium and thick white wing-bar in flight, also different voice. Juvenile similar to adult, but with scaly upperparts due to pale fringes to coverts and mantle feathers. **Voice** A soft disyllabic and rising *hu-it* is commonly heard in the archipelago.

Kentish Plover *Charadrius alexandrinus* — L 15–17 cm, WS 42–45 cm
Resident breeder (T, GC, F, L, g), possibly extinct (T). Favours coastal intertidal lagoons with sandy edges for nesting, but outside the breeding season also along rocky shorelines, saltpans and in arid coastal plains. **ID** Summer male shows pale grey-brown upperparts and dark legs and bill, white supercilium and forehead, a thin black breast collar clearly broken in the centre, and a variable amount of rufous on nape. Summer female has brown head markings, diffuse breast-side patches and buff supercilium. Winter adult recalls summer female, but very little or no rufous on crown and nape. In flight all plumages show conspicuous thick white wing-bar and black tail with white external sides. Juvenile similar to Common and Little Ringed Plover juveniles, but combination of dark legs and broken breast collar is diagnostic. **Voice** Song-flight a *tjekke-tejekke-tejekke…* also a soft *pit* and a *prrr* when alarmed. **Tax.** Nominate ssp. *alexandrinus* occurs in the region.

Lesser Sand Plover *Charadrius mongolus* — L 19–21 cm, WS 45–58 cm
Vagrant. Sexes differ slightly in summer. **ID** Summer male shows rufous breast-band with black border, black mask, white throat and chin, white underside and brown upperparts. Summer female has a duller breast-band and brown where male shows black. Winter adult has a reduced breast-band (two large patches on the sides almost meeting in the centre), no rufous and black markings, forehead white and narrow white supercilium. Juvenile shows sandy fringes to coverts. Confusion likely with slightly smaller Kentish Plover but lacks white collar, and toes project beyond the tail in flight. **Voice** Similar to Ruddy Turnstone, a sharp *chitik* and a short *drrit*.

ad breeding

ad non-breeding

juv

Little Ringed Plover

ad breeding

ad non-breeding

juv

Common Ringed Plover

ad ♂ breeding

ad ♀

Kentish Plover

juv

ad breeding

pamirensis

juv

Lesser Sand Plover

PLATE 28: SNIPES, WOODCOCK AND DOWITCHER

Jack Snipe *Lymnocryptes minimus*   L 18–20 cm, WS 33–36 cm

Irregular winter migrant (all islands). A clear preference for freshwater ponds and reservoirs. **ID** Sexes similar. A small wader similar in plumage pattern and structure to Common Snipe but smaller, with greenish tinge to mantle and scapulars, lack of pale median crown-stripe, shorter bill (not twice length of head), streaks on breast and flanks (not barring), face with split creamy supercilium and black crescent below the eye. In flight wedge-shaped tail is sometimes visible and while foraging and feeding characteristically bounces as it walks; does not have the typical erratic zigzag flight of Common Snipe. **Voice** A soft *scah* when alarmed.

Common Snipe *Gallinago gallinago*   L 23–28 cm, WS 39–45 cm

Regular winter migrant (all islands). Favours freshwater reservoirs and ponds with vegetation, but sometimes also around brackish reservoirs. **ID** A dumpy brown wader with barred chest and flanks, and long straight bill. Flight is erratic and zigzagging, showing a prominent white trailing edge to the wing and pale bands on the underwing. The pale crown-stripe separates it from Eurasian Woodcock. Confusion also possible with Jack Snipe (which see) and vagrant Wilson's Snipe, which has darker underwing; see also Long-billed Dowitcher. **Voice** Most often heard is a harsh *scaap* given in flight.

Eurasian Woodcock *Scolopax rusticola*   L 33–38 cm, WS 55–65 cm

Resident breeder (P, H, Go, T, GC) and recorded elsewhere (F, L, a). Favours laurel forest, but also occurs in suboptimal habitats such as open areas in secondary mixed forests and banana plantations near the coast. **ID** Sexes similar. Adult has short legs, long bill (one-and-a-half times the head size) and complex plumage pattern, belly is barred and has a rufous tinge, unlike snipes. Similar to Common Snipe, but in all plumages differs by diagnostic broad transverse dark brown bands (not stripes) on crown and no conspicuous pale stripes on upperparts, also different habitat type. In flight is pot-bellied and shows rufous rump and no white trailing edge to wings. Crepuscular habits. **Voice** Often gives a *scaap*, not unlike Common Snipe. Male during roding gives an intermittent high-pitched *chissick* mixed with guttural notes *aurk-aurk-aurk*.

Long-billed Dowitcher *Limnodromus scolopaceus*   L 24–26 cm, WS 46–52 cm

Vagrant. Prefers brackish pools, also tidal mudflats but tends to avoid saltpans. **ID** A medium-sized wader similar to Common Snipe and Bar-tailed Godwit. In all plumages shows a broad distinct supercilium, rather long grey-green slightly decurved bill and greenish legs. First-winter is grey overall but adult in summer is mainly reddish. Winter adult near-identical to Short-billed Dowitcher (not recorded in Canary Islands), but slightly greyer body, longer bill and plain grey tertial centres, lacking buff markings as in Short-billed, are diagnostic. Juvenile has shorter bill and no pale markings on dark-centred tertials. **Voice** Diagnostic flight and contact call is a *kik* when flushed, but also a *keeek*, sometimes repeated.

Jack Snipe
ad

Common Snipe
ad

Eurasian Woodcock
ad

Long-billed Dowitcher
juv
ad win
ad sum

PLATE 29: GODWITS AND CURLEWS

Black-tailed Godwit *Limosa limosa* — L 37–42 cm, WS 63–74 cm

Regular winter migrant and seasonal visitor (all islands). Favours freshwater lakes and reservoirs when available but also on brackish lagoons on some islands. **ID** Sexes similar. Winter adult has pinkish bill with dark tip, inconspicuous and short white supercilium and is plain grey overall with black-and-white tail. Summer adult has orange or chestnut (depending on ssp.) head, neck, chest and bill-base, greyish upperparts and white barred belly and white ventral region. Juvenile recalls adult in summer, but chest and belly unbarred, black centres to mantle and scapular feathers, and pale fringes to tertials. Confusion likely with Bar-tailed Godwit but in flight all plumages differ in broad white wing-bar contrasting with black tail, square white rump, and toes projecting conspicuously beyond the tip of tail. **Voice** A repeated *kip*.

Bar-tailed Godwit *Limosa lapponica* — L 37–41 cm, WS 70–80 cm

Seasonal visitor (all islands). Favours sandy beaches with rocky coastline as foraging and feeding sites, occasionally on freshwater reservoirs and saltpans. **ID** Winter adult similar to adult Black-tailed in grey overall plumage with white underside, but shorter legs and shorter bill, which is slightly upcurved, streaked on upperparts, longer supercilium reaching behind the eye and barred tail. Summer adult similar to adult Black-tailed Godwit, but all-dark bill, unbarred belly and all rufous underside are diagnostic. Juvenile similar to juvenile Black-tailed, but bill size and shape diagnostic, and is less orange-buff and has pale notching on tertials and streaks on wing-coverts. In flight all plumages have diagnostic barred tail. **Voice** A *kik* or a disyllabic *kiv-ik* in flight.

Whimbrel *Numenius phaeopus* — L 40–46 cm, WS 76–89 cm

Regular winter migrant and seasonal visitor (all islands). Prefers rocky coastlines for wintering, but also on sandy beaches and golf courses. **ID** Sexes similar. A large wader, similar in size to Eurasian Oystercatcher but all brown with an eyestripe, long legs and long decurved bill. Confusion likely with Eurasian Curlew but shows a diagnostic dark brownish crown with a pale median stripe, a much shorter bill (though beware of shorter-billed juvenile Eurasian Curlew), black eye-stripe, and toes do not project beyond the tail-tip in flight. Juvenile similar to adult but in autumn shows fresh plumage whereas adult plumage is worn. In flight shows a white wedge on rump/back. **Voice** In Canary Islands often utters a series of 6–8 whistles *wewewewewewe*....

Eurasian Curlew *Numenius arquata* — L 48–57 cm, WS 89–106 cm

Seasonal visitor (all islands). Favours pastures, arable fields, semi-desert coastal scrub near freshwater reservoirs and ponds. **ID** Female is larger and longer-billed than male. Confusion likely with Whimbrel, but separated by plain head with no dark crown or buff median stripe (note that some individuals may have a hint of this last feature), larger size and much longer bill, more than three times the head length. Juvenile similar to adult, but bill is shorter and therefore can easily be confused with Whimbrel. In flight shows a finely barred tail and a white wedge as in Whimbrel, but Curlew separated by bill size and the amount of dark feathers on the upper hand, just five outer primaries rather than all primaries and some secondaries in Whimbrel. **Voice** A far-carrying *tutututu* and a *coour-lee*.

ad sum

ad win

Black-tailed Godwit

ad sum

Bar-tailed Godwit

ad

Whimbrel

ad win

ad

ad

Eurasian Curlew

PLATE 30: SANDPIPERS I

Spotted Redshank *Tringa erythropus* L 29–33 cm, WS 61–67 cm

Irregular winter migrant and seasonal visitor (all islands except H and Go). Favours freshwater and brackish reservoirs in winter, but also associated with saltpans. **ID** Sexes similar. A medium-sized wader similar to smaller Common Redshank. Winter adult similar to Common Redshank, but at close range shows greyer, paler plumage overall and diagnostic prominent white supercilium in front of the eye; also black lores, and longer bill with black upper and red lower mandibles. Juvenile similar to juvenile Common Redshank, but has two-coloured bill as in winter adult, darker plumage overall and is uniformly barred on ventral region (white ventral region on Redshank). In flight all plumages can easily be separated from Common Redshank by the lack of broad white trailing edges to the upperwing and instead only a white wedge on the back. Summer adult has black plumage and legs, contrasting with bright red lower mandible and fine white speckles on upperparts created by notches in tertials and wing feathers. **Voice** Most often heard in flight is a *chewit*.

Common Redshank *Tringa totanus* L 24–27 cm, WS 47–53 cm

Regular winter migrant and seasonal visitor (all islands). In the archipelago in winter favours freshwater reservoirs, as well as saltpans and brackish lagoons. **ID** Sexes similar. Winter adult has brownish upperparts, inconspicuous pale supercilium in front of eye, reddish bill-base with dark tip, red legs, mottling on breast and flanks, and white speckles on wings. Juvenile is brown overall with buff tinge on chest (also deeply streaked), white ventral regions, yellowish-orange legs and bill base, and neat buff fringes to feathers creating a scaly pattern on upperparts. Summer adult is brownish on head, neck and upperparts, and streaked on breast and flanks, with white supercilium in front of the eye contrasting with black lores and reddish bill-base. In flight all plumages easily separated from Spotted Redshank (which see) by the broad white trailing edge to the upperwings and more compact shape in the air. **Voice** When alarmed may utter a *tli-tli-tli* and in flight gives a *teu-hu* or *teu-hu-hu*.

Marsh Sandpiper *Tringa stagnatilis* L 22–25 cm, WS 55–59 cm

Vagrant. Prefers gullies with running water, saltpans and freshwater and brackish lagoons and reservoirs. **ID** Sexes similar and size as Common Redshank. Smaller, more elegant and delicate than Common Greenshank, which has same structure and leg colour. Marsh Sandpiper has diagnostic needle-thin straight bill, never upturned as in Common Greenshank. Winter adult similar to adult winter Common Greenshank in having grey upperparts and white underside. Juvenile similar to juvenile Common Greenshank, but less finely streaked on centre of breast. Compared to Greenshank in flight the toes project farther beyond the tail-tip, but this is difficult to observe at long range. Summer adult is dark grey with black spots on upperparts and white underside with some neat bars on flanks; legs vary from dull yellow to greenish (as in Common Greenshank, but never reddish as in Redshank). **Voice** Most typical call in flight is a soft *keeuw*.

Common Greenshank *Tringa nebularia* L 30–34 cm, WS 55–62 cm

Regular winter migrant and seasonal visitor (all islands). Prefers freshwater reservoirs, but also on saltpans and brackish reservoirs. **ID** Summer adult is finely streaked on head and foreneck and is deeply streaked on chest, with white belly and ventral region. Upperparts have a variable amount of dark-centred feathers contrasting with greyish-brownish feathers, legs vary from grey to green, and bill is long, slightly upturned with a diagnostic greenish base and black tip. Winter adult as summer adult but greyer above with white forehead and no streaks on white centre of breast. Juvenile similar to adult in winter, but darker on upperparts and neatly streaked on breast. In flight toes project slightly beyond the tail-tip. Shows a lot of white on back due to white rump and finely barred tail. **Voice** A rising *chew-chew-chew* repeated in flight and on the ground.

Lesser Yellowlegs *Tringa flavipes* L 23–25 cm, WS 59–64 cm

Vagrant. Favours freshwater ponds and reservoirs, also on brackish ponds and lagoons. **ID** Sexes similar. An all brownish wader with bright yellow legs, fine dark bill and diffuse streaks on the chest. In flight has a white rump and no white wedge on back and the yellow feet project well beyond the tail. Confusion likely with Marsh and Wood Sandpipers (which see) and vagrant Greater Yellowlegs. Separated from the latter by smaller Redshank-sized, delicate build with thinner, two-coloured straight bill, diffuse streaks on chest, and voice. Confusion also possible with Common Greenshank, but separated by diagnostic yellow legs and the lack of white wedge on back, best seen in flight. **Voice** A harsh *kiew-kiew* or a single *kiew*.

Spotted Redshank
juv
ad win
ad sum
ad sum
Marsh Sandpiper
ad win
juv
Common Redshank
juv
ad win
ad sum
juv
Common Greenshank
ad win
ad sum
ad win
Lesser Yellowlegs
juv
ad sum

PLATE 31: SANDPIPERS II

Green Sandpiper *Tringa ochropus* L 21–24 cm, WS 57–61 cm

Regular winter migrant and seasonal visitor (all islands). Favours freshwater reservoirs but also in gullies with running brackish water and sewage pools. **ID** Sexes similar. Winter adult is very dark overall with breast and upperparts appearing black in strong light. Summer adult has more heavily streaked head and breast (breast-band ends abruptly), clean white underside, diagnostic greyish-green legs, longish bill, and white supercilium restricted to lores. Juvenile resembles adult, but finely buff-spotted upperparts have a scaly pattern similar to Wood Sandpiper. In flight all plumages show very dark underwings contrasting with white rump and tail with three broad black bars. Confusion likely with Common and Wood Sandpipers. Separated from the former by the lack of white gap near the shoulder, lack of wing-bar in flight and from the latter by the green leg-colour (not yellowish). **Voice** A *klu-uweet-wit-wit* and a sharp *wit-wit-wit* when alarmed.

Wood Sandpiper *Tringa glareola* L 19–21 cm, WS 56–57 cm

Seasonal visitor (all islands). Favours freshwater reservoirs, but also brackish lagoons. **ID** Sexes alike. An elegant wader that in all plumages shows a white supercilium contrasting with a black eye-stripe. Winter adult has grey-brown head, neck and upperparts, which are mottled white, white underside and yellow legs. Summer adult as winter adult but darker overall. Juvenile distinguished by buff pattern on upperparts and diffuse breast. In flight all plumages show narrow black bars on tail, white rump and dark upperwing that contrasts with pale underwing (dark on Green Sandpiper, which has grey-green legs in all plumages). Often bobs rear body as in Common Sandpiper. Confusion possible with Lesser Yellowlegs (which see). **Voice** A high-pitched *chiff-iff-iff*.

Common Sandpiper *Actitis hypoleucos* L 19–21 cm, WS 38–41 cm

Regular winter migrant and seasonal visitor (all islands). Prefers freshwater reservoirs in winter, but also rocky coastlines, saltpans, brackish lagoons and sewage farms. **ID** Sexes similar. Behaviour on the ground and in flight aid identification. On the ground bobs rear body continuously while foraging and feeding and flies with unique pulsating wing-beats on stiff wings. Summer adult is brown above and white below with diagnostic white gap near the shoulder, only shared by vagrant Spotted Sandpiper. Separated from Spotted by longer tail (compared to wingtips), less yellowy legs, no pale base to bill, and no black spots on chest, breast or flanks. Juvenile similar to adult, but wing feathers and tertials buffier due to pale tips and edges. Shows a white wing-bar in flight and no clear white rump. **Voice** A series of whistles *swee-swee-swee*, rising and varying in intensity.

Spotted Sandpiper *Actitis macularius* L 18–20 cm, WS 37–40 cm

Vagrant. Prefers freshwater reservoirs, but also rocky coastline in low tide and, brackish reservoirs and saltpans. **ID** Winter adult similar to Common Sandpiper, but has shorter tail (in relation to wingtips), deeper yellow legs, pale base to the bill diagnostic and wing-bar seen in flight that does not extend to inner wing (less white than on Common, but difficult to assess without a photo). Juvenile similar to winter adult, but plain tertial fringes. In spring (i.e. from end March onwards) easily separated from Common Sandpiper when black spots on underside start to become visible. **Voice** Unlike Common Sandpiper most characteristic calls are a disyllabic *teet-teet* and a monosyllabic *peet*.

Green Sandpiper

ad sum

ad win

juv

Wood Sandpiper

ad sum

juv

ad win

Common Sandpiper

ad sum

juv

ad win

Spotted Sandpiper

ad sum

juv

ad win

PLATE 32: SANDPIPERS III

Red Knot *Calidris canutus*   L 23–26 cm, WS 47–53 cm

Seasonal visitor and irregular winter migrant (all islands except Go). Prefers to winter on muddy and sandy areas near freshwater reservoirs, but also saltpans. **ID** Sexes alike. Winter adult has diagnostic greenish legs, short bill, plain grey overall with white supercilium, grey streaks on chest, flanks and undertail-coverts. Summer adult has black bill and legs, reddish-orange face and underside diagnostic, and rusty feathers on upperparts with black tips. Could be confused with summer adult Curlew Sandpiper (which see). Juvenile recalls winter adult, but has scaly mantle and buff tinge on chest. In flight all plumages show a white wing-bar and a pale grey rump. **Voice** A *kikkik* when flushed and a soft *knut*.

Sanderling *Calidris alba*   L 18–21 cm, WS 40–45 cm

Regular winter migrant and seasonal visitor (all islands). Prefers natural sandy beaches when available, but also saltpans. **ID** Sexes similar. In all plumages differs from similar-sized Dunlin in diagnostic lack of hind toe. Winter adult, the plumage most likely to be seen in Canary Islands, has pale grey upperparts with white fringes to scapulars and coverts, pure white underside, and supercilium contrasting with short dark bill and black legs. Summer adult has black and rufous upperparts, reddish-rufous head and chest with fine dark spotting, white underside, dark legs and bill. Adult in spring similar to summer adult, but only slightly rufous-tinged on head and chest. Juvenile similar to winter adult, but has darker crown and a broken breast collar; scapulars and wing-covert feathers have dark centres with three spear-like marks. **Voice** A sharp *klit* given in flight.

Semipalmated Sandpiper *Calidris pusilla*   L 13–15 cm, WS 34–37 cm

Vagrant. Prefers sandy beaches and tidal mudflats during the non-breeding period. **ID** Confusion likely with Little Stint, but bill stouter. Half-webbed toes are diagnostic for separating it from all other *Calidris* species except vagrant Western Sandpiper (not recorded in Canary Islands). Summer adult is greyish on upperparts with black centres to scapulars, and fine streaks on chest creating a neat breast-band; does not have the typical pale 'V' on back of adult Little. Winter adult difficult to separate from Little and the best identification feature is the half-webbed toes and the harsh *tchrp* call, sometimes similar to Little. Juvenile similar to juvenile Little, but supercilium not split, has rufous-tinged crown and upper scapulars, generally lacks white 'V' on back, and primary projection is shorter. **Voice** Most typical call is a harsh *chruup* or *tchrp*, but sometimes also a *kriit* similar to Little.

Little Stint *Calidris minuta*   L 12–14 cm, WS 34–37 cm

Seasonal visitor and irregular winter migrant (all islands except Go). Prefers saltpans, freshwater reservoirs and rocky shoreline. **ID** Sexes alike. Winter adult is smaller than Dunlin, lacks the diagnostic pale 'V' on mantle, has grey on head, chest and upperpart feathers, which have black centres and white tips. Juvenile has crown, mantle and wing feathers with black centres, wing-coverts have rufous fringes and the pale 'V' on the mantle is both conspicuous and diagnostic. Summer adult also shows a diagnostic pale 'V' on mantle to separate from other *Calidris*, has rufous head, mantle, fringes to scapulars and chest, which also has fine dark streaking; black bill and legs, white underside and split supercilium. In flight all ages have grey tail with broken white rump; all-white in similar Temminck's Stint which also has yellowish legs. **Voice** A high-pitched *stit* given singly or repeated in flight.

Temminck's Stint *Calidris temminckii*   L 13–15 cm, WS 34–37 cm

Vagrant. Prefers tidal mudflats, saltpans and freshwater reservoirs. **ID** Sexes similar. Winter adult is mainly grey-brown on head, chest and upperparts (not just grey as in Little), no white supercilium, yellow legs, and white underside. Summer adult has a variable amount of rufous on mantle created by the rufous fringes to black-centred feathers (visible at long range), brownish-grey crown and chest, and yellow legs. Juvenile is browner overall with grey-brown head and breast-band, pale legs and a characteristic pattern on scapulars and wing-coverts (dark and pale fringed). In flight all plumages show white outer tail feathers (grey on Little and vagrant Least Sandpiper). Recalls a miniature Common Sandpiper due to the white gap near carpal area. Also similar to Little Stint, but in all plumages legs are diagnostically yellow. **Voice** A high-pitched trill *tirr* or *tirrrr-r-r*, sometimes repeated.

Red Knot

ad sum / ad win / juv

Sanderling

ad sum / ad win / juv

Semipalmated Sandpiper

ad sum / ad win / juv

Little Stint

ad sum / ad win / juv

Temminck's Stint

ad sum / ad win / juv

PLATE 33: SANDPIPERS IV

White-rumped Sandpiper *Calidris fuscicollis* L 15–18 cm, WS 40–45 cm

Vagrant. Prefers freshwater reservoirs, but also tidal pools and rocky shorelines. **ID** Sexes alike. Winter adult as smaller winter Dunlin, but longer bill, a white rump divided by black line and long primary projection extending well beyond tail-tip. Has a tern-like structure with short legs and long wings, with white rump in all plumages. Summer adult in fresh plumage looks greyish with pale supercilium, is finely streaked on breast and flanks, and has white stripes on mantle, a decurved black bill with brownish base on lower mandible, black legs and diagnostic long primary projection. Juvenile is rufous on upperparts, shows a white 'V' on mantle. Best separated from other *Calidris* species by long primary projection, except for vagrant Baird's Sandpiper which does not have a full white rump. **Voice** An insect-like *theeet* or *tzreet* given singly or repeated in flight.

Baird's Sandpiper *Calidris bairdii* L 14–17 cm, WS 40–46 cm

Vagrant. Prefers coastal rocky shorelines but also on freshwater reservoirs. **ID** Sexes similar. Winter adult similar to summer adult, but paler overall on upperparts. Summer adult is grey-buff on upperparts with irregular and variable number of black centres to scapulars, and buff breast with fine streaks. Juvenile is buff overall with pale spot above lores often visible, while white fringes to upperpart feathers give a neat scaly pattern (no white 'V' on mantle); also has white chin, all-black bill and long primary projection. Confusion likely with adult summer Sanderling and adult late summer Little Stint (which see). Differs from similar vagrant White-rumped Sandpiper in black and white rump (not all white). **Voice** A soft *kreep* is sometimes given in flight.

Pectoral Sandpiper *Calidris melanotos* L 19–23 cm, WS 42–49 cm

Vagrant. Prefers freshwater reservoirs, but also found on saltpans and golf courses and brackish water dams. **ID** Sexes alike and similar to a miniature Ruff. In all plumages shows yellow to grey-greenish legs and neat gorget, ending abruptly, of fine streaks meeting at a point at centre of breast. Summer adult has inconspicuous supercilium, decurved bill with pale base, sharp contrast between finely streaked breast and white underside, yellowish legs, greyish scapular feathers with black centres and longer primary projection than Ruff or Dunlin. Juvenile recalls adult but differs in overall plumage coloration; mantle with white stripes, more rufous on crown, scapulars and tertials. Winter adult unlikely in the region. **Voice** A flight call *krrrt*.

Curlew Sandpiper *Calidris ferruginea* L 18–23 cm, WS 42–46 cm

Seasonal visitor (all islands). During migration found in tidal muddy areas, saltpans, brackish coastal lagoons, rocky coastline, but also on freshwater reservoirs. **ID** In all plumages separated from Dunlin by white rump, toes projecting beyond tail-tip in flight, more elegant appearance with longer neck and legs, and longer and thinner bill. Winter adult has grey upperparts and white underside like most other *Calidris* species outside the breeding season, but combination of long thin down-curved bill, long legs, conspicuous white supercilium (particularly in front of eye) and white rump are diagnostic. Summer adult is uniform reddish overall, but when moulting from summer to winter becomes less uniform on chest and underside. Juvenile recalls adult, but upperparts have uniform scaly patterning. Has prominent supercilium and often creamy coloration on chest. **Voice** A soft *kirrip* may be heard in flight.

White-rumped Sandpiper

Baird's Sandpiper

Pectoral Sandpiper

Curlew Sandpiper

PLATE 34: SANDPIPERS V

Dunlin *Calidris alpina* L 17–21 cm, WS 32–36 cm

Regular winter migrant and seasonal visitor (all islands). Favours brackish lagoons, saltpans, freshwater reservoirs and rocky coastline at low tide. **ID** Winter adult is mainly grey on upperparts contrasting with white underside, inconspicuous supercilium, pale grey breast-band and no complete white rump. Summer adult has rufous on crown, mantle and scapulars – variation from rufous to red-brown depending on race – fine black streaks on chest and black belly patch. Confusion likely with similar but larger Curlew Sandpiper but in all plumages distinguished by black and white rump and black belly-patch or conspicuous and variable black spots on belly-sides, and shorter bill (but this is variable). Juvenile similar to summer adult, but crown gingery, has white 'V' on mantle, and black spots on belly sides do not reach the wings (but the amount of spotting variable). **Voice** Most characteristic flight-call when flushed is a rasping shrill *kreeep*.

Purple Sandpiper *Calidris maritima* L 19–22 cm, WS 37–42 cm

Vagrant. Prefers rocky coastlines, foraging at low tide. **ID** Sexes alike. Winter adult is slate-grey overall, showing notable contrast with bright orange-yellow legs and bill-base, and has slate-grey mottling on breast and flanks. Dunlin-sized, but easily separated from this and other *Calidris* species by yellowish legs and bill-base. In structure resembles a fat, short-legged Dunlin but in all plumages is much darker overall. Summer adult is dark grey-brown with scaly pattern on upperparts (whitish-rufous feather edges) and thick blackish streaks on breast and flanks; the combination of yellowish-grey legs and hint of yellowish bill-base is diagnostic. Juvenile similar to adult in summer, but rustier on crown and mantle. **Voice** Most typical flight-call is a liquid *kut*.

Buff-breasted Sandpiper *Calidris subruficollis* L 18–20 cm, WS 43–47 cm

Vagrant. Favours freshwater reservoirs, but also frequents golf courses with tall grass. **ID** Sexes alike. Similar in size to Dunlin and confusion only likely with much larger juvenile Ruff. Summer adult and winter is creamy-buff overall with conspicuous pale eye-ring on plain face, short dark bill, yellowish legs and some spotting on flanks. Juvenile as adult, but neatly scalloped patterning on mantle created by pale fringes to feathers. Separation of all plumages from juvenile Ruff straightforward by smaller size, long primary projection, spotted flanks and lack of white on rump in flight ('V'-shaped white patch in Ruff), no white wing-bar and toes projecting far beyond tail-tip. **Voice** May utter a rolled *prrreet* when not breeding.

Ruff *Calidris pugnax* L ♂ 29–32 cm, ♀ L 22–26 cm, WS ♂ 54–60 cm, ♀ 46–49 cm

Seasonal visitor (all islands). Prefers freshwater reservoirs but also in brackish dams. **ID** Males much larger than females. Male in breeding plumage has diagnostic crest and variable-coloured ruff (black, white, orange, chestnut, etc.), as well as orange legs, pinkish bill, heavy spotting on chest, white underside, orange skin on face, and brownish upperparts. Summer adult female with black bill and pale bill surround is grey overall with orange legs and variable black spotting on foreneck and chest. Winter adults of both sexes similar to summer female, but with orange bill-base. Juvenile similar to winter adult, but overall buffier with scaly patterning on upperparts created by white fringes to scapular and wing-coverts; also has long tertials reaching tail-tip, all-dark bill and yellowish legs. Confusion likely with Buff-breasted Sandpiper (which see). **Voice** A *kuk* call given in flight.

Dunlin

alpina
ad sum — ad win — juv

Purple Sandpiper

ad sum — ad win — juv

Buff-breasted Sandpiper

ad — juv

Ruff

ad ♂ win — ad ♀ — ad ♂ sum — juv

PLATE 35: SANDPIPERS VI

Ruddy Turnstone *Arenaria interpres*   L 21–25 cm, WS 50–57 cm
Regular winter migrant and seasonal visitor (all islands). Favours rocky shorelines at low tide for foraging, also in harbours. **ID** Sexes similar. Summer adult has rufous-orange back and scapular fringes, white underside, black-and-white head pattern, and orange legs. Winter adult is similar to summer adult, but has blackish upperparts, brownish head and neck, bold, broad dark breast-band orange legs and white underside. Juvenile similar to adult in winter, but scaly pattern on upperparts created by pale fringes to scapulars and wing feathers. In flight shows a contrasting plumage created by the white wing-bar, white tail with a black terminal band, and long white patch on mantle. Combination of wedge-shaped bill, short orange legs and stocky shape makes this medium-sized wader unmistakable. **Voice** Most characteristic call in flight is a rattling *tuk, tuk-ituk-tuk* or disyllabic *chit-uk*.

Wilson's Phalarope *Phalaropus tricolor*   L 22–24 cm, WS 39–43 cm
Vagrant. Favours saltpans, freshwater reservoirs and brackish intertidal lagoons. Unlike congeners it is not pelagic during the winter. **ID** Sexes similar in winter but differ in summer. Winter adult is pale grey above and white below, at long range appears almost white with diagnostic yellow legs (dark in congeners), and has a grey stripe on side of neck visible at close range. Juvenile or first-winter similar to winter adult, but some juvenile unmoulted brown feathers still retained. In flight pale grey upperparts contrast with conspicuous white rump, and yellow toes project beyond the tail tip (cf. vagrant Lesser Yellowlegs). In non-breeding plumage the lack of black on hindcrown separates Wilson's from Grey and vagrant Red-necked Phalaropes. Summer adult male has grey crown, chestnut sides to neck, orange breast collar, brownish-grey upperparts with dark centre to scapulas and wing-coverts, and white underside. Summer adult female is similar to male but larger and brighter and has grey crown but blackish-chestnut sides to neck, orange breast collar, slate-grey upperparts and white underside. **Voice** May utter a soft *chew* while in the air.

Grey Phalarope *Phalaropus fulicarius*   L 20–22 cm, WS 40–44 cm
Seasonal visitor and irregular winter migrant (central and eastern Canarian seas). Pelagic. **ID** Sexes similar in winter but differ in summer. Winter adult has a stout bill, is pale grey above and white below, with a conspicuous black mask and nape patch, and a broad white wing-bar visible in flight. Juvenile browner on upperparts and whiter on the underside with a tinge of buff on chest. Summer adult unmistakable due to contrast of red plumage with darker upperparts, white face patch and yellow bill. Female is slightly larger and brighter than male. In flight and over the sea can be mistaken for White-faced Storm-petrel, which has rounder wings and legs and toes projecting beyond the tail. Confusion at sea also likely with Sanderling, but face mask diagnostic. **Voice** Unlikely to be heard in the region. [Alt: Red Phalarope]

Ruddy Turnstone

Wilson's Phalarope

Grey Phalarope

PLATE 36: COURSER, PRATINCOLE AND AUKS

Cream-coloured Courser *Cursorius cursor*   L 24–27 cm, WS 51–57 cm

Resident breeder (F, L), occasional breeder (T) and recorded elsewhere (Go, GC, g). Prefers sandy but also stony semi-desert with sparse low shrub cover. **ID** Sexes similar. In flight black primaries on upperwing contrast with overall sandy-buff colour, all-black underwings contrast with chestnut leading edge and thin white trailing edge. Adult is all sandy-buff, conspicuous blue-grey patch on rear crown ending as a 'V' on nape, where the white supercilium and the black eye-stripe also meet. Short black decurved bill. Juvenile similar to adult, but finely spotted on the upperparts and lacking the blue-grey patch. Tends to run rather than fly. **Voice** A typical *whit, whit…chew…* on the ground and while in the air. **Tax.** The ssp. *bannermani* has been described for the Canaries, but is poorly differentiated and not recognised today.

Collared Pratincole *Glareola pratincola*   L 24–28 cm, WS 60–70 cm

Seasonal visitor (all islands). While in the archipelago often rests on golf courses. **ID** In flight adult shows conspicuous white rump and white trailing edge to wing, contrasting with black primaries and brownish upperparts; diagnostic chestnut underwing restricted to secondaries and secondary coverts. Summer adult has yellowish chin, black-bordered throat, black eye, dark legs, black bill with conspicuous red base, white ventral region, brownish plumage overall with yellowish tinge on the lower chest. Winter adult has no yellowish tinge on chest and is less neatly patterned on throat; lacks red on bill base. Tail often extends beyond wingtip. Juvenile recalls adult in structure, but black centres to upperpart feathers create a scaly pattern, and has dark speckles on chest and yellowish throat – can appear all black in strong light. **Voice** A typically high-pitched flight call *kit* or *kitik*.

Atlantic Puffin *Fratercula arctica*   L 28–34 cm, WS 50–60 cm

Vagrant. Highly pelagic while in the region. **ID** Winter adult, the plumage most likely in the region, has dusky face and smaller and less colourful bill than summer adult, which is easily identified by large colourful parrot-like bill. Black-and-white-head, black upperparts, white underside and orange webbed feet. Juvenile bill half size of adult's. In flight all plumages have dark axillaries and no white trailing edge as in Little Auk. Confusion likely with Common Guillemot but toes do not project beyond the tail-tip. **Voice** Unlikely to be heard in the region.

Little Auk *Alle alle*   L 19–21 cm, WS 34–38 cm

Vagrant. Pelagic away from breeding colonies. **ID** Adult in winter similar to adult in summer, but with white throat and neck. Adult in summer has a small black stubby bill, black head, neck and upperparts contrasting with white below, the upper half of a white eye-ring and white edges to the scapulars. Confusion only likely with much larger first-year Atlantic Puffin, which has less rapid whirring wing-beats. In flight, shows dark underwing in all plumages, as in Atlantic Puffin; white trailing-edge and thighs diagnostic. **Voice** Mainly silent away from the breeding colonies. [Alt: Dovekie].

Common Guillemot *Uria aalge*   L 38–46 cm, WS 61–73 cm

Vagrant. Highly pelagic outside the breeding season. **ID** Adult in winter is similar to adult in summer, but has a white patch near ear-coverts, white throat and foreneck, and dark streaks on the flanks; also dusky underwings in flight. Adult in summer is brownish on the head and upperparts, and white on the underparts, with a long black bill; some birds show a narrow white eye-ring and line behind the eye. The extent of dark streaking on the flanks and dusky axillaries are both important features for separation from other species. First-summer recalls adult, but white on throat is variable and juvenile feathers are brownish due to wear. **Voice** Unlikely to be heard in the region. [Alt: Common Murre].

Cream-coloured Courser

ad

juv

Collared Pratincole

ad

juv

Atlantic Puffin

ad win

ad win

Little Auk

ad win

Common Guillemot

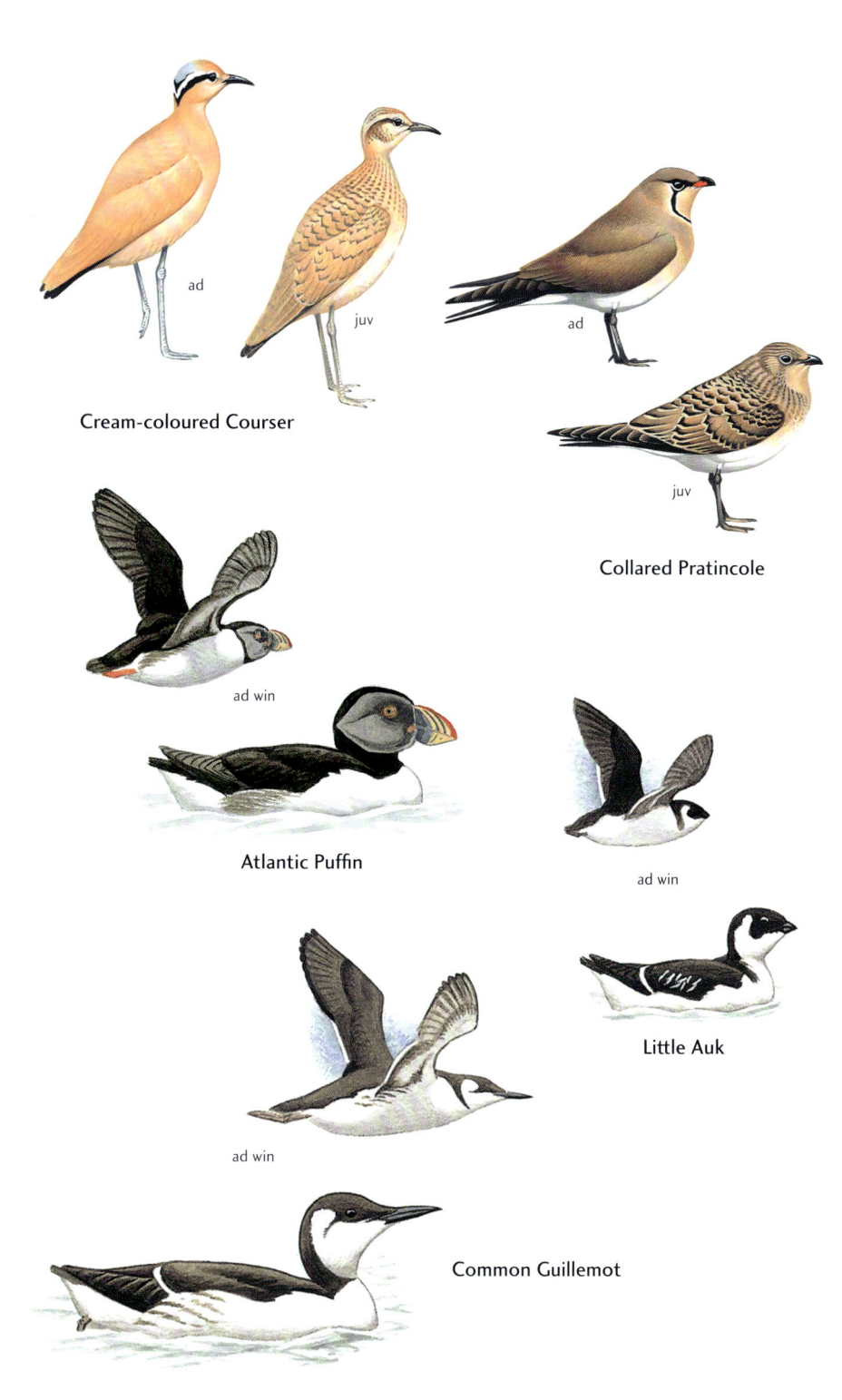

PLATE 37: GULLS I

Mediterranean Gull *Ichthyaetus melanocephalus* L 36–37 cm, WS 100–110 cm

Irregular winter migrant and seasonal visitor (all islands). While in Canary Islands prefers coastal areas. **ID** Sexes similar. Three age-classes. Summer adult separated from Black-headed by black hood (not brownish), stout bright red bill with black vertical stripe, and no black on primary tips making hand look all white. Winter adult similar to summer adult, but hood reduced to a dark mask. Juvenile has scaly back with dark legs and bill. First-winter has dark mask, black bill and legs, and in flight pale grey panel on secondaries and plain underwing. Second-winter similar to adult in winter, but has variable black marks on primary tips. **Voice** May give a *kyow* while in the air.

Laughing Gull *Leucophaeus atricilla* L 36–41 cm, WS 105–120 cm

Vagrant. In natural range prefers saltmarshes, beaches and rocky coastline as in the Canary Islands. **ID** Sexes similar. Three age groups. Summer adult has black hood, white eye-crescents, dark grey upperparts, dark legs, long, dark red bill, and inconspicuous white mirrors on primary tips. Winter adult similar to summer adult, but hood reduced to a variable-sized black mask. First-winter has long black bill and black legs, dirty grey breast-band and black mask. Confusion possible with vagrant Franklin's Gull. In flight has dark axillaries (white on Franklin's Gull) and dirty sides to tail (neat terminal band on Franklin's). Second-winter similar to adult in winter, but with greyish hindneck and variable black markings on tail-tip. **Voice** A high-pitched *ha-ha-ha...* laughter-like call.

Franklin's Gull *Leucophaeus pipixcan* L 32–36 cm, WS 85–95 cm

Vagrant. When in Europe often associates with similar Black-headed Gull. In natural range favours coastal areas as in the archipelago. **ID** Sexes alike. Two age-classes. Similar to Laughing Gull (which see). Summer adult separated from Laughing by shorter and brighter red bill and legs, and large white mirrors on wingtips. Winter adult similar to summer adult, but hood restricted to nape and ear-coverts (black mask). First-winter similar to first-winter Laughing but has smaller proportions, shows white axillaries and neat tail band in flight. Second-winter similar to adult, but with more black on wing-tips. **Voice** A soft *kruk* may be heard in the region.

Sabine's Gull *Xema sabini* L 27–32 cm, WS 90–100 cm

Passage migrant (central and eastern Canarian seas). Highly pelagic when passing through the Canary Islands. **ID** Sexes similar and two age-classes. Summer adult has a dark grey hood, black bill with pale yellowish tip, dark legs, grey upperparts and black wingtips with five mirrors. Winter adult similar to summer adult, but no hood and variable amount of black on nape and hindneck. Juvenile has brownish crown, hindneck and upperparts, dark forked tail. Confusion likely with Kittiwake and Little Gull (which see). In flight all plumages lack black carpal bar, a diagnostic feature separating Sabine's from other smaller gulls in non-adult final plumage (juvenile and first-winter Little Gull and Kittiwake). **Voice** Sometimes gives a tern-like *krrrr* while migrating.

Mediterranean Gull

Laughing Gull

Franklin's Gull

Sabine's Gull

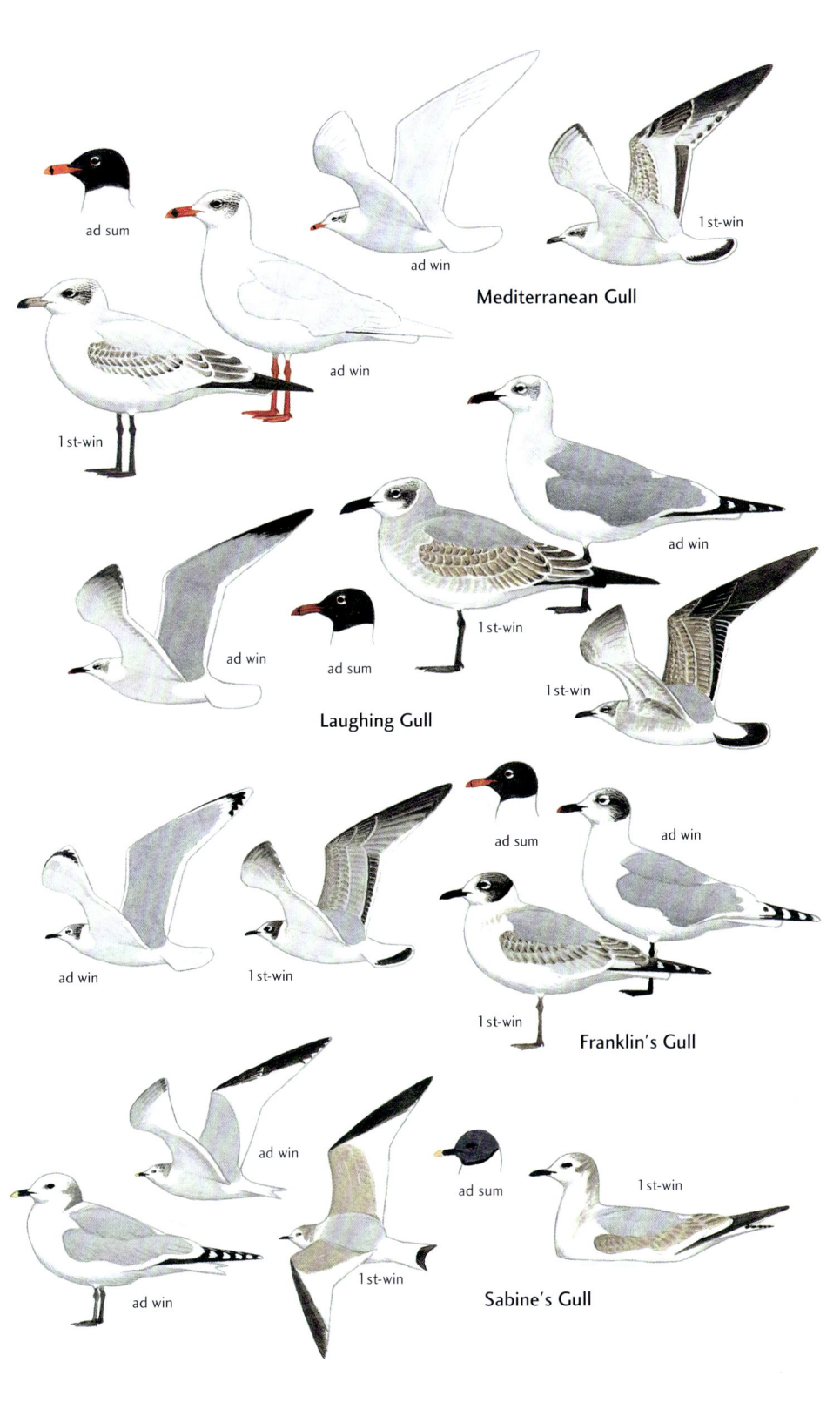

PLATE 38: GULLS II

Little Gull *Hydrocoloeus minutus* — L 25–27 cm, WS 75–80 cm
Vagrant. Prefers inshore coastal waters and freshwater or brackish lagoons when not breeding. **ID** Sexes similar. Three age-classes. Summer adult has black head and bill contrasting with pale grey upperparts, white underside and reddish legs. Winter adult similar, but black on head restricted to rear crown and ear-coverts, and legs pinkish-red. In flight both winter and summer adults have black underwing, and white trailing edge extends from secondaries to tips of primaries. Juvenile is blackish on crown, ear-coverts, bill, mantle and in flight shows a grey secondary bar and a dark 'M' across wings. First-winter similar to winter adult, but with black carpal bar and outer primaries and black tail-tip. Second-winter variable, with black markings on wing-tip and paler axillaries than adult. **Voice** Most common call is a tern-like *kik-kik-kik....*

Black-headed Gull *Chroicocephalus ridibundus* — L 34–37 cm, WS 100–110 cm
Regular winter migrant and seasonal visitor (all islands). Favours freshwater reservoirs but also near coastal waters and harbours in the archipelago. **ID** Sexes similar. Two age-classes. Summer adult has brownish hood, white crescents, and dark red bill and legs. Winter adult similar to summer adult, but hood absent, and has black ear-spot and black line above the eye, red bill with dark tip, and brown-red legs. Juvenile has brown-ginger upperparts, yellowish-pink legs and pink bill with dark tip. First-winter similar to winter adult, but has dark centres to tertials and wing-coverts, and legs are yellowish-pink. First-summer hood not fully developed and thus some have white mixed in; also has neat pattern on upperwing. Note the diagnostic white leading edge to the outer wing, only shared with Slender-billed Gull and vagrant Bonaparte's Gull. **Voice** Most typical call is a high-pitched scream *karrr* or *kreeay*, but also a sharp *kek-kek* when foraging.

Audouin's Gull *Ichthyaetus audouinii* — L 48–52 cm, WS 125–140 cm
Irregular winter migrant and seasonal visitor (all islands except P and H). Prefers beaches and coastal areas. **ID** Sexes alike. Four age-classes. Summer adult has diagnostic dark red bill, dark iris and grey-green legs. Juvenile brownish overall with scaly pattern on upperparts and separated from juvenile Yellow-legged and Lesser Black-backed Gulls by pale bill with black tip, U-shaped white rump contrasting with black tail, black-and-white on axillaries and dark legs. First-winter as juvenile, but whiter on throat and underside, greyer on mantle. Second-summer similar to adult, but upperwing hand all black and black terminal band on tail still unmoulted. Second-winter has a variable amount of black on head and sometimes a tail-band is present, bill is not yet reddish. **Voice** Similar to Yellow-legged Gull but deeper.

Slender-billed Gull *Chroicocephalus genei* — L 42–44 cm, WS 100–110 cm
Vagrant. Prefers sandy beaches, freshwater and brackish reservoirs and lagoons while in the archipelago. **ID** Sexes similar. Two age-classes. Confusion possible with Black-headed. Summer adult lacks hood, has pinkish-tinged underside, darker red bill and legs, whitish iris and white head. Winter adult as summer adult but often a pale ear-spot visible. Juvenile less brownish than juvenile Black-headed and ear-spot inconspicuous; no black tip on pinkish bill. First-winter similar to summer adult, but has brown centres to wing-coverts, very small black tip to bill and diagnostic pale iris (dark on Black-headed). **Voice** A *krerrr*, harder than Black-headed Gull.

Little Gull

ad sum

1st-win

ad win

1st-win

ad win

Black-headed Gull

ad win

ad sum

1st-win

ad win

1st-win

Audouin's Gull

1st-win

ad

1st-win

ad

Slender-billed Gull

ad win

ad sum

1st-win

1st-win

PLATE 39: GULLS III

Ring-billed Gull *Larus delawarensis* L 41–49 cm, WS 112–124 cm

Vagrant. Favours coastal areas but also freshwater reservoirs. **ID** Sexes similar. Three age-classes. Confusion likely with Common Gull. Summer adult differs in yellow bill with a broad vertical black stripe visible at long range, yellowish legs (not greenish), light iris (not dark) and in flight only a small white mirror in wingtip is visible (larger in Common). Winter adult as winter adult Common with thin vertical stripe on bill, but pale not dark iris. First-winter separated from first-winter Common by paler grey upperparts, stouter bill, pale thin fringes to tertials and in flight a less clear cut band on tail. Second-winter shares with second-winter Common Gull the greenish legs and greenish bill with thick vertical stripe, but shows paler grey upperparts, pale iris and a variable amount of black on terminal tail-band (usually absent in Common). In flight Ring-billed has a less clear cut white trailing edge to wing. **Voice** May give a mellow *kowk*.

Common Gull *Larus canus* L 40–46 cm, WS 99–108 cm

Vagrant. Prefers coastal waters near harbours. **ID** Sexes alike. Thee age-classes. Winter adult has a pale bill with a thin vertical stripe similar to vagrant Ring-billed Gull (which see). Summer adult has yellow bill, yellow-green legs, grey upperparts contrasting with white head and underside. Confusion also possible with adult summer Black-legged Kittiwake, which has short dark legs. In flight adult has a prominent white trailing edge to wing, and a large white mirror on black wing-tip. Juvenile brownish overall with neat scaly pattern on upperparts. First-winter has grey bill with black tip, pinkish legs, grey upperparts and brownish wing feathers. Second-winter similar to adult, but has thick vertical stripe on greenish bill, greenish legs, all-grey upperparts and a small white mirror is often visible when bird on the ground or in the air. **Voice** Most common call is a *gleeoo*, given on the ground or in flight during the non-breeding period. [Alt: Mew Gull.]

Lesser Black-backed Gull *Larus fuscus* L 48–56 cm, WS 117–134 cm

Regular winter migrant and seasonal visitor (all islands) and occasional breeder (mc, a). Prefers offshore coastal waters, harbours, freshwater reservoirs, but also frequents rubbish dumps. Breeding only on isolated islets in colonies of Yellow-legged Gull. **ID** Sexes similar. Four age-classes. Winter adult similar to summer adult, but legs are orange (yellow on Yellow-legged Gull, ssp. *atlantis*) and head and neck are heavily streaked (not so heavily on nape of ssp. *atlantis*). Juvenile/first-winter is brown overall and often shows a dark eye-surround. Narrow pale tips to tertials (all dark in ssp. *atlantis*) and in flight an all-dark hand and white rump with a bold black terminal band. Second-winter as first-winter, but with greyish mantle, brown wings and streaks on crown, neck and chest, pinkish legs and black terminal band on tail, which is retained. Third-winter much like winter adult, but still some hint of black terminal band on tail. Summer adult has deep orange bill with a red dot, yellow legs, white head and underside, and black upperparts. Ssp. *fuscus* and *graellsii* both occur in the Canary Islands, the former having a black mantle and upperwing and the latter dark grey mantle and upperwing contrasting with black wing-tip and white mirror (similar to Yellow-legged Gull, ssp. *atlantis*). **Voice** Almost identical to Yellow-legged Gull.

Yellow-legged Gull *Larus michahellis* L 52–58 cm, WS 120–140 cm

Resident breeder (all islands). Prefers nesting on coastal cliffs and foraging offshore following fishing boats, but also found on arable land looking for grasshoppers and in rubbish dumps near the coast. **ID** Sexes alike. Four age-classes. Summer adult has white head and underside contrasting with dark grey upperparts, small mirrors on black wingtip, yellow bill with red dot, yellow iris with red orbital ring, and yellow legs. Winter adult similar to summer adult, but thin streaks on crown. Juvenile/first-winter varies from light to dark plumage, but separated from other similar-sized gulls by all-dark centres to tertials and in flight by neat terminal band on tail and clean white rump. Second-winter often has variable number of grey feathers on upperparts, yellow legs, and pale bill with dark tip. Third-winter similar to adult, but still with some blackish feathers on tail and primary coverts. **Voice** Most typical call is a *keeow* followed by an anxious *gag-ag-ag*. **Tax.** The subspecies *atlantis* occurs in the Canary Islands.

Ring-billed Gull

1st-win · ad win · 2nd-win · ad win · 1st-win

Common Gull

1st-win · ad win · 2nd-win · 1st-win · ad win

Lesser Black-backed Gull

1st-win · ad win *nominate* · ad win *graellsii* · ad win *nominate* · ad win *graellsii*

Yellow-legged Gull

1st-win · ad win *atlantis* · 1st-win · ad win *atlantis*

PLATE 40: GULLS IV

Great Black-backed Gull *Larus marinus*   L 61–74 cm, WS 144–166 cm

Irregular winter migrant and seasonal visitor (T, GC, F, L). Prefers harbours and rocky coastal areas. **ID** Sexes similar. Four age-classes. Winter adult with some fine streaks around the eye and hindneck, similar to summer adult. Summer adult has white head and underside, yellow iris with red orbital ring, yellow bill with red dot, black upperparts, pale fleshy legs, and black primaries with large mirrors. Confusion likely with Lesser Black-backed Gull but larger size, pink legs and large white mirrors. Juvenile/first-winter separated from Lesser Black-backed by heavy bill, neat plumage overall, broad pale tips to black-centred tertials and in flight by conspicuous pale window and narrow black terminal band on tail. Second-winter similar to juvenile/first-winter, but wing-coverts less squared and often has pale bill-base. Third-winter similar to adult, but not all wing-coverts are black and bill is often pale with dark subterminal band. **Voice** A deep *oow-oow-oww*.

Iceland Gull *Larus glaucoides*   L 52–60 cm, WS 123–139 cm

Vagrant. Prefers coastal waters and harbours during the non-breeding period and while in the archipelago. **ID** Sexes similar. Four age-classes. Summer adult has white head and underside, yellow eye, greenish-yellow bill with red dot, pale grey upperparts and reddish legs. Winter adult as summer adult, but heavily streaked brown on head and neck. Juvenile/first-winter is much paler overall, particularly on upperparts, than juvenile/first-winter Yellow-legged Gull and compared to Glaucous often has an all-dark bill; longer primary projection gives Iceland a more elegant structure. In spring the first-winter plumage is faded to white and the bill turns pale at base, similar to Glaucous in this period. Second-winter is all-white, bill often greenish with dark tip. Third-winter similar to adult, but some greyish feathers on upperparts are visible. **Voice** As Yellow-legged Gull.

Glaucous Gull *Larus hyperboreus*   L 63–68 cm, WS 138–158 cm

Vagrant. During the non-breeding period favours coastal areas around fishing villages. **ID** Sexes similar and four age-classes, with diagnostic whitish primaries as in Iceland Gull (which see). Adult best told from Iceland by larger size and short projection of primaries beyond the tail tip. Winter adult similar to summer adult, but head and neck are heavily streaked. Summer adult has white head and underside, yellow bill with red dot, yellow orbital ring (reddish on Iceland), pale grey upperparts and white primaries. Juvenile/first-winter is pale uniform brown with buff-white wingtips and diagnostic pink bill with dark tip (almost all dark on Iceland). In spring first-winter becomes almost all-white. Second-winter similar to first-winter, but blotchier on breast, iris yellow and bill often with a pale tip. Third-winter similar to adult, but less evenly patterned on upperparts and bill is often not entirely yellow. **Voice** Deeper than Yellow-legged Gull.

Black-legged Kittiwake *Rissa tridactyla*   L 37–42 cm, WS 93–105 cm

Seasonal visitor and irregular winter migrant (all Canarian seas). Mainly offshore when in the archipelago and in flocks following fishing boats. **ID** Sexes similar. Three age-classes. Has a diagnostic shearwater-like gliding flight. Summer adult has white head and underside, yellowish bill, black eye and dark legs. Winter adult as summer adult, but has a conspicuous dark ear-spot and grey hindneck. In flight upperwing is two-toned grey with a black triangle on wingtip. Juvenile/first-winter recalls juvenile/first-winter Little Gull, but upperparts grey and often with a dark ear-spot and a black half-collar on neck. In flight similar to Little with black 'M' across upperparts, but lacks dark cap, mantle is plain grey and the absence of a grey secondary bar creates a much whiter upperwing. Second-winter similar to adult, but some blackish feathers on carpal bar are retained, and has black on bill. **Voice** Mainly silent in the archipelago.

Great Black-backed Gull

1st-win

ad win

1st-win

Iceland Gull

ad win

1st-win

1st-win

2nd-win

ad win

Glaucous Gull

2nd-win

1st-win

1st-win

ad win

Black-legged Kittiwake

ad win

1st-win

1st-win

ad win

PLATE 41: TERNS I

Gull-billed Tern *Gelochelidon nilotica* L 35–42 cm, WS 76–86 cm
Seasonal visitor (all islands). Favours fresh and brackish reservoirs when in the archipelago. **ID** Sexes similar. Summer adult has black cap on crown extending to nape, grey above and white below, dark legs and all-black bill. Winter adult as summer adult but lacks the black cap and has a conspicuous dark mask visible at long range. In flight adult separated from adult Sandwich by pale grey rump with white sides, and dark trailing edge to outer primaries visible from below and above. Juvenile similar to juvenile Sandwich in all-black bill and dark legs, but has pale crown and upperparts. First-winter as first-winter Sandwich, but with dark mask, pale grey rump and plainer upperwing with dark trailing edge visible on outer primaries. Tends to plunge-dive less often than Sandwich. **Voice** Most frequent calls include a metallic *kak-kak*, and a nasal *ger-erk* similar to Sandwich Tern.

Caspian Tern *Hydroprogne caspia* L 48–55 cm, WS 96–111 cm
Vagrant. Favours sand spits, sheltered coastal waters and saltpans. **ID** Sexes alike. Summer adult has black cap and shaggy crest, huge red bill with black tip, grey upperparts and white underside, and dark legs. Winter adult similar to summer adult, but cap less neat and with white streaks. Juvenile similar to adult in winter, but crest less shaggy, bill less deep red and with dusky tip, and has pale legs and scaly pattern on upperparts. First-winter has a plain upperwing and black outer tail feathers. First-summer similar to adult in winter, but with variegated pattern on wings and tail. Beware that juvenile Red-billed Tropicbird can resemble Caspian Tern at long range. In all plumages has thick red bill with a dark tip and black patch underneath wingtips. **Voice** A disyllabic *kra-krah* and a heron-like *kraah*.

Sandwich Tern *Thalasseus sandvicensis* L 37–43 cm, WS 85–97 cm
Regular winter migrant and seasonal visitor (all islands). Favours coastal waters near rocky coasts, harbours and fishing ports. **ID** Sexes alike. Slightly larger than Common Tern. Summer adult has black crown and shaggy crest, black bill with yellow tip (often visible at long range), dark legs, pale grey upperparts and white underside (washed pinkish-creamy). Winter adult as summer adult, but with white forecrown. In flight adult has white rump and inconspicuous dark wedge on wingtip (more visible later in the summer) and broad white trailing edge (narrow on Common and Arctic Terns). Juvenile has black crown, short dark bill, scaly upperparts, white underside and dark legs. First-winter resembles adult in winter, although wing-coverts and tertials have dark centres and bill all dark, usually lacking yellow tip. In flight shows greyish wings with darker hand and black on outer tail feathers. **Voice** A *kreeer* and a deep *kirruk* can be heard in the region.

Little Tern *Sternula albifrons* L 21–25 cm, WS 41–47 cm
Vagrant. Prefers sand spits along the coast and shallow inshore islets. **ID** Sexes similar. Summer adult has black cap contrasting with white forehead, is grey above and white below, has yellow bill with dark tip, yellowish-orange legs and in flight long wings with three black outer primaries. Winter adult as summer adult, but bill all black and only rear half of cap is black showing a white forecrown. Juvenile/first-winter has black cap, whitish forehead, black bill with pale base, yellowish legs, and scaly pattern on upperparts contrasting with white underside. In flight has black carpal bar and white triangular patch on secondaries and primaries. **Voice** Sometimes a continuous *kirrikikki, kirrikikki…*, also a sharp *kik-kik* and an alarm call *kyik*.

Sooty Tern *Onychoprion fuscatus* L 42–45 cm, WS 72–80 cm
Vagrant. Highly pelagic away from breeding grounds. **ID** Black-and-white tern similar in size to Sandwich Tern, but most likely to be confused with Bridled Tern (unrecorded in Canaries). Adult in summer told from Bridled by white forehead patch not reaching behind the eye and very thin loral stripe; also has black mantle and upperparts, but latter feature in strong light is unreliable. Juvenile has all-dark plumage contrasting with white belly and undertail-coverts, pale spots on mantle and wing coverts, and darkish axillaries. In flight, confusion of juvenile likely with adult Black Tern, which is much smaller and has paler axillaries and upperwing. **Voice** Unlikely to be heard.

Gull-billed Tern

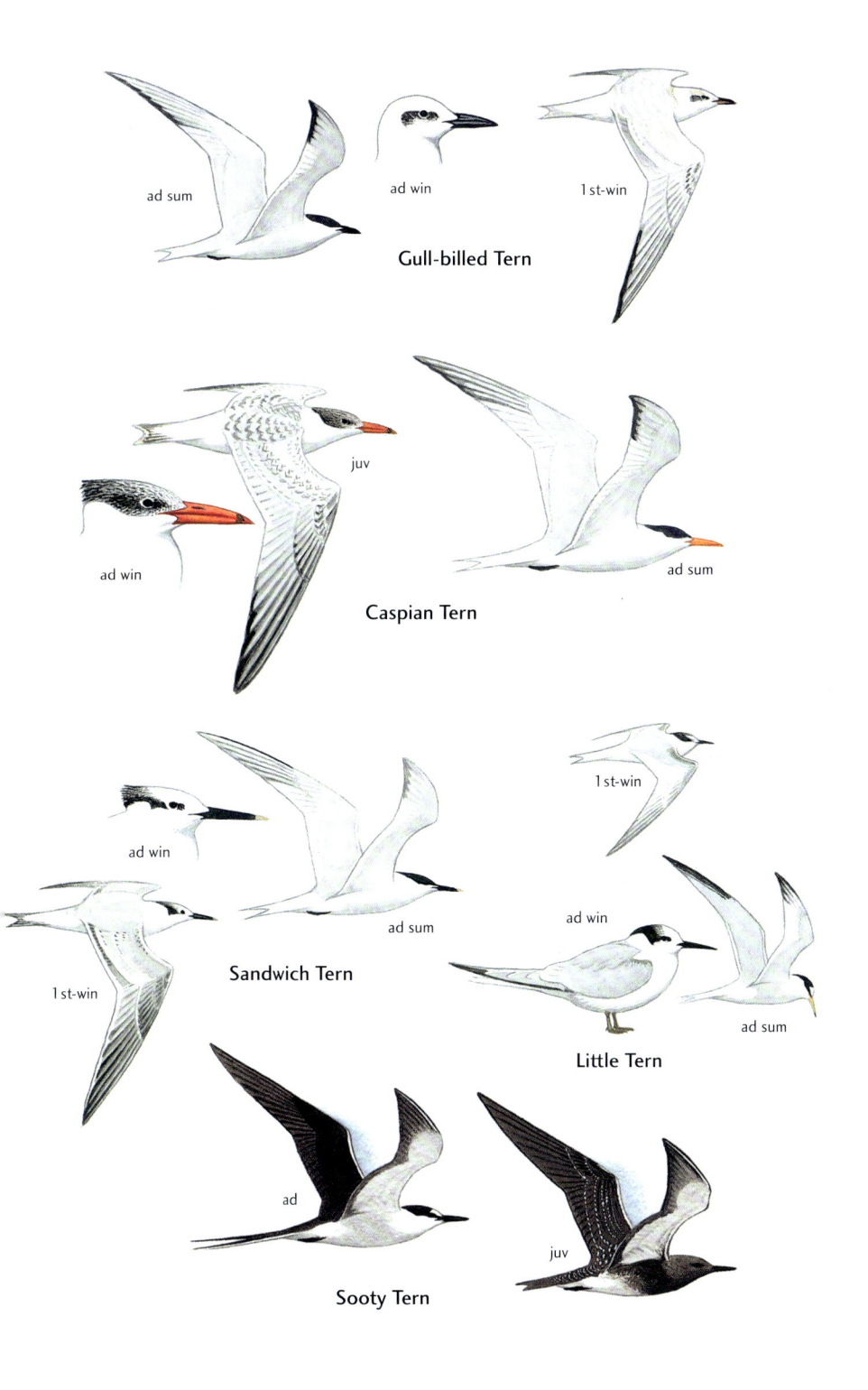

ad sum, ad win, 1st-win

Caspian Tern

ad win, juv, ad sum

Sandwich Tern

ad win, ad sum, 1st-win

Little Tern

1st-win, ad win, ad sum

Sooty Tern

ad, juv

PLATE 42: TERNS II

Common Tern *Sterna hirundo*   L 34–37 cm, WS 70–80 cm

Migrant breeder in summer (P, H, Go, T, GC) and seasonal visitor (F, L). Prefers offshore islets for breeding when available, also found near harbours and in calm waters. **ID** Sexes alike. Summer adult has pale grey upperparts and underside and black cap. Can be separated from Arctic by two-tone bill (red with black tip), longer red legs, wingtips projecting beyond tail and broader trailing edge to 4–6 primaries (narrower in Arctic). In flight adult from below shows diagnostic whiter patch on inner primaries and has a more compact silhouette than Arctic. Winter adult similar to summer adult, but white underside, all-black bill, white forecrown and dark carpal bar visible in flight. Juvenile told from juvenile/first-winter Arctic and Roseate Terns by brownish upperparts contrasting with white underside when recently fledged, and in flight shows diagnostic broad carpal bar and darker bar on secondaries. **Voice** A repetitive *kirri-kirri-kirri…* and flight calls include a high-pitched scream *kreeer*, but also a sharp *kik*. **Tax.** Nominate ssp. *hirundo* occurs in the Canary Islands.

Arctic Tern *Sterna paradisaea*   L 33–39 cm, WS 66–77 cm

Passage migrant (central and eastern Canarian seas). Away from breeding colonies mainly along coasts and at sea during passage. **ID** Sexes similar. Summer adult like Common Tern but bill dark red with no black tip, very short red legs, darker grey upperparts and dirtier grey underside, and wingtips do not project beyond tail-tip. Winter adult similar to summer adult, but bill all black, has white on forecrown and streamers shorter. In flight longer tail streamers than Common and conspicuous white patch on all primaries (not just on inner primaries as in Common). Juvenile/first-winter similar to juvenile/first-winter Common with white forehead and dark bill with red base (although sometimes all black), but in flight lacks the secondary black bar (has all-white secondaries), shows inconspicuous black carpal bar (broad on Common) and has a diagnostic triangular white patch created by secondaries and inner primaries visible on upperwing. First-summer similar to winter adult. **Voice** A disyllabic *kree-eer* as Common Tern.

Roseate Tern *Sterna dougallii*   L 33–36 cm, WS 67–76 cm

Occasional breeder (H) and vagrant. Associated with coastal areas during the non-breeding period and with isolated islets during the single breeding attempt. **ID** Sexes alike. Summer adult has black cap, very pale grey upperwings, white underside with a pinkish tinge, variable bill colour ranging from all black to black with reddish base, red legs and white inner primaries (dark on Common and Arctic). Winter adult as summer adult, but has black bill, white forecrown and black carpal bar. In flight very white overall with 2–4 inconspicuously darker primaries, and long tail contrasting with short wings. Juvenile similar to juvenile Sandwich Tern, but much smaller, dark cap (often white forehead), black bill and legs contrasting with scaly pattern on upperparts. Similar in size to Common and Arctic Terns, but differs in structure with shorter wings that produce a slightly different flight action with faster wing-beats. **Voice** A rasping *kraak* and a disyllabic Sandwich Tern-like *cher-vrik*. **Tax.** Nominate ssp. *dougallii* occurs in the archipelago.

Whiskered Tern *Chlidonias hybrida*   L 24–28 cm, WS 57–63 cm

Seasonal visitor (all islands except H, Go). Prefers freshwater reservoirs. **ID** Sexes alike. Summer adult is grey overall with black cap, deep red bill and legs, white cheeks and white ventral region. Winter adult as summer adult, but very pale grey overall, with white forecrown, reddish legs and dark bill with red base. Confusion likely with Black and White-winged Terns (which see). Juvenile often lacks dark carpal bar in flight, and mantle tinged rufous with scaly pattern. **Voice** Unlikely to be heard in the region, but in flight may utter a short and repetitive *kek*.

Black Tern *Chlidonias niger*   L 22–26 cm, WS 56–62 cm

Vagrant. Prefers freshwater reservoirs but also seen along the coast. **ID** Similar in size to Whiskered Tern, but adult in summer unmistakable due to all-black head, bill, legs and underside contrasting with white ventral region and pale grey upperparts. Winter adult as summer adult in shape, but black helmet covering crown and ear, black bill, grey upperparts and dark breast patch are diagnostic when separating from congeners. Juvenile similar to winter adult, but has darker breast patch and buff fringes to mantle and wing feathers. In flight grey rump and dark outer primaries, underwing all pale (white rump and black-and-white underwing in vagrant White-winged Tern). **Voice** Most characteristic call is a weak *kik* or *kik-kik* in flight.

White-winged Tern *Chlidonias leucopterus*   L 20–24 cm, WS 50–60 cm

Vagrant. Associated with coastal areas in the Canary Islands. **ID** Winter adult separated from Black Tern by inconspicuous black markings on crown (lacking black helmet), faint ear-spot, pale grey upperparts and white underside with no dark breast patch. Summer adult as summer adult Black Tern in plumage coloration, but tail is less forked and has white rump, a variable amount of black on underwing-coverts (depending on moult stage) and dark grey mantle. Juvenile best told from juvenile Black Tern by the lack of a dark breast patch and from juvenile Whiskered Tern by the lack of rufous and scaly pattern on mantle. In flight white rump diagnostic, but adult winter Whiskered Tern can look very pale in strong light. **Voice** A loud *kreek* unlike congeners. [Alt: White-winged Black Tern]

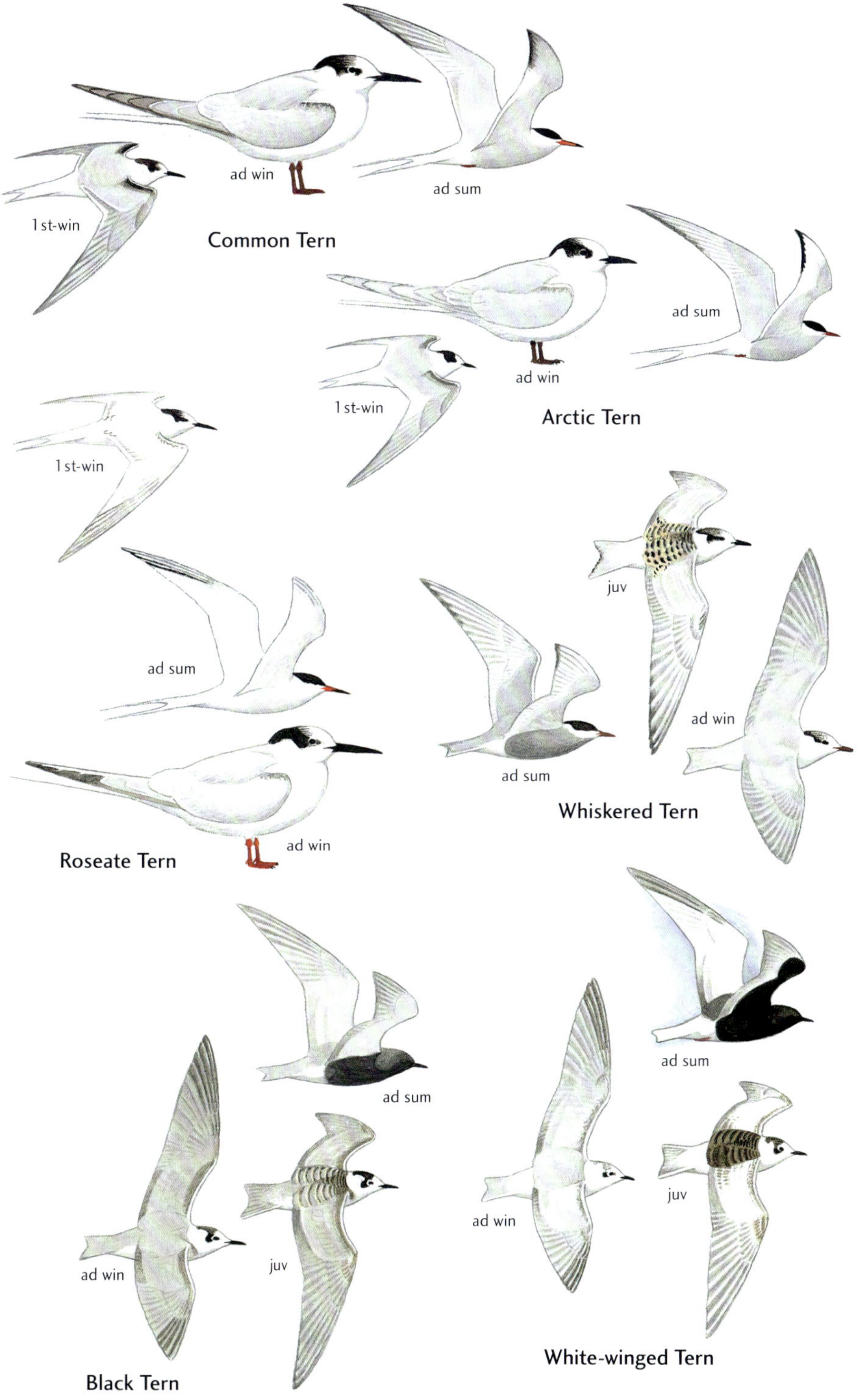
1st-win
ad win
ad sum
Common Tern
ad sum
ad win
1st-win
Arctic Tern
1st-win
ad sum
ad win
Roseate Tern
juv
ad sum
ad win
Whiskered Tern
ad sum
ad win
juv
Black Tern
ad sum
ad win
juv
White-winged Tern

PLATE 43: SKUAS

Pomarine Skua *Stercorarius pomarinus* L 46–51 cm (tail included), WS 125–135 cm
Seasonal visitor (all Canarian seas). Pelagic and rarely approaches the shoreline. **ID** Sexes similar, occurs in pale and dark morphs with pale being commoner. Summer adult similar to Arctic Skua, with dark cap, yellow ear-coverts and nape, white neck and breast (dark breast-band often present), dark upperparts, but diagnostic spoon-shaped central tail feathers and pale bill-base. Winter adult normally lacks the spoon-shaped feathers, so is more difficult to separate from congeners. Juvenile all brown, and often separable from congeners by pale base to heavy bill and from juvenile Great Skua by presence of pale bars on rump and ventral region. Due to larger size than congeners (except Great) flight action more relaxed and steady. **Voice** Unlikely to be heard in the region. [Alt: Pomarine Jaeger]

Long-tailed Skua *Stercorarius longicaudus* L 48–53 cm (tail included), WS 105–115 cm
Passage migrant (central and eastern Canarian seas). Pelagic when not breeding and while passing through the Canary Islands. **ID** Sexes similar. The most elegant of all skuas and slightly smaller than Arctic. Summer adult has diagnostic elongated, pointed central tail feathers that are *c*. 29 cm long (18 cm in Arctic). Summer adult has black cap, yellowish tinge to ear-coverts, grey upperparts contrasting with white underside and in flight lacks conspicuous white wing flashes, which are restricted to the base of a few outer primaries. Juvenile variable and best told from congeners by short bill (half black), no pale tips to primaries and less extensive white wing-flashes in flight. **Voice** Relatively silent away from breeding colonies. [Alt: Long-tailed Jaeger]

Arctic Skua *Stercorarius parasiticus* L 41–46 cm (tail included), WS 110–120 cm
Seasonal visitor (central and eastern Canarian seas). Pelagic when not breeding. **ID** Sexes alike and several morphs. In size between larger Pomarine and smaller Long-tailed. In flight shows a sharp division between white wing flashes and the rest of the wing. Summer adult pale and dark morphs have diagnostic elongated, pointed central tail feathers that are *c*. 18 cm long (29 cm in Long-tailed); pale morph has black cap, yellowish tinge to the ear-coverts and neck, dark grey-brown upperparts, all-white underside and dark legs, and often a pale bill-surround. Juvenile is very variable and best told by slight projection of central tail feathers, difficult to observe at long range. **Voice** Unlikely to be heard in the region. [Alt: Parasitic Jaeger]

Great Skua *Stercorarius skua* L 53–58 cm (tail included), WS 135–145 cm
Seasonal visitor (all Canarian seas). Prefers to winter near the coast. **ID** Sexes similar. Summer adult is brown overall with dark cap, very heavy bill, yellowish stripes on neck and mantle, and dark legs. In flight shows conspicuous white wing-flashes on upper and underwing created by white on primary bases. Juvenile and first-year plumage is reddish-brown overall, especially on underside, and on average the wing-flash is smaller. Lighter and darker birds occur in all ages. Confusion most likely with larger gulls, and juvenile Pomarine Skua, which has bars on rump and vent, light grey legs and pale base to bill. Could also be confused with vagrant South Polar Skua (which see). **Voice** Mostly silent away from breeding grounds and therefore unlikely to be heard in the Canary Islands.

South Polar Skua *Stercorarius maccormicki* L 51–54 cm, WS 125–135 cm
Vagrant. Highly pelagic away from the breeding grounds. **ID** Sexes similar; two morphs. Slightly smaller and more elegant than Great Skua, due to slimmer body. Occurs in pale and dark morphs, sometimes intermediate. In most plumages lacks the mottled aspect of Great, never shows any rufous in plumage and in paler birds a conspicuous pale nape is often visible even at long range. Dark morph recalls Great Skua, but often a hint of paler neck-collar visible, although this is difficult to observe at long range at sea. Juvenile recalls adults of respective morphs, but generally shows bluish lower mandible (greyer or all dark in juvenile Great). Pale morph has head and underside pale buffish with no clear brown crown-patch, as in Great Skua, contrasting with darker wings. **Voice** Unlikely to be heard in the region.

ad pale morph

juv intermediate morph

Pomarine Skua

ad pale morph

Arctic Skua

ad

juv

juv intermediate morph

Long-tailed Skua

South Polar Skua

ad

Great Skua

ad dark morph

ad pale morph

juv

PLATE 44: PIGEONS I

African Collared Dove *Streptopelia roseogrisea*   L 29–30 cm, WS 45–50 cm

Introduced (all islands except H). Prefers human settlements in towns and tourist resorts near the coast and always associated with man. **ID** Sexes similar. A domesticated form that escaped from captivity is today mixed with Eurasian Collared. Differs from Eurasian Collared by slightly smaller size, overall paler white and sandy plumage, rounder head shape, whitish vent and undertail-coverts and darker tail when spread; broader black half-collar on neck and buff-brown primaries (not black). In flight shows blue-grey wash to greater wing-coverts and a broken white terminal band to tail. Juvenile lacks the black half-collar on neck. Beware of hybrids *roseogrisea* x *decaocto* **Voice** Gives a typical laugh *kook r-r-r-r-r-rOOoooooooo* with strong rolling 'r' sound, unlike Eurasian Collared. **Tax.** The nominate ssp. *roseogrisea* occurs in the Canary Islands.

Eurasian Collared Dove *Streptopelia decaocto*   L 31–34 cm, WS 48–56 cm

Resident breeder (all islands). Favours non-native habitats at low altitude such as gardens with tall and dense canopy trees, but also in tamarisk woodland on eastern Canary Islands. **ID** Sexes similar. Adult is uniform buff-grey overall with slightly darker brownish upperparts, bluish primary and secondary coverts, a narrow black half-collar on neck, and grey vent and undertail-coverts. In flight display, the spread tail shows a conspicuous broad white terminal band. Juvenile similar to adult, but lacks the narrow black half-collar on neck. Confusion likely with African Collared Dove (which see). Hybrids also occur. **Voice** Most characteristic call is a repeated trisyllabic *koo-KOO-ku*. **Tax.** Nominate ssp. *decaocto* is present in the region.

European Turtle Dove *Streptopelia turtur*   L 25–27 cm, WS 49–55 cm

Migrant breeder in summer (all islands). Found from low semi-desert scrub near the coast to pine and laurel montane forest, but also near cultivated areas at mid elevation. **ID** Confusion likely with Laughing Dove in flight as the diagnostic orange collar of this species is not visible, but uniform brown back important to identification. Laughing also lacks red skin around the eye, dark centres to wing-coverts and black-and-white striped patch on neck. Sexes similar. Adult has blue-grey crown, nape and hindneck, orange eye surrounded by conspicuous red bare skin, black-and-white striped patch on neck, uniform buff throat, pinkish-tinged breast, brown mantle, bright orange scapulars and wing-coverts with all-dark centres, and bluish alula and inner primary-coverts. Juvenile similar to adult, but neck patch absent. In flight the bluish panel contrasts with orange wing-coverts, and conspicuous white tail-band contrasts with a black subterminal band. **Voice** A characteristic *toorrr toorr* is always heard. **Tax.** Nominate ssp. *turtur* occurs in the archipelago.

Laughing Dove *Streptopelia senegalensis*   L 23–26 cm, WS 40–45 cm

Resident breeder (all islands). Colonisation process assisted by introduction (T) but possibly natural too. Prefers rural towns and villages, also in palm trees and tamarisk woodland in eastern Canary Islands. **ID** Sexes alike. Adult has black eye, brownish-pink head and hindneck, dark brown upperparts contrasting with blue-grey along the external part of the wing, white belly and ventral region, and a diagnostic orange collar with black dots forming a necklace. Confusion likely with European Turtle Dove in flight, but no black centres to wing feathers. Laughing shows white restricted to the outer tail-feathers and very little black, whereas Turtle has a neat but thin white terminal band and a black subterminal band (best seen in flight display). **Voice** A variable rising and falling laughing call *ha-ha-hoo-hoo hoo-hoo-hoo*. **Tax.** Most likely ssp. in the archipelago is *phoenicophila*.

African Collared Dove

Eurasian Collared Dove

European Turtle Dove

Laughing Dove

PLATE 45: PIGEONS II

Bolle's Pigeon *Columba bollii* L 35–37 cm, WS 65–68 cm

Endemic. Resident breeder (P, H, Go, T). Inhabits primary and secondary laurel forest. **ID** Sexes similar. Adult has blue-grey head, foreneck and ventral region, red bill with a hint of yellow on tip, yellow eye with red eye-ring, dark slate-grey upperparts and rump, black tail with pale grey subterminal band (black-grey-black), vinous breast patch, and green gloss restricted to hindneck. Juvenile similar to adult, but brownish-tinged on upperparts. In flight and in strong light the diagnostic pale grey subterminal band of Bolle's is easy to see against a dark background from above and below, and even with the naked eye at a long range. Confusion possible with Laural Pigeon (which see). **Voice** A very low-pitched Common Wood Pigeon-like *ruor ruor ruor rup*, accentuated on the last note and sometimes repeated two or more times. **Tax.** Monotypic. An early coloniser to the Canary Islands and closely related to Common Wood Pigeon.

Laurel Pigeon *Columba junoniae* L 37–38 cm, WS 64–67 cm

Endemic. Resident breeder (P, H, Go, T) and currently being introduced (not reintroduced) on GC where it is not known to have occurred in the past and where only 8–16% of the original thermophile forest is left today as suboptimal patches. Mainly associated with thermophilous woods. **ID** Sexes and ages similar. Confusion likely with Bolle's Pigeon (which see) and most likely to be detected in flight which is slower with more flapping on blunter wings, while Bolle's tends to fly very fast over the forest canopy. In poor light conditions Laurel can look almost black, with a conspicuous white tail tip, best seen on circular flight display. Adult has greyish head, green glossy patch on hindneck, vinous upper mantle and breast, slate-grey tail with broad off-white terminal band (conspicuous during display flight), whitish bill with a hint of red at the base, and yellow eye with red eye-ring. Juvenile similar to adult, but paler brown above and rufous-cinnamon below; green gloss on neck is often missing. **Voice** A loud and rising *up-poooo* and a crooning *pu-pu-pooo*. **Tax.** Monotypic. An old lineage that could have colonised the Canaries a long time ago from Africa. [Alt: Thermophile Pigeon]

Rock Dove *Columbia livia* L 31–34 cm, WS 63–70 cm

Resident breeder (all islands). Uses a wide array of habitat types, and mainly breeds on coastal but also inland cliffs. **ID** Sexes alike. Impossible to separate from its domestic descendants. Adult has bluish head, shimmering green vinous neck patch, pale grey upperparts and wing-coverts, two broad black wing-bars and black narrow terminal tail-band. Juvenile as adult, but plumage duller and brownish-tinged; dark bars on wings and tail are less noticeable (all features only visible at close range). In flight shows a small white rump patch, thick black trailing edge to wing, and a pale underwing. **Voice** A cooing *oh-hoo-oorh*. **Tax.** Nominate ssp. occurs in the region.

Common Wood Pigeon *Columba palumbus* L 40–42 cm, WS 75–80 cm

Seasonal visitor (all islands, not H or Go). No noticeable habitat preference when visiting the islands. **ID** Sexes alike. Adult has blue-grey head, yellow eye, yellow bill with red base, pale grey upperparts contrasting with vinous-pink breast, white ventral region, long tail and diagnostic large green-white neck patch. In flight shows diagnostic broad white transverse bands on upperwings that are visible at very long range, plain underwing and a broad black terminal band to the tail that can be seen from above and below (as in Bolle's Pigeon). Juvenile lacks white neck patch, but unlikely to be observed in region. **Voice** A mellow *ooo-cooh-coo-coo-coo*, unlikely to be heard in the archipelago. **Tax.** Nominate ssp. occurs in the Canary Islands.

ad

Bolle's Pigeon

ad

ad

Laurel Pigeon

ad

ad

Rock Dove

ad

ad

Common Wood Pigeon

PLATE 46: CUCKOOS AND NIGHTJARS

Great Spotted Cuckoo *Clamator glandarius* L 35–39 cm, WS 58–61 cm
Seasonal visitor (all islands except Go). Does not favour a particular habitat while visiting the archipelago, but reported from semi-desert scrub and arable land. **ID** Sexes similar, but juvenile easily told by a black cap with a hint of a crest, red eye-ring, yellow throat and upper breast, white underside, and black upperparts with wing-coverts and flight feathers tipped white; and in flight by rusty-brown patch on primaries, less visible from below. Adult has a grey crown with a hint of a crest, an all-black bill, reddish eye-ring, black on nape, lemon-yellow throat extending to upper breast, white underside and vent, and dark grey upperparts; also note heavy white spotting on tips of wing-coverts and flight feathers. **Voice** Unlikely to be heard in the Canary Islands.

Common Cuckoo *Cuculus canorus* L 32–36 cm, WS 54–60 cm
Seasonal visitor (all islands except H). While in the archipelago reported from arable land to semi-desert scrub. **ID** Sexes differ and two morphs in the female. Adult male has pale grey upperparts, head and breast contrasting with finely barred white underside, diagnostic yellow feet, yellowish iris and eye-ring, and black bill with yellow base. Adult female grey morph recalls adult male, but has variable amount of yellowish tinge on breast and often dark barring on throat; rufous morph (not illustrated) is almost entirely black-barred. Juvenile similar to adult female, but best separated by white nape patch. In flight grey-looking individuals recall Eurasian Sparrowhawk. **Voice** Unlikely to be heard while in the archipelago.

European Nightjar *Caprimulgus europaeus* L 24–28 cm, WS 52–59 cm
Vagrant. Semi-desert areas with scattered trees and bushes. **ID** Confusion likely with Red-necked Nightjar. Sexes similar. At rest adult male is mainly grey, particularly on the neck, dark carpal bar and thick white upperwing-covert bar are diagnostic for separating from Red-necked; white patch on throat sides is not present in female. In flight adult male shows three white spots near the wingtip, visible from above and below, inconspicuous or absent in adult female and first-autumn male. The latter also lacks the white on tail corners shown by adults of both sexes. **Voice** Unlikely to be heard in the region.

Red-necked Nightjar *Caprimulgus ruficollis* L 30–34 cm, WS 60–65 cm
Vagrant. Prefers semi-desert scrub. **ID** Confusion likely with European Nightjar. Adult at rest has diagnostic rufous-red neck collar, throat and upper breast, dark grey carpal bar, four creamy discontinuous wing-bars and a white patch at throat sides. In flight both sexes show three white spots near the wingtips and white patches on tail corners (as in European, but slightly larger), although the rufous-red neck collar is the most important feature. Juvenile resembles adult, but the rufous-red neck collar is less marked. In flight best told from European by larger size, longer tail and rufous underwing and belly. **Voice** Unlikely to be heard in the region.

Great Spotted Cuckoo

ad

juv

Common Cuckoo

ad ♂

juv

European Nightjar

ad

ad

Red-necked Nightjar

ad

ad

PLATE 47: OWLS

Western Barn Owl *Tyto alba* L 33–35 cm, WS 85–93 cm
Resident breeder (all islands). In the west and central Canaries prefers the lowlands, while on eastern Canaries is associated with mountainous areas with caves and coastal cliffs, and absent from sandy plains. **ID** Sexes similar. Confusion possible with Long-eared Owl, but note heart-shaped white face, dark eyes, variable upperparts ranging from yellowish with grey feathers intermixed to all dark grey, variable unstreaked underside ranging from white to yellow-orange depending on subspecies. In flight legs are often dangling. **Voice** A hissing scream *shrrreeeeee* with a tremolo when flying. **Tax.** Nominate (P, H, Go, T, GC) and ssp. *gracilirostris* (F, L, g, mc, a) which is darker orange-buff overall.

Eurasian Scops Owl *Otus scops* L 19–20 cm, WS 53–63 cm
Vagrant. In the archipelago often recorded in parks and gardens. **ID** Sexes similar. Two morphs. Overall plumage coloration varies from rufous-brown to grey-brown, but always heavily streaked on the underside, short ear-tufts are visible when relaxed. Has white line on back, and yellow eyes. Close-up shows an intricate plumage pattern, but seems more uniform at longer range. In flight separated from Long-eared by the lack of yellowish-orange primary patches, but sometimes white spots on primaries are detectable. **Voice** A repetitive *tyuu* but unlikely to be heard in the region.

Long-eared Owl *Asio otus* L 31–37 cm, WS 86–98 cm
Resident breeder (P, H, Go, T, GC) and occasional breeder (F, L). Uses a wide array of habitats from semi-desert coastal scrub to pine and laurel forests, also in pastures and grasslands. **ID** Sexes similar. Adult has orange-red iris, rusty-buff-orange face, heavily streaked underside and dark brown upperparts, and finely barred orange-yellow tail. In flight diagnostic yellow-orange upperwing primary patches on two-coloured underwing; also shows finely barred tail and a yellow-orange upperwing patch restricted to the base of the primaries. Confusion possible with Barn and Short-eared Owl (which see). **Voice** Male utters a typical cooing and repeated *hoo-hoo-hoo*, female a nasal *paah*. **Tax.** The local form is usually considered to be an endemic subspecies, *canariensis*. [Alt: Northern Long-eared Owl]

Short-eared Owl *Asio flammeus* L 33–40 cm, WS 95–105 cm
Irregular winter migrant and seasonal visitor (all islands except H). Favours arable cereal fields but also in grassy fields and set-aside land. **ID** Sexes similar. Differs from Long-eared by yellow eyes, also pink-buff face, boldly barred tail, big yellow spots on wing-coverts giving an overall yellowish aspect, and black primary projection. In flight shows a lot of yellowish on primaries and secondaries on upperwing, not just on primary bases (as in Long-eared), and 2–3 black bands on wing-tips. The underwing is similar to Long-eared, but less two-toned and with conspicuous black wing-tips (not present in Long-eared). From below the thick tail bands are visible and the streaking does not reach the belly as in Long-eared. **Voice** Unlikely to be heard in the Canary Islands.

Western Barn Owl

ad nominate

ad *gracilirostris*

Long-eared Owl

ad grey morph

ad *canariensis*

Eurasian Scops Owl

Short-eared Owl

ad

ad

PLATE 48: SWIFTS

Chimney Swift *Chaetura pelagica* L 12–13 cm, WS 31–32 cm
Vagrant. Favours towns and villages while in the archipelago. **ID** Sexes similar. Adult is all dark with diagnostic cigar-shaped body and square-ended tail with thin 'needle' feather tips, only visible in the hand. Juvenile resembles adult, but less contrast between throat and breast. Differs from other swifts of the region by a quicker and fluttery flight action, similar to a bat. Confusion likely with Plain Swift when moulting tail (which see). **Voice** Unlikely to be heard in the Canary Islands.

Plain Swift *Apus unicolor* L 14–15 cm, WS 38–39 cm
Migrant breeder in summer (all islands); most leave in the autumn, but wintering grounds imperfectly known. Recent geolocator studies have shown that some birds winter in Liberia. Favours coastal and inland cliffs for nesting and unfinished houses in towns and villages. **ID** Similar to Common Swift in structure but contrast between throat and head much less obvious (in Common white throat almost reaches the lower cheeks) even in good light conditions. Confusion also possible with Pallid Swift (call diagnostic), which is much bigger with conspicuous white throat and two-coloured contrast on upperwing (pale and darker brown). Flight action more fluttering with quicker wing-beats than Common or Pallid. While in the air sometimes shows a pale grey throat, but this is only visible at certain angles (especially head-on) and in good light against a dark background. Beware of individuals carrying white nest material or food boluses. **Voice** Higher-pitched than Pallid.

Pallid Swift *Apus pallidus* L 16–17 cm, WS 42–46 cm
Migrant breeder in summer (T, L, g) but recorded elsewhere too (P, H, Go, GC, F, mc). Favours buildings in towns and cities for nesting but also in crevices of coastal cliffs. **ID** Sexes alike. Larger than Plain Swift but similar size to Common. Flight silhouette differs from other all-dark swifts in being less elegant with broader head, less pointed wings, and less forked tail. While in the air shows a large white throat patch, visible at long range, and the strong contrast between outer primaries and the rest of the wing is diagnostic, seen from below and above. Flight action less fluttering and slower than other all-dark swifts. **Voice** A scream *srreeeu*, harsher than Common and Plain Swift. **Tax.** The ssp. *brehmorum* occurs in the archipelago.

Common Swift *Apus apus* L 16–17 cm, WS 42–48 cm
Seasonal visitor (all islands). Found in any type of habitat. **ID** Sexes alike. Adult is overall black with a distinct white throat patch reaching the lower cheek, but difficult to see in strong light. Confusion likely with Plain and Pallid Swifts, but separated by flight silhouette with long, narrow and more sickle-shaped wings, although this is difficult to appreciate on single birds. When seen from below, the contrast between dark shoulders and lighter flight feathers is an important feature. Juvenile has whitish feather fringes and whiter throat, but this is difficult to observe during the first winter in the field. **Voice** A characteristic high-pitched scream *srreeeee*, less harsh than Pallid but similar to Plain.

Alpine Swift *Tachymarptis melba* L 20–22 cm, WS 54–60 cm
Seasonal visitor (all islands). Occurs in a wide array of habitats while visiting the archipelago. **ID** Sexes similar. A large brown swift with diagnostic white belly patch and white throat, the latter sometimes difficult to observe at long range. Flight action slow with much gliding and less wing-beating. Flight silhouette can resemble Eurasian Hobby and is similar to Pallid and less elegant than other smaller all-dark swifts. Juvenile as adult in fresh plumage. **Voice** A high-pitched rising and falling *tryhihihihihihihi* might be heard in the region.

Little Swift *Apus affinis* L 12–13 cm, WS 34–35 cm
Vagrant. Uses a wide array of habitats for foraging. **ID** Sexes similar. A dark swift with a white throat contrasting with dark underside and a diagnostic unforked square tail and broad white rump extending to the flanks. Silhouette less elegant than other all-dark swifts of similar size, mainly due to broad short wings. Confusion likely with Northern House Martin but different flight action with stiff wings and an unforked tail are important identification features. **Voice** A high-pitched insect-like *siksiksiksiksik...* may be heard in the region.

Chimney Swift
ad

Plain Swift
ad

Pallid Swift
ad

ad

Common Swift
ad
ad

Alpine Swift
ad

Little Swift
ad

PLATE 49: ROLLER, KINGFISHER, BEE-EATERS, HOOPOE, WOODPECKERS

European Roller *Coracias garrulus*   L 29–32 cm, WS 52–57 cm

Seasonal visitor (all islands). While in the archipelago found in arable land and semi-desert scrub. **ID** Unmistakable. Sexes similar. Adult has black bill, pale turquoise-blue head, wing-coverts and underside, contrasting with rufous-cinnamon mantle and inner secondary coverts and ultramarine rump. Juvenile as adult, but much paler overall and whiter on face and throat. In flight adult shows a marked contrast between blue wing-coverts and black flight feathers; tail ultramarine to light blue (brown centre) and with black tips to outer rectrices. **Voice** A loud *rak-rak* may be heard in the region.

Common Kingfisher *Alcedo atthis*   L 16–17 cm, WS 24–26 cm

Vagrant. Both freshwater and brackish reservoirs, also near sheltered coastlines. **ID** Sexes differ. Adult male has light brilliant blue on back and tail, is mainly bright blue-green on crown and wings, deep orange on underside, and with white throat and all-black bill. Adult female as male, but base of bill reddish on lower mandible. Flies in straight lines with very rapid wing-beats over the water. Juvenile similar to adult, but duller and greener. **Voice** A combination of calls *tseee ti-tee ti-tee…*, but most likely a *tsee* call note.

European Bee-eater *Merops apiaster*   L 25–29 cm, WS 36–40 cm

Seasonal visitor (all islands). Found in a wide array of habitats when visiting the islands. **ID** Sexes alike. Adult has red-brown crown, upper mantle and wing-coverts, yellow on shoulder and throat, deep blue underside, black eye-stripe, and red eye. Juvenile is similar to adult, but has greenish on mantle and wing-coverts. In flight has rusty-red underwing and a black trailing edge to the wing, which is broader on secondaries. Confusion possible with vagrant Blue-cheeked Bee-eater, which is overall green with a uniform black trailing edge to the wing and diagnostic deeper reddish on the underwing. **Voice** Utters a far-carrying *pruup* call while in the air.

Blue-cheeked Bee-eater *Merops persicus*   L 28–32 cm, WS 35–39 cm

Vagrant. In natural range favours riparian areas, but also dry country with scattered trees and bushes. **ID** Similar in size and shape to European Bee-eater, but longer tail projection and longer bill give Blue-cheeked a more elegant look. Beware that both species share black trailing-edge (uniform in Blue-cheeked) and rusty-red underwing, and in strong light the differences in throat coloration is difficult to discern, although European looks pale-throated and Blue-cheeked dark-throated. Adult is deep green overall with a dark eye-line, red eye, light blue eye-stripe and cheek, and yellow-and-red throat. In flight, underparts are green, not bluish like European, and has deeper rusty-red on underwing. Juvenile similar to adult, but has red-brown throat patch and browner plumage on the upperparts. **Voice** A characteristic flight-call *priip*, often heard as disyllabic *pri-ip*, unlike the *pruup* of European.

Eurasian Hoopoe *Upupa epops*   L 26–28 cm, WS 44–48 cm

Resident breeder (all islands). Prefers semi-desert scrub at low and mid elevation, but also frequents man-made habitats such as golf courses and cultivated areas. **ID** Sexes similar, but female slightly duller overall, when directly compared to the male. Adult has a thin, slightly downcurved bill, an erectile buff, black-tipped crest, buff head and throat, dusky coloration on upper mantle, black-and-white striped lower mantle and wings, white belly and vent, and black tail. In flight, almost butterfly-like, the black-and-white pattern on the upper- and underside of its very broad wings is diagnostic; tail black with white subterminal band. **Voice** Most often heard is an unmistakable *poo-poo-poo*. **Tax.** Nominate ssp. occurs in the archipelago.

Northern Wryneck *Jynx torquilla*   L 16–18 cm, WS 25–27 cm

Seasonal visitor (P, T, F, L). No clear habitat preference while visiting the archipelago. **ID** Sexes similar. Adult has cryptic plumage, short pointed bill and brownish eye-stripe, grey above with a dark brown line along centre of crown extending to lower back, yellowish-buff finely barred throat contrasting with white underside (also barred); tail has evenly spaced bars and a white terminal band. Juvenile, unlikely to be observed in the region, similar to adult, but slightly duller and browner. Confusion possible with Great Grey Shrike which shows in flight a white patch at base of primaries contrasting with black wing-coverts and flight feathers. **Voice** A repetitive *quee-quee-quee-quee-quee…*, but difficult to hear in the region.

Great Spotted Woodpecker *Dendrocopos major*   L 22–23 cm, WS 34–39 cm

Resident breeder (T, GC). A pure pine forest specialist in Tenerife, but less so on Gran Canaria. **ID** Sexes differ. Adult male has a black crown and red patch on nape, white ear-coverts, forehead, throat and underside (which are tinged brownish on ssp. *canariensis*), and red vent. White scapular patches conspicuous in both male and female and particularly when seen in typical strongly undulating flight. Adult female told from adult male by lack of red on nape. Juvenile similar to adult, but full crown is red, although this disappears during post-juvenile moult in early autumn. Both sexes show diagnostic black-and-white plumage, unlikely to be confused with any other species in the region. **Voice** Drums frequently for half to one second and most typical call is a loud *pik*. **Tax.** Two subspecies (ssp. *thanneri*, Gran Canaria and ssp. *canariensis*, Tenerife), but sometimes only *canariensis* recognised for the Canary Islands.

European Roller

Common Kingfisher

European Bee-eater

Blue-cheeked Bee-eater

Eurasian Hoopoe

Northern Wryneck

ad ♂
thanneri

ad ♂
canariensis

Great Spotted Woodpecker

PLATE 50: FALCONS I

Lesser Kestrel *Falco naumanni*   L 27–33 cm, WS 63–72 cm

Seasonal visitor (T, GC, F, L, g). Prefers arable land with cereal crops when available but also semi-desert scrub when migrating. **ID** The most diagnostic feature at close range for both sexes and all ages are the pale claws, but this is sometimes difficult to observe. A small raptor, very similar to Common Kestrel but adult male at long range lacks black spots on mantle and wing-coverts and lacks a dark moustachial stripe; shows a slate-grey upperwing panel on secondaries, and a few small spots on chest and breast. First-summer males still have some spots on upperparts, but not on mantle or lesser and median coverts. Adult female and juvenile similar to Common Kestrel but in the Canary Islands the longer wings can aid identification. **Voice** A *kee-kee-kee…* similar to Common Kestrel but slightly faster, also a trisyllabic contact call *chay-chay-chay*.

Common Kestrel *Falco tinnunculus*   L 31–37 cm, WS 68–78 cm

Resident breeder (all islands). Occurs from flat semi-desert to lush mountainous laurel forest, pine forest and the high alpine zone. **ID** Sexes differ. Adult male has grey head with conspicuous black moustachial stripe, finely spotted reddish-brown upperparts, creamy underside with dense spotting, yellow cere and feet, grey tail with dark terminal band, and black claws. First-summer males can sometimes be identified by the dark barring on uppertail and rump. Female differs from male in brown streaked head with inconspicuous moustachial stripe, brownish uppertail finely barred black, and less reddish on mantle and upperparts. Juvenile similar to adult female, but has a yellowish tinge above and breast with thicker streaks. In flight hovers frequently when hunting, with tail spread open like a fan. Confusion is likely with Eurasian Sparrowhawk, but narrower wings diagnostic. **Voice** Most typical call is a repetitive *kee-kee-kee-kee…*. **Tax.** Two subspecies in the Canary Islands: ssp. *canariensis* (P, H, Go, T, GC) and spp. *dacotiae* (F, L, g, mc, a).

Red-footed Falcon *Falco vespertinus*   L 28–34 cm, WS 65–76 cm

Vagrant. Prefers open grasslands and cereal crops near patches of woodland areas when available. **ID** Sexes differ. Adult male is dark grey overall with contrasting red eye-ring, cere, feet and ventral region. Silvery-grey on primaries on the upperwing, and the all-dark underwing is diagnostic when in the air. Adult female has rufous crown, finely striped underside, heavily barred blue-grey upperparts, orange feet and cere, and tail with a dark subterminal band. Juvenile can be confused with juvenile Eleonora's Falcon or Eurasian Hobby, but evenly spaced bars on uppertail is an important feature, also whiter cheeks, less prominent moustachial stripe, and a dark trailing edge visible in flight (only shared by Eleonora's). Has the tendency to land on the ground regularly when foraging for insects. **Voice** A whinnying *kew-kew-kew-kew…* may be heard in the region.

Merlin *Falco columbarius*   L 26–33 cm, WS 55–69 cm

Irregular winter visitor and seasonal visitor (all islands except P and Go). Prefers open arable land and grasslands. **ID** Sexes differ. Adult male has orangey-buff, finely dark-streaked underside, blue-grey upperparts, and white throat, orangey nape, and yellow feet and eye-ring. In flight shows diagnostic black terminal band to the tail, visible from below and from above, as well as dark outer wings. Adult female is dark brown overall with flight and tail feathers barred buffish on top, a double moustachial stripe, and heavy streaking on chest and breast. Juvenile difficult to separate from adult female in the field. Confusion likely with Peregrine or Barbary Falcon but also with smaller Eurasian Sparrowhawk. **Voice** Unlikely to be heard in the region.

ad ♀
ad ♂
ad ♂
ad ♀
Lesser Kestrel

ad ♀
ad ♂
dacotiae
ad ♂
canariensis
ad ♂
ad ♀
Common Kestrel

ad ♀
juv
ad ♂
ad ♀
ad ♂
juv
Red-footed Falcon

ad ♀
ad ♂
ad ♂
ad ♀
Merlin

PLATE 51: FALCONS II

Eurasian Hobby *Falco subbuteo* L 29–35 cm, WS 70–84 cm
Seasonal visitor (all islands except H and P). In the region near the coast and inland in habitats ranging from coastal semi-desert scrub to open pine and dense laurel forest. **ID** Sexes similar. Adult has thin moustachial stripe and is dark grey on upperparts, uppertail and crown, heavily streaked on chest, breast, flanks and belly, has red vent and 'trousers', white on throat and cheeks, and yellow feet and eye-ring. The long pointed wings, at long range, give a scythe-like silhouette in flight. Often hunts dragonflies in the air. Juvenile browner and buff overall and differs from adult in lacking the red 'trousers' and vent (buff). Confusion possible with juvenile Red-footed or Eleonora's Falcons. The latter is larger and shows more contrast between the wing-coverts and flight feathers on the underwing, whereas the former has evenly spaced bars on the uppertail and whiter cheeks. **Voice** Unlikely to be heard when around the Canary Islands.

Eleonora's Falcon *Falco eleonorae* L 36–42 cm, WS 87–104 cm
Migrant breeder in summer off N Lanzarote (mc, a), but also recorded elsewhere (all islands except P and Go). In the archipelago breeds on offshore islets near mainland migratory routes of small birds (their main prey). **ID** Sexes similar but two morphs, the pale form more common. Adult dark morph is all dark, but as in the adult pale morph shows a contrast between the black underwing-coverts and the greyish flight feathers in flight. Adult pale morph has dark brown crown, upperparts and tail, dark moustachial stripe, white cheeks, yellow cere, feet and eye-ring, white throat, chestnut chest and belly, and vent with heavy black stripes. In flight the adult pale morph has dark underwing-coverts that contrast with greyish flight feathers, a diagnostic feature separating adult Eleonora's from adult Eurasian Hobby which is slightly smaller. Juvenile has buff fringes to mantle feathers and upperwing-coverts, and buff cheek, crown and throat, similar to juvenile Red-footed and juvenile Eurasian Hobby. **Voice** A nasal *kyair-kyair-kyair...* in flight near the breeding colonies.

Barbary Falcon *Falco pelegrinoides* L ♂ 33–37 cm, ♀ 36–39 cm, WS ♂ 76–86 cm, ♀ 89–98 cm
Resident breeder (all islands). Prefers coastal sea cliffs bordering semi-desert scrub for nesting (less so inland cliffs), but also near pine and laurel forest to high alpine scrub. **ID** Sexually dimorphic and female slightly larger. Similar to Peregrine, but adult male paler bluish-grey on the upperparts, rufous nape, and rufous tinge to the underside and underwing, finely barred on breast. Thinner moustachial stripe diagnostic. In flight has darker terminal band to the tail (pale rump on this species), darker 'hands' contrasting with paler secondary coverts and secondaries. Juvenile has brownish upperparts and light streaking on underside, bluish-green eye-ring and cere. Differs from juvenile Peregrine by less heavy streaking on underside, thinner moustachial stripe and lack of thick dark streaks on 'trousers'. **Voice** A harsh *kek-kek-kek...* can be heard near the nest. **Tax.** Some authorities still consider it as a subspecies of Peregrine Falcon. Nominate ssp. *pelegrinoides* occurs in the Canary Islands.

Peregrine Falcon *Falco peregrinus* L ♂ 38–45 cm, ♀ 46–51 cm, WS ♂ 89–100 cm, ♀ 104–113 cm
Vagrant. Prefers semi-desert areas when visiting Canary Islands. **ID** Similar to resident Barbary Falcon (which see). Adult has yellow eye-ring and cere, dark bluish-grey upperparts and light underside, strongly barred on chest and breast. In strong light the head can appear all black with diagnostic broad moustachial stripe (thinner in Barbary). Juvenile has brownish crown and upperparts, heavy streaking on underside, buff tinge on chest and belly, and bluish-green eye-ring and cere. **Voice** Silent away from breeding grounds. **Tax.** Ssp. unknown in the Canary Islands.

Eurasian Hobby

Eleonora's Falcon

Barbary Falcon

Peregrine Falcon

PLATE 52: PARAKEETS, ORIOLE AND TITS

Rose-ringed Parakeet *Psittacula krameri* — L 38–42 cm, WS 42–48 cm
Introduced (T, GC, F, L) and recorded elsewhere (P). Associated with low altitude urban areas, in gardens with exotic palms and trees, never found in native forests. **ID** Sexes differ. Adult male is pale green overall with long blue tail, bluish wash on rear crown, red upper mandible and black lower mandible, yellow iris, red eye-ring and black-and-red collar. Adult female similar to male, but lacks the black-and-red collar and the bluish wash on the rear of crown. Flight is fast and direct, yellow underwing-coverts sometimes visible. Confusion likely with smaller Monk Parakeet or Nanday Parakeet (which see). **Voice** A loud high-pitched scream *kee-a* is given in flight. **Tax.** Hybrids between spp. *borealis* and *manillensis*, both from Asia, have been recorded in the archipelago.

Nanday Parakeet *Aratinga nenday* — L 35–36 cm, WS 58–60 cm
Introduced (T). Associated with gardens holding exotic palms and trees. Never detected in native woodland. **ID** Sexes alike. Adult with black crown, bill and front of cheeks, all contrasting with the intense green of the rest of the body, a pale-blue chest-band and red thighs. In flight the green on the underwing-coverts and body contrast with black head, undertail and flight feathers. Both the primaries and the upperside of the tail are blue. Juveniles have less light blue on the chest and a shorter tail. **Voice** Similar to Rose-ringed Parakeet.

Monk Parakeet *Myiopsitta monachus* — L 29–33 cm, WS 32–35 cm
Introduced (P, T, GC, F). Associated with city gardens with exotic trees and palms. **ID** Sexes alike and confusion possible with Rose-ringed but has grey forehead, throat and breast, horn-coloured bill, ultramarine wing feathers and black eye. Also beware of other introduced parakeets such as Nanday Parakeet, in which both sexes have a black hood contrasting with all-green plumage. In flight conspicuous blue wings diagnostic, making identification straightforward even at a long distance. **Voice** Can be told from Rose-ringed by rolling *rrr* sounds in call.

Eurasian Golden Oriole *Oriolus oriolus* — L 22–25 cm
Seasonal visitor (all islands). **ID** Sexes differ. Adult male has reddish bill and bluish legs, bright yellow overall with black wings, lores and tail. Adult female/first-summer male as adult male, but faint to prominent streaks on white breast, yellowish flanks, variable amount of olive on head and upperparts, and black wings with variable olive fringes to feathers. Juvenile similar to adult female, but no yellow on flanks and off-white underside, dull olive-green upperparts, pinkish bill. **Voice** Unlikely to be heard while visiting the region.

African Blue Tit *Cyanistes teneriffae* — L 11–12 cm
Resident breeder (all major islands). Prefers laurel forest, when available, but also pine forest, gullies with lush scrub vegetation, parks and gardens. On semi-desert islands associated with mixed palm and tamarisk areas, but also on hillsides with semi-desert scrub. **ID** Sexes similar and five subspecies. The nominate has blue-black and white head, blue upperparts and yellow underside (indistinct white tips to tertials). Ssp. *ombriosus* like nominate, but greenish mantle and whitish wing-bar and tips to tertials. Ssp. *palmensis* as nominate, but generally dark greyish overall with white wing-bar and tips to tertials, also diagnostic white centre to belly. Ssp. *ultramarinus* (formerly *degener*) as nominate, but paler overall with pale grey head and upperparts and conspicuous white wing-bar and tips to tertials. The recently described ssp. *hedwigae* (not illustrated) is almost identical to nominate. Juvenile similar to adult, but with olive-grey and yellow head pattern, olive upperparts, bluish wings, white wing-bar on greater coverts, white tips to tertials, and yellow throat and underside. Has habit of hanging upside down, although some ssp. more than others. **Voice** Song is a subspecies-variable melodious and liquid *tsi-tsi-sirrrrr-r-r-r-r*. Most typical call shared by all races is a *churrrrr* often given when alarmed. **Tax.** Five subspecies considered today in the Canary Islands: nominate (Go, T), *palmensis* (P), *ombriosus* (H), *hedwigae* (GC), *ultramarinus* (F, L). Taxonomy under revision by SOC.

Rose-ringed Parakeet
ad ♂

Nanday Parakeet
ad

Monk Parakeet
ad

Eurasian Golden Oriole
ad ♂
ad ♀

African Blue Tit
ad *palmensis*
ad *ombriosus*
ad *ultramarinus*
ad *teneriffae*
juv *teneriffae*

PLATE 53: SHRIKES AND CROWS

Red-backed Shrike *Lanius collurio* L 16–18 cm
Vagrant. Favours forest edges and open areas with thorny scrub. **ID** Sexes differ. Adult male has reddish-brown mantle and wings and pinkish underside, pale grey head and nape, black mask and white throat. In flight shows black 'T'-shaped pattern on tail (similar to wheatears), grey rump and inconspicuous white bases to primaries. Adult female as adult male but duller, with dark brown mantle, brown-grey crown, brownish mask and dirty buff vermiculated underside. First-winter as adult female, but more vermiculated overall on upperparts. **Voice** May give a *shak* or a *churruk churruk*. Song unlikely to be heard in the archipelago.

Great Grey Shrike *Lanius excubitor* L 22–26 cm
Resident breeder (T, GC, F, L, g, mc, a). Prefers semi-desert scrub but also the alpine zone, avoiding the forests. **ID** Sexes alike. Adult with conspicuous black face-mask, thin indistinct white supercilium. Otherwise grey above and white below, black wings with white on primary bases, and black-and-white tail. Strong black hooked bill. Flight direct and very low, difficult to follow. Often sits on high perches when looking for prey. Juvenile similar to adult, but has a brownish tinge to upperparts and best told by a brownish wing-bar on greater coverts. **Voice** Most typical call is a harsh *shree*, ringing toward the end and a liquid *gle-gle*. Song a mixture of squeaks, trills and chattering phrases. **Tax.** The ssp. *koenigi* occurs in the archipelago; this form is sometimes considered to be a subspecies of Southern Grey Shrike *L. meridionalis*.

Woodchat Shrike *Lanius senator* L 17–19 cm
Seasonal visitor (all islands). Prefers scrubby areas as well as tamarisk woodland. **ID** Sexes differ. Adult male has buff spot near the base of bill, red-brown crown extending to nape, black mask, forehead and mantle, off-white underside, white scapular patch, black wings with white fringes to median and greater coverts and tertials, white on primary bases, whitish rump and black tail with white edges. Adult female as adult male, but has greyish mantle and often vermiculated flanks, orange crown and nape and black mask. Juvenile/first-winter as adult, but with grey vermiculations, particularly on flanks and breast. **Voice** May give a *greeek* similar to Nightingale. Song unlikely to be heard in the archipelago.

Red-billed Chough *Pyrrhocorax pyrrhocorax* L 37–41 cm, WS 68–80 cm
Resident breeder (P). Prefers cultivated areas, pine forests and deep gullies, avoiding primary laurel forest. **ID** Sexes alike. Adult is all glossy black with long reddish legs and slightly decurved red bill. Juvenile resembles adult, but duller overall and bill less reddish. Often performs acrobatic flights. In flight, silhouette differs from Northern Raven in having a short square tail (not wedge-shaped), also broader, deeply fingered wings and darker coverts contrasting with rest of wing. **Voice** Most typical call is a *cheee-aw* scream that is given in flight or on the ground. **Tax.** The ssp. *barbarus* occurs in the archipelago.

Carrion Crow *Corvus corone* L 44–51 cm, WS 84–100 cm
Vagrant. Associated with urban areas. **ID** Sexes similar. Smaller in size and different shape than Northern Raven. Adult entirely black with a stout bill. Differs from Northern Raven by flight silhouette showing broader and shorter wings and a square-ended tail, never wedge-shaped. Flight action less powerful than in Northern Raven, and has shallower wing-beats. Juvenile as adult, but duller and with less glossy plumage overall. **Voice** An often-repeated *kraaa*, but may give Raven-like *konk*.

Northern Raven *Corvus corax* L 56–67 cm, WS 115–130 cm
Resident breeder (all islands), but on the endangered list. Prefers semi-desert scrub, cultivated areas and forests including pine and laurel. **ID** Sexes similar. Adult in certain light conditions can show a metallic bluish-lilac to green sheen but generally all black at a distance, also thick bill with elongated feathers on throat. Flight silhouette diagnostic with relatively narrow wings and five fingers in the hand, and a wedge-shaped tail. Confusion in flight likely with Common Buzzard, which has a different tail shape. **Voice** A characteristic call *tok-tok-tok* and a honking *pruuk-pruuk*. **Tax.** The subspecies *canariensis* occurs in the Canary Islands.

Red-backed Shrike
ad ♂
ad ♀
juv

Great Grey Shrike
ad
koenigi
juv

Woodchat Shrike
ad ♂
juv

Red-billed Chough
ad

Carrion Crow
Northern Raven

Carrion Crow
ad

Northern Raven
ad

PLATE 54: LARKS

Bar-tailed Lark *Ammomanes cinctura*   L 13–14 cm
Vagrant. Favours semi-desert and sandy and rocky plains with low shrub cover. **ID** Sexes similar. Adult has a small pinkish bill, is almost uniform sandy-coloured, but darker grey-brown above, with rufous wings and rufous tail with a diagnostic black terminal band. In flight the dusky tips to the primaries create a hint of a trailing edge, and the tail pattern is difficult to discern in strong light and often only clearly visible when alighting. Juvenile shows pale fringes to back feathers, no dusky primary tips and narrow dark spots on crown. **Voice** A buzzing *preet*, also a typical *jupp* and a high-pitched *see-ou*; all unlikely to be heard in the region.

Greater Hoopoe-Lark *Alaemon alaudipes*   L 19–22 cm
Vagrant. Favours sand dunes with scattered bushes. **ID** Sexes differ. Adult male has long and slightly decurved bill, grey head, white supercilium, black eye-stripe and moustachial stripe, white throat, heavy dark spots on chest, sandy upperparts, black centres to coverts, whitish underside and has long pale legs. Adult female as adult male, but has faint dark spot on chest and on average is smaller with shorter bill. Juvenile lacks any chest markings and shows pale scales on upperparts; bill shorter and pinker. Conspicuous black-and-white wing pattern and black rectrices diagnostic in flight. **Voice** A *too* and a buzzing *zeee* when alarmed.

Calandra Lark *Melanocorypha calandra*   L 17–20 cm
Vagrant. Prefers semi-desert plains with sparse vegetation and grassy fields and open cultivated areas. **ID** Sexes similar. Adult has heavy yellowish-brown bill, is greyish-brown above with dark streaks, off-white below, underside unmarked, but the dark patch (less marked in autumn) on side of breast is diagnostic. Confusion likely with Greater Short-toed Lark and Eurasian Skylark, but the former has no white trailing edge and the latter no black patch on breast-side. Juvenile unlikely to be observed in the archipelago due to complete post-juvenile moult. In flight diagnostic all black underwing, even at long range. **Voice** Mainly silent in the region.

Greater Short-toed Lark *Calandrella brachydactyla*   L 14–16 cm
Seasonal visitor (P, T, F, L, g). Prefers semi-desert steppes in dry flat areas. **ID** Sexes alike. Similar to Lesser Short-toed Lark but no streaks on chest, long tertials cloaking primary tips diagnostic, a dark patch on breast-side (sometimes lacking), rufous-tinged crown and a strong but pointed bill. Confusion possible with Eurasian Skylark but no white trailing edge to the wing, best seen in flight, and different voice. Juvenile unlikely to be observed in Macaronesia, but shows a scaly pattern on upperparts. **Voice** May give a *dreet-it-it*, but mainly silent while in the archipelago.

Lesser Short-toed Lark *Alaudala rufescens*   L 13–14 cm
Resident breeder (GC, F, L, g), extinct from Tenerife. Favours semi-desert flat areas with low shrub cover. **ID** Sexes similar. Adult has short stubby bill and a tiny crest, greyish-brown upperparts with heavy streaking on crown, cheeks, back and breast. Confusion possible with larger Eurasian Skylark and similar-sized Greater Short-toed Lark. Told from the latter by streaking on entire breast, lack of black patch on breast-side, and longer primary projection. Separated from Eurasian Skylark by different flight-call, stubbier bill, and lack of clear white trailing edge to the wings in flight. Juvenile has pale scaling and dark mottling on upperparts. **Voice** The song is given during a circular flight or from the ground, and consists of melodious phrases interspersed with mimicry of other species in the area. Most common flight-call is a monosyllabic *chirrup* or *prrrt*, not unlike Eurasian Skylark. **Tax.** Two subspecies usually recognised: nominate *rufescens* on Tenerife (now extinct) and *polatzeki* elsewhere.

Eurasian Skylark *Alauda arvensis*   L 16–18 cm
Regular winter migrant and seasonal visitor (all islands except P). Prefers stubble fields, but also winters in semi-desert areas and abandoned pastures on terraces. **ID** Sexes alike, but male can erect a small crest that is usually flattened and not visible. In flight easily told from any other lark by the combination of a white trailing edge to secondaries, grey-white underwing and white outer tail feathers, although the white edge on the secondaries can become inconspicuous with wear. Confusion likely with resident Lesser Short-toed Lark (which see) and separated on the ground from smaller Greater Short-toed Lark by the lack of black patch on breast sides and long primary projection. Juvenile similar to adult in first autumn and unlikely to be separable in the region. **Voice** Most characteristic flight-call is a liquid *chirrrip* similar to Lesser Short-toed Lark.

Bar-tailed Lark

ad tail

Greater Hoopoe-Lark

Calandra Lark

Greater Short-toed Lark

polatzeki

Lesser Short-toed Lark

Eurasian Skylark

PLATE 55: SWALLOWS AND MARTINS

Sand Martin *Riparia riparia*   L 12–13 cm, WS 26–29 cm
Seasonal visitor (all islands). While visiting the archipelago not associated with any particular habitat. **ID** Sexes similar. Adult has diagnostic grey-brown breast-band visible even at long range, is grey-brown above and white below and shows a forked tail. Confusion likely with vagrant Eurasian Crag Martin, which lacks breast-band, and shows conspicuous white windows on tail feathers and dark ventral region. Juvenile similar to adult, but at close range buff fringes to upperpart feathers, particularly on the tertials and wing-coverts. **Voice** Contact flight-call is a rasping *tschrrr* or *brrtt*, easy to hear in the region.

Eurasian Crag Martin *Ptyonoprogne rupestris*   L 14–15 cm, WS 32–34 cm
Vagrant. Prefers coastal and open lowlands. **ID** Sexes similar. Adult has dusky ventral region, dark-streaked throat, and lack of clear breast-band, all features to separate from similar Sand Martin (which see). In flight also differs by strong contrast between the darker underwing-coverts and the rest of the wing and, more importantly, conspicuous white windows visible in spread tail. Juvenile similar adult, but told by buff fringes to wing-coverts, tertials and mantle feathers. **Voice** A monosyllabic flight contact call *prrit* or a disyllabic *pri-tit* might be heard.

Barn Swallow *Hirundo rustica*   L 13–19 cm, WS 32–34 cm
Seasonal visitor (all islands) and occasional breeder (GC). All kinds of open country, such as abandoned pastures, cereal crops and semi-desert scrub, and often near freshwater ponds and reservoirs. **ID** Sexes similar. Adult has deep red forehead and throat visible at close range, is glossy blue-black on the upperparts, with white underside including vent and glossy blue-black breast-band. Juvenile as adult, but buffier on forehead and throat and shorter tail streamers. In flight, spread tail shows small white windows on outer tail feathers, visible from above or from below. Confusion likely with Red-rumped Swallow (which see). **Voice** A flight call *witt* or *witt-witt* is commonly heard.

Red-rumped Swallow *Cecropis daurica*   L 14–18 cm, WS 32–34 cm
Seasonal visitor (all islands). In the archipelago prefers open areas such as cereal crops and abandoned pastures in flat terraces, but also near freshwater ponds and reservoirs, often associated with flocks of other hirundines. **ID** Sexes alike. Similar in shape, but slightly smaller than Barn Swallow, with a diagnostic black ventral region or vent, rusty-brown nape and ear-coverts, buff underside with diffuse dark streaks. Juvenile as adult, but has buff fringes to upperpart feathers, shorter tail streamers, buff-brown on head and white-buff rump similar to Common House Martin (which see). In flight when seen from above adult separated from Barn Swallow by the rusty-red rump and from below by the diagnostic squared-off black vent. **Voice** A sparrow-like *threet* may be heard in the region.

Common House Martin *Delichon urbicum*   L 12.5 cm, WS 26–29 cm
Seasonal visitor (all islands). Prefers areas away from dense forests but while visiting the islands can be detected in any kind of habitat. **ID** Sexes similar. Adult has glossy blue-black head and upperparts contrasting with large white rump-patch and white throat and underside including the vent; tail is only moderately forked. Juvenile similar to adult, but duller and brownish overall with dusky throat and pale tips to tertials. At long range and in strong light upperparts and tail appear all black. Confusion possible with vagrant Little Swift (Plate 48), which has black underside contrasting with white throat. **Voice** A rolling *prrt* or disyllabic *pri-pit* can be heard while in the air.

Sand Martin
ad

Eurasian Crag Martin
ad

Barn Swallow
ad

Red-rumped Swallow
ad

Common House Martin
ad

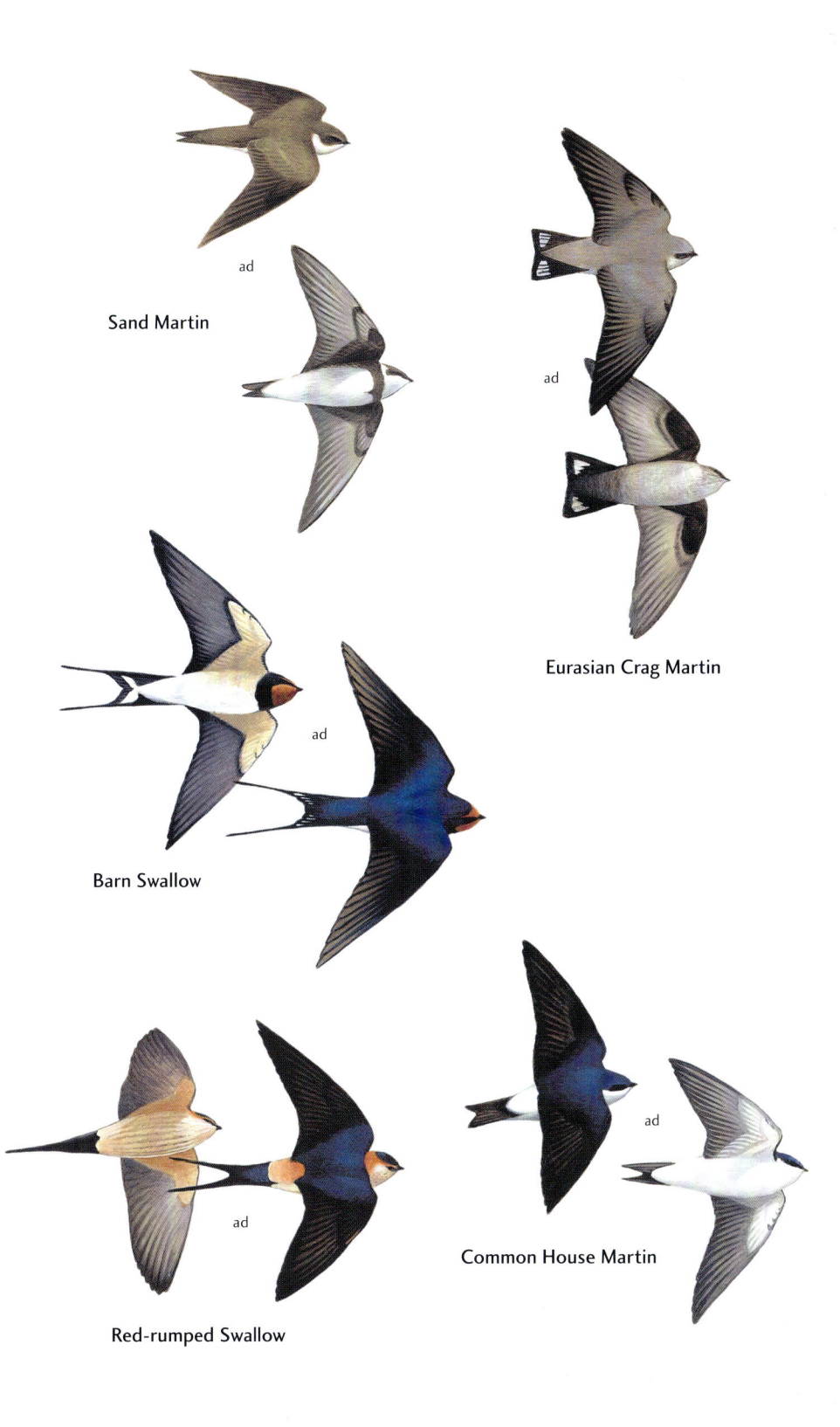

PLATE 56: LEAF WARBLERS

Yellow-browed Warbler *Phylloscopus inornata* L 9–10.5 cm
Vagrant. Prefers gardens with trees when available. **ID** Sexes similar. Adult has long broad yellowish supercilium, black eye-stripe, moss-green head and upperparts, off-white underside, short black bill with pinkish lower mandible, two yellowish wing-bars, white tips to tertials, and pinkish-brown legs. Just slightly larger than Goldcrest and best detected by its call. **Voice** Contact call a high-pitched disyllabic *tswe-eeet*. Song unlikely to be heard in the islands.

Western Bonelli's Warbler *Phylloscopus bonelli* L 10.5–12 cm
Seasonal visitor (all islands except P and Go). Prefers any shrubby habitat with trees when visiting the archipelago. **ID** Sexes alike. Adult easily identified by the combination of thin white eye-ring, yellowish rump best seen in flight, pale greyish head and mantle, pale lores, indistinct supercilium (but this variable), yellow-green fringes to wing-coverts and flight feathers, pale greyish edges to tertials, yellow edges to outer tail feathers, and brownish legs. Confusion possible with Common Chiffchaff and Willow Warbler, but separated from these by lack of yellowish tinge on face, throat, belly and flanks. **Voice** May give a disyllabic *pr-eee*. Song unlikely to be heard in the region.

Wood Warbler *Phylloscopus sibilatrix* L 11–12.5 cm
Seasonal visitor (all islands except H). Prefers areas with trees when visiting the islands. **ID** Sexes similar. Summer adult is green on the upperparts and white on the underside, with lemon-yellow throat, ear-coverts and breast-sides. Confusion likely with Willow Warbler but broader chest and shorter tail. Plumage differences also aid separation as Wood Warbler has darker green head and upperparts, deeper yellow supercilium, throat and chest, clean white underside, slightly longer primary projection, pale fringes to tertials and yellowish fringes to flight and outer tail feathers. **Voice** May utter a mellow *pew*. Song unlikely to be heard in the region.

Common Chiffchaff *Phylloscopus collybita* L 10–12 cm
Regular winter migrant (F, L) also reliably (ringed) recorded in winter elsewhere (T). Prefers areas with trees, such as tamarisk woodlands or thickets, hotel gardens, parks and golf courses. **ID** Two subspecies have been suggested in the archipelago, nominate *collybita* and *abietinus*; but the variation on the amount of yellowish wash on underside sometimes makes separation impossible. Nominate *collybita* is greenish-brown above, off-white below with variable amount of yellow on underside, and dark brown to grey-black legs. Race *abietinus* similar to *collybita*, but paler and greyer above. **Voice** Most typical call is a *hoeet* similar to Canary Islands Chiffchaff. Song by wintering birds is a combination of *chif-chaf* notes, repeated much more slowly than in Canary Islands Chiffchaff.

Canary Islands Chiffchaff *Phylloscopus canariensis* L 10–11 cm
Endemic. Resident breeder (P, H, Go, T, GC). Favours laurel forests, but distributed from sea-level to alpine zone, where prefers areas with shrubs but also in parks and gardens. **ID** Similar in plumage to Common Chiffchaff, but structurally different with longer tarsus and bill, shorter primary projection. Sexes similar. Adult has variable amount of yellow on the underside (which is generally dark buff-tinged on flanks), brownish-green upperparts, indistinct pale supercilium, and dark legs. Confusion possible with Willow and Wood Warbler (which see). **Voice** Song is clearly faster and louder than Common Chiffchaff. Most typical call is a monosyllabic whistle *hoeet*.

Willow Warbler *Phylloscopus trochilus* L 11–12.5 cm
Seasonal visitor (all islands). Found anywhere with trees, often in tamarisk woodlands, but also parks and gardens when visiting the archipelago. **ID** Sexes alike. Adult has yellowish tinge to face and chest, long primary projection (equal to length of tertials), brown-green upperparts with a tinge of greyish, whitish supercilium, and brownish-pink legs. Juvenile similar to adult, but underside often completely yellow. Confusion likely with Common Chiffchaff, which has shorter primary projection and bill, more uniform facial markings, thinner darker supercilium, paler lores and eye-stripe. **Voice** Song may be given in the islands and consists of a descending series of very delicate and mellow *swee* notes. Most typical call is a *hoeet*.

Yellow-browed Warbler

Western Bonelli's Warbler

Wood Warbler

Common Chiffchaff
ad nominate
ad abietinus

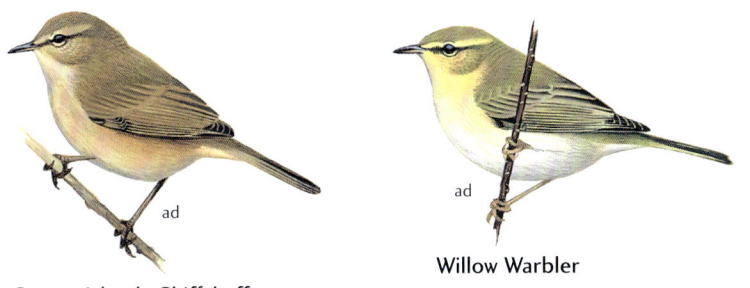

Canary Islands Chiffchaff

Willow Warbler

PLATE 57: REED AND BUSH WARBLERS

Sedge Warbler *Acrocephalus schoenobaenus*   L 11.5–13 cm

Seasonal visitor (all islands except P and H). Favours freshwater ponds with reeds, but also dry wadis with tamarisk woodland, when visiting the archipelago. **ID** Sexes similar. Adult has diagnostic buff supercilium contrasting with black crown-stripes, dark lores, may show a hint of pale median crown-stripe, olive-brown overall, brownish-pink legs. Confusion likely with similar-sized Eurasian Reed Warbler, but has shorter bill and is conspicuously marked on head. Juvenile similar to adult, but generally finely spotted on chest. **Voice** Song unlikely to be heard in Canary Islands, but can give a harsh *trrrr* and a *tuk*, often repeated as a series: *tuk-tuk-tuk-tutututututuktuk*.

Eurasian Reed Warbler *Acrocephalus scirpaceus*   L 12.5–14 cm

Seasonal visitor (all islands). Favours areas near freshwater or brackish water reservoirs, but also attracted to gardens and golf courses when visiting the archipelago. **ID** Sexes similar. Adult is uniform brown on the upperparts, and has inconspicuous supercilium in front of the eye, dark lores, both crown and mantle often tinged olive-grey, dark legs, and reddish-brown rump. Confusion possible with Great Reed Warbler but smaller, lacks dark tip to the lower mandible, primary projection is not as long as tertial length, lacks a pale supercilium and has less dark lores. Told from Sedge Warbler by the lack of conspicuous buff supercilium and dark stripes on crown, darker legs and longer bill. Separated from Western Olivaceous Warbler by the latter's habit of flicking tail downwards; also Common Reed lacks pale outer tail feathers, and does not have square-ended tip to tail. **Voice** May give a *chur* or *tscherr*, but song unlikely to be heard in the archipelago.

Great Reed Warbler *Acrocephalus arundinaceus*   L 16–20 cm

Vagrant. Prefers freshwater reservoirs with reeds and tall waterside vegetation, also attracted to golf courses. **ID** Sexes alike. Adult is larger and less elegant than Eurasian Reed, has stouter bill with a diagnostic dark spot at tip of lower mandible, more prominent pale supercilium and darker lores, a longer, more-rounded tail, longer primary projection, brownish-grey or pinkish-grey legs and at close range often visible grey streaks on chest. Shares overall coloration with Eurasian Reed Warbler; brown upperparts and buff-white underside, but during the summer greyer-brown above and yellowish-brown below. **Voice** Most typical call includes a *krek*, *gurg* and *chak*. Eurasian Reed Warbler-like phrases can be heard in spring, but louder, *karra-karra-karra*, *geek-geek*, *gurk-gurk*, *seep-seep*, *karra-karra*….

Western Olivaceous Warbler *Iduna opaca*   L 12–14 cm

Vagrant. Associated with open shrub habitat, but also tamarisk woodlands, parks, gardens and golf courses. **ID** Sexes similar. Adult lacks any yellow coloration on face, throat and underside. Similar to Eurasian Reed Warbler but brownish-green rump (not reddish-brown), square tail tip with whitish outer webs to outer tail feathers (only apparent under good viewing conditions), brownish-grey upperparts, broader bill base and the habit of constantly flicking tail downwards. **Voice** Typical calls include an alarmed *trrrrr*, and a repetitive contact call *chuck*. [Alt: Isabelline Warbler]

Common Grasshopper Warbler *Locustella naevia*   L 12.5–13.5 cm

Seasonal visitor (T, GC, F, L, a). Prefers herbaceous areas and coastal scrub, attracted to golf courses with freshwater ponds. **ID** Sexes similar. Adult has variable fine streaking on throat and upper breast, is grey-brown overall with a tinge of olive on the dark-streaked upperparts and off-white below, also diagnostic dark streaks on vent useful to separate from the *Acrocephalus* warblers recorded in the archipelago. Also told from Sedge Warbler by lack of prominent pale supercilium. **Voice** May utter a *thik*, but song unlikely in the region.

Melodious Warbler *Hippolais polyglotta*   L 12–13 cm

Seasonal visitor (T, GC, F, L, g). Often found in tamarisk woodland. **ID** Like congeners has the typical broad-based bill (pinkish-orange on lower mandible), steep forehead, and square-ended tail with white outer tail feathers. Summer adult is grey-green above with a tinge of brown and deep yellow below, and has brownish legs, short primary projection (never the length of tertials) and pale lores. During the autumn the yellowish coloration is restricted to lores, throat and upper breast. Juvenile similar to adult, but in fresh autumn plumage can show pale edges to secondaries, worn in the adult. Confusion likely with vagrant Icterine Warbler but no pale wing panel (less obvious in autumn), shorter primary projection and overall less grey and more brownish plumage. Confusion possible with Willow Warbler (which see). **Voice** May give a harsh *trrrr*, a soft *tuck* or a chattered *chret-chet*. Song unlikely to be heard in the region.

Icterine Warbler *Hippolais icterina*   L 12–13.5 cm

Vagrant. Favours areas of trees with dense understorey. **ID** Adult similar to Melodious Warbler but separated by less bright yellow underside, primary projection equal in length to tertials, lack of brownish tinge to upperparts (grey-green), grey legs and diagnostic whitish wing-panel created by the pale edges to tertials and secondaries which is less obvious in autumn. Told from Willow Warbler by slightly larger size, pale lores, lack of long supercilium and dark eye-stripe, square-ended tail with pale outer tail feathers, and dark legs. **Voice** A sharp *tek-tek* when alarmed.

Sedge Warbler

Eurasian Reed Warbler

Great Reed Warbler

Western Olivaceous Warbler

Common Grasshopper Warbler

Melodious Warbler

Icterine Warbler

PLATE 58: *SYLVIA* WARBLERS I

Eurasian Blackcap *Sylvia atricapilla* L 13.5–15 cm
Resident breeder (P, H, Go, T, GC) and regular winter migrant (F, L). Prefers laurel forests, parks and gardens, but also in tamarisk woodland in the eastern islands. **ID** Sexes differ. Adult male has a diagnostic small black cap on crown never reaching below the eye, dark grey body, white vent, and lacks white outer tail feathers. Adult female/juvenile male similar to adult male, but cap rusty-brown. A melanistic form, recorded on some islands, is all dark grey with a black hood extending to form a breast-band. **Voice** A characteristic call *tek*. Song combines melodious phrases, rising and falling in pitch towards the end. **Tax.** Resident breeding ssp. is *heineken*; winter migrants are nominate.

Garden Warbler *Sylvia borin* L 13–14.5 cm
Seasonal visitor (all islands except P and H). Favours forest areas with dense understorey, parks, gardens and riparian woodland when visiting the archipelago. **ID** Sexes similar. Adult has diagnostic short bill and mild expression, is olive to brownish-grey on the upperparts contrasting with stout pale grey bill and strong lead-grey legs; shows an indistinct supercilium and eye-ring. Often has grey on the side of neck. Long primary projection, pale buff underside and off-white vent. **Voice** May utter a *chek* call, often repeated. Song unlikely to be heard in the region.

Spectacled Warbler *Sylvia conspicillata* L 12–13 cm
Resident breeder (all islands). Uses a wide array of habitats from coastal semi-desert scrub to alpine zone, but never associated with woodland areas. **ID** Sexes differ. Adult male has brown upperparts, rusty-brown wings, white throat, blue-grey head, black lores, a conspicuous broken white eye-ring, uniform brownish-pink breast, and white vent. Adult female and first-year similar to adult male, but brownish head, paler lores and whitish-buff underside. Most likely to be confused with female Sardinian Warbler, which has red orbital ring and warm brown wings and mantle. Separated from Common Whitethroat and Subalpine Warbler by very black centres to rusty-brown tertials (tawny-brown in Subalpine). African vagrants similar to Spectacled include African Desert and Tristram's Warblers. **Voice** Song similar to that of Sardinian, but with 2–3 introductory whistled notes. Most typical call is a rattled *trrrrrrr*. **Tax.** Formerly, Macaronesian birds were considered to be ssp. *orbitalis* but the species is now best treated as monotypic.

Subalpine Warbler *Sylvia cantillans* L 12–13 cm
Seasonal visitor (all islands except H). While visiting found anywhere with any degree of shrub cover. **ID** Sexes differ. Summer male has red orbital ring and iris, white moustachial stripe, lead-grey head and upperparts, pinkish to rusty-orange throat and breast. Summer female has red orbital ring, faint moustachial stripe, lead-grey head, white eye-ring, pinkish-buff throat and breast, brownish upperparts, and greyish-brown or greyish-pink legs. First-winter female has brown head and upperparts, thin white eye-ring, white throat and diagnostic tawny-brown edges to tertials contrasting with wide dark centres. Confusion likely with Common Whitethroat and Spectacled Warbler (which see). Summer adult male told from vagrant spring Tristram's Warbler by lack of rusty-brown wings and vent and lack of red eye-ring. Confusion of adult female likely with resident male Spectacled Warbler, but the latter has rusty-brown wings. **Voice** Calls include a low rattling *trrrrt* and a *tek*. Song unlikely to be heard in the region. **Tax.** Western birds from Iberia, NW Africa and the Canaries are sometimes separated as Western Subalpine Warbler *S. inornata*.

nominate

ad ♂ ad ♀

Eurasian Blackcap

ad

Garden Warbler

ad ♂ ad ♀

Spectacled Warbler

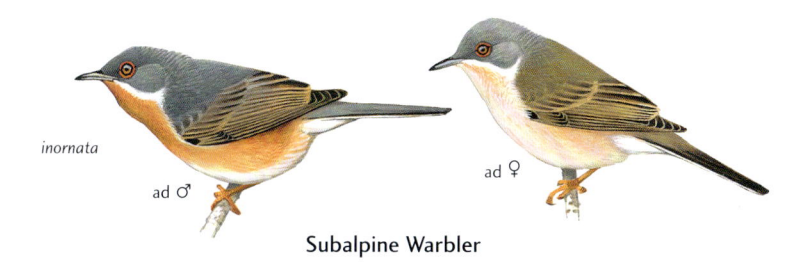

inornata

ad ♂ ad ♀

Subalpine Warbler

PLATE 59: *SYLVIA* WARBLERS II

Sardinian Warbler *Sylvia melanocephala* L 13–14 cm
Resident breeder (all islands). Prefers gullies and hillsides below 1,000 m, with a well-developed shrub layer, but also tamarisk woodlands in the eastern islands. **ID** Sexes differ. Adult male has red eye-ring and iris, dark grey upperparts, wings and underside, black head, and white throat and outer tail feathers. Adult female as adult male, but warm brown upperparts, wings and flanks, and white throat, grey head, paler red eye-ring. First-winter similar to adult, but outer tail feathers are less white; juvenile all brown before first moult. Confusion likely with Lesser Whitethroat or Western Orphean Warbler (which see). **Voice** Most frequent call is a machine-gun like *cha-cha-cha-cha...*. Song mixed in with rattling *trr-trr*, unlike Spectacled. **Tax.** Formerly, Canarian birds were separated as ssp. *leucogastra*, but are now best included in nominate *melanocephala*.

African Desert Warbler *Sylvia deserti* L 11.5–12.5 cm
Vagrant. Prefers sandy deserts with scattered bushes. **ID** Sexes similar. Adult has golden-buff head, upperparts and wings, whitish underside and diagnostic conspicuous yellow iris, bill and legs. Similar to resident Spectacled Warbler, but separated by the lack of rusty colour on wings, an important first field mark; also plain tertials and central tail feathers. **Voice** May utter a *djerrr-r-r-r-r* similar to African Blue Tit, and a high-pitched *chee-chee-chee*. Song unlikely to be heard in the islands.

Western Orphean Warbler *Sylvia hortensis* L 15–16 cm
Vagrant. Prefers coastal scrub but also gardens. **ID** Sexes differ. Summer male has a diagnostic pale iris (only attained towards the third year of life), white throat, dirty white underside, blackish head not contrasting greatly with grey upperparts, and a dark squared-off tail with white outer tail feathers. Summer female as adult male but iris variable and not diagnostic, browner on upperparts and black on head restricted to ear-coverts. Confusion likely with Lesser Whitethroat (which see). First-year resembles adult female, but browner above and with dark iris. **Voice** Calls includes *tak* similar to Blackcap and a *churrrr*. Song unlikely to be heard in the archipelago.

Lesser Whitethroat *Sylvia curruca* L 11.5–13.5 cm
Vagrant. Prefers parks, gardens and areas with high shrub cover. **ID** Sexes similar. Adult has dark grey-brown upperparts in summer and paler in the autumn, dark grey tail with white outer tail feathers, grey head, dark ear-coverts and dark legs. Confusion possible with female Sardinian Warbler, but separable by lack of red orbital ring, dark ear-coverts, dark legs, grey-brown upperparts (not warm brown) and whitish underside. **Voice** May utter a sharp *tek* or *tuk*. Song unlikely to be heard in the archipelago.

Common Whitethroat *Sylvia communis* L 13–15 cm
Seasonal visitor (all islands except P). Uses all sort of scrubby habitats when visiting the archipelago but prefers semi-desert scrub. **ID** Sexes differ. Adult male has brown mantle, white throat, pinkish underside, grey head, white eye-ring, dark tail with pale outer tail feathers and yellow legs. Adult female/first-summer male as adult male, but white eye-ring is inconspicuous and head is brown like mantle. First-winter has darker iris than adult female. Confusion likely with resident Spectacled Warbler, but is larger and in all plumages has rusty-brown tertials with a yellowish tinge and extensive dark centres, longer primary projection, and no black on lores of male. **Voice** May utter a *churrrrr-rrr-rrr* when alarmed and a short *churr*. Song unlikely to be heard in the archipelago.

ad ♀
nominate

Sardinian Warbler
ad ♂

African Desert Warbler
ad

Western Orphean Warbler
ad ♂
ad ♀

Lesser Whitethroat
ad

Common Whitethroat
ad ♂
ad ♀

PLATE 60: GOLDCREST, STARLING AND ROCK THRUSHES

Goldcrest *Regulus regulus*   L 8.5–9.5 cm
Resident breeder (P, H, Go, T). Favours mixed dense tree-heath woodlands and laurel forest, but also in pine forests. **ID** Sexes differ. Adult male has white wing-bars on median and greater coverts, white-tipped tertials, dark legs and longish bill, green above and buff-pink below, has thick, black-bordered crown-stripe that is yellow at the front and orange near the nape but orange colour only visible when erect, greyish tinge above the eye. Female as adult male, but no orange in crown. Both sexes differ from mainland races in deeper pinkish-buff underparts and broad lateral crown stripes meeting on the forehead. Juvenile before post-juvenile moult has grey crown and ear-coverts. **Voice** Song consists of a high-pitched and rapid *ze-zezeezee-ze-zezezee* ending in *zueet*. Calls include a trisyllabic *zee-zee-zee*. **Tax.** Two subspecies in the archipelago, differing only in song types: ssp. *ellenthalerae* (P, H) and ssp. *teneriffae* (Go, T); taxonomically unresolved and under review by SOC.

Common Starling *Sturnus vulgaris*   L 19–22 cm
Resident breeder (T, GC) and regular winter migrant (all islands). Prefers towns and villages, parks and gardens for breeding and overwintering. **ID** Sexes alike. Summer male at close range has a metallic green or violet sheen but normally appears all black with yellow bill and reddish legs, some whitish spots and blue-grey base to bill. Summer female as male, but has whitish base to bill and more conspicuous whitish spots. Winter adult has an all-dark bill and much more pale spotting than in summer. First-winter has grey head and dark body, heavily marked with pale spots. Juvenile is grey-brown overall with black bill, pinkish-brown legs and no pale spotting. **Voice** Song is a complicated series of warbles, clicks and drawn-out whistles *wheeeeoooooo*, often with mimicry. May give a *tcheerrr* call. **Tax.** The nominate ssp. *vulgaris* occurs in the archipelago.

Common Rock Thrush *Monticola saxatilis*   L 17–20 cm
Vagrant. Favours rocky hillsides with dense shrub layer. **ID** Sexes differ. Summer male has deep orange-rufous breast and underside including vent, light blue head and upper mantle, and white back. White patch on back shows well in flight. In adult male in autumn/winter, rusty-red tail contrasts with densely vermiculated black-brown plumage, and there is a tinge of orange on breast, flanks and underside. Summer female as adult male in autumn. **Voice** Characteristic calls are a low *chak-chak* and a distinctive *diu*. Song unlikely to be heard in the Canary Islands. [Alt: Rufous-tailed Rock Thrush]

Blue Rock Thrush *Monticola solitarius*   L 21–23 cm
Vagrant. Favours open areas of semi-desert. **ID** Sexes differ. Often perches on rocks, in silhouette shows characteristic long and strong bill. Summer male deep blue overall and can look all black at long range. Summer female is uniform dark brown above, vermiculated below and with a dark brown tail, not rusty-red as in Common Rock Thrush. First-year similar to respective adult, but male has broader pale feather-fringes than adult male. **Voice** Typical calls are a hard *chak-chak*, a soft *see* and a staccato *uit-uit*. Song unlikely to be heard in the archipelago.

ad ♂ *teneriffae* ad ♀ juv

Goldcrest

ad sum juv

Common Starling

ad ♂ ad ♀

Common Rock Thrush

ad ♂ ad ♀

Blue Rock Thrush

PLATE 61: THRUSHES

Ring Ouzel *Turdus torquatus*   L 23–24 cm
Irregular winter migrant (all islands except GC). Prefers alpine areas but also in tamarisk woodland. **ID** Sexes differ. Adult male has diagnostic conspicuous white crescent on chest, black overall with yellow, dark-tipped bill, pale fringes to wing-coverts and tertials. Female as male, but browner overall and with brownish-white crescent on chest. First-winter similar to adult female, but with inconspicuous pale crescent, often not visible in the field and therefore separated from Common Blackbird by pale fringes to wing-coverts. **Voice** May give a Common Blackbird-like *tak-tak-tak* when alarmed.

Common Blackbird *Turdus merula*   L 23.5–29 cm
Resident breeder (P, H, Go, T, GC), also recorded occasionally in winter (F, L). Prefers laurel forest, also in humid pine forests, cultivated areas at mid-elevations, parks and large gardens near the coast. **ID** Sexes differ. Adult male is all black with a conspicuous orange-yellowish bill and yellow eye-ring. First-winter male shows brown unmoulted flight feathers, a very dark almost all-black bill, and a less obvious yellow eye-ring. Adult female is similar to adult male, but sooty- or olive-brown overall with some fine streaks on chest, inconspicuous pale throat and dark yellow bill. Juvenile similar to female, but paler brown with pale spots overall, particularly on upperparts, and dark bill. **Voice** Song melodious with flute-like notes. Most often heard call is a *chuk-chuk-chuk*, but also a sharp *chik-chik-chik* and in flight can give a high-pitched *seee*. **Tax.** Birds on the Canaries and Madeira are separated as ssp. *cabrerae*.

Fieldfare *Turdus pilaris*   L 22–27 cm
Vagrant. Favours open farmland and gardens. **ID** Sexes similar. Adult has grey head with a pale supercilium, dark yellow bill, yellowish throat and ochre chest and flanks with dark chevrons and dark brown mantle. Pale grey rump visible in flight, as are the clean whitish axillaries only shared with vagrant Mistle Thrush. First-year similar to adult, but told by the pale spots on wing-coverts. **Voice** Song unlikely to be heard in the region. Call in flight is a *chuck-chuck-chuck…chack-chack-chack*, also a thin *seeh*.

Redwing *Turdus iliacus*   L 19–23 cm
Irregular winter migrant (T, F, L, a). Prefers semi-desert areas, tamarisk woodland and gardens. **ID** Sexes alike. Similar to Song Thrush but prominent white supercilium, yellow bill with dark tip, darker brown-grey upperparts, no arrowhead-shaped spots on breast and rusty-red flanks. Juvenile has buff streaking on upperparts and more rounded spots on underside, and some show whitish spots at tips of tertials. In flight rusty-red axillaries and underwing easily detected at distance and important for separation from congeners. **Voice** A flight-call *seeeh* and when alarmed may give a *chup* or a rattled *chittick*. Song unlikely to be heard in the Canary Islands.

Mistle Thrush *Turdus viscivorus*   L 26–29 cm
Vagrant. Prefers parks and gardens. **ID** Sexes alike. Adult is brownish-grey above and heavily spotted below. Confusion likely with similar Song Thrush, but tends to stand more upright and is clearly larger in size and overall paler, with rounded-shaped spots, face whiter. In flight white axillaries and white corners to outer tail feathers are diagnostic, although the latter are sometimes difficult to observe in the field. First-winter similar to adult, but identified by pale fringes to the greater coverts. **Voice** A *kerrr* given in flight and a *tuck-tuck-tuck*. Song unlikely to be heard in the region.

Song Thrush *Turdus philomelos*   L 20–22 cm
Regular winter migrant (all islands). Prefers areas with trees such as coniferous forest edges and on semi-desert islands prefers tamarisk woodland and gardens. **ID** Sexes similar. Adult is spotted below with a tinge of yellow-buff on chest and flanks, plain brown above. The arrowhead-shaped spots on the belly are an important field mark to separate from larger vagrant Mistle Thrush, which has round spots. Confusion also likely with Redwing (which see). In flight shows short tail and rusty-buff axillaries, but mainly detected by flight call. **Voice** A very low *zip* given in flight and a high-pitched *chick* when alarmed.

Ring Ouzel
ad ♀
ad ♂

Common Blackbird
ad ♀
cabrerae
ad ♂

Fieldfare
ad

Redwing
ad

Mistle Thrush
ad

Song Thrush
ad

PLATE 62: ROBINS, NIGHTINGALE AND BLUETHROAT

Rufous-tailed Scrub Robin *Cercotrichas galactotes* — L 15 cm
Vagrant. Prefers semi-desert areas with some bushy cover. **ID** Sexes similar. Confusion likely with adult female Bluethroat, but thicker and longer bill, pale legs (not blackish) and distinctive tail pattern. Separated from Common Nightingale (similar size and shape) by conspicuous creamy supercilium, black lores rufous-buff above (not warm brown), buff fringes to flight feathers, and diagnostic black-and-white spots on tips of outer tail feathers (visible when tail spread). Tends to move tail up and down. Juvenile similar to adult, but less conspicuous spots at tips of tail feathers. **Voice** May give a harsh *teck-teck* or a single call *tseet*. [Alt: Rufous Scrub Robin]

European Robin *Erithacus rubecula* — L 12.5–14 cm
Resident breeder (P, H, Go, T, GC) and regular winter migrant (F, L). Breeds in both laurel and pine forest areas, also in rural areas but avoids semi-desert habitat. Winters mainly in tamarisk woodland and where palm trees are present. **ID** Sexes alike. The olive-brown upperparts (including tail and wings) contrast with reddish-orange face and breast, whitish underside and some slate-grey feathering along the forehead and breast sides. First-winter as adult, but before the post-juvenile partial moult is brown overall, heavily mottled with buff, lacking reddish on breast, and some with a rusty wing-bar. Ssp. *superbus* has darker olive-brown upperparts, darker breast, and the bib can sometimes look reddish compared to nominate birds. Ssp. *marionae* differs from the nominate genetically. **Voice** A characteristic *tic-tic-tic* call. Song a series of melodious warbling phrases with much mimicry of other birds present in the area. **Tax.** Three subspecies in the archipelago: ssp. *superbus* (T), a recently described ssp. *marionae* (GC) and nominate (P, H, Go, F, L).

Common Nightingale *Luscinia megarhynchos* — L 15–16 cm
Seasonal visitor (T, GC, F, L, g, a). Prefers woodlands with dense understorey, and also riparian areas of dense scrub. **ID** Sexes alike. Slightly larger than European Robin. A very plain and often difficult to observe bird. Adult is reddish-brown on tail and rump, black eye with conspicuous white eye-ring, warm brown on the upperparts, whitish-buff below. First-year similar to adult, but greater coverts tipped buff. **Voice** Characteristic song unlikely to be heard in the region, but may give a high-pitched *seeeeee* or a guttural *grrrrr*. Other possible calls include *tacc-tacc* and *tucc-tucc*.

Bluethroat *Luscinia svecica* — L 13–14 cm
Vagrant. Prefers scrubby waterside undergrowth and reedbeds or canes while in the archipelago. **ID** Sexes differ. Summer male is grey-brown above, has prominent pale supercilium, deep blue throat with red dot (nominate) or white dot (*cyanecula*), red collar and whitish underside. Adult female/first-year female similar to adult male in summer, but has white throat and breast with dark malar stripe and some may show a hint of blue on breast. First-winter male has smaller blue patch on throat, forming a neat collar. In all plumages has a conspicuous white supercilium and a diagnostic reddish-rusty patch at the base of the tail, this latter character easy to spot when the bird is flushed. **Voice** Song unlikely, but may give *hweet* or *tuck tuck* calls.

Rufous-tailed Scrub Robin

ad

European Robin

ad *superbus*

ad nominate

Common Nightingale

ad

Bluethroat

ad ♂ nominate

ad ♂ *cyanecula*

ad ♀ nominate

ad ♀ *cyanecula*

PLATE 63: FLYCATCHERS

Spotted Flycatcher *Muscicapa striata*   L 13.5–15 cm
Seasonal visitor (all islands). Found anywhere with trees, for example parks and gardens, when visiting the islands. **ID** Sexes similar. Adult is off-white below, greyish-brown above with inconspicuous dark streaks on crown, throat and chest, strong bill and short black legs. First-winter similar to adult, but has conspicuous buff wing-bar on greater coverts and pale fringes to wing feathers. Slightly larger than European Pied Flycatcher and less slender in shape. Constantly flicks tail when perched. **Voice** May give a thin *zeee* and a loud *chick*, and when alarmed often a *zee-zucc*. Song unlikely to be heard in the region.

Red-breasted Flycatcher *Ficedula parva*   L 11–12 cm
Vagrant. Favours areas with trees, such as parks and gardens. **ID** Sexes differ. Summer male has conspicuous orange-red throat patch restricted to upper chest, grey sides to neck and greyish tinge to head and nape, pale brown upperparts and wings, white underside, black-and-white tail, black bill and legs. Adult female/first-summer male similar to adult male, but no orange patch or grey on head and sides of neck. Second-summer male as adult male, but orange patch restricted to throat, no grey on head or neck and has darker brown upperparts and wings. First-winter similar to adult female, but underside buff, pale tips to greater coverts and buff edges to tertials. **Voice** May give a rattle consisting of *chick* notes, sometimes just given singly or twice. Song unlikely to be heard in the archipelago.

European Pied Flycatcher *Ficedula hypoleuca*   L 12–13.5 cm
Seasonal visitor (all islands). Anywhere with trees, at both low or high altitudinal areas. **ID** Sexes differ. Summer male has black bill and legs, is black-and-white overall, with black head and upperparts, white underside, a variable amount of white on forehead (often two dots), pale patch on rump, white wing-patch covering inner greater coverts, inner secondaries and fringes to tertials, thin white line at tip of primary coverts, and dark tail with white on outer tail feathers. Adult female as male, but with brown head and upperparts, off-white below, brownish wings, white wing-patch restricted to intersection between tertials and inner greater coverts, which are tipped white (wing-bar), and inconspicuous white line at tip of primaries. First-winter as adult female, but shows a buff wing-bar on median coverts and a buff-cream wing-bar on greater coverts. **Voice** May give a *bit* or a *wheet* that are often combined.

Collared Flycatcher *Ficedula albicollis*   L 12–13.5 cm
Vagrant. Favours parks and gardens with trees. **ID** Sexes differ. Summer male similar to European Pied Flycatcher, but with complete white collar, large white patch at base of primaries and normally conspicuous white on rump. First-summer male as adult male but small white patch on base of primaries. Summer female similar to female European Pied Flycatcher, but with a large patch at base of primaries reaching almost to edge of wing. First-winter similar to adult female, but some have a second wing-bar on median coverts. **Voice** Song unlikely to be heard in the Canaries.

Spotted Flycatcher

Red-breasted Flycatcher

European Pied Flycatcher

Collared Flycatcher

PLATE 64: REDSTARTS AND STONECHATS

Black Redstart *Phoenicurus ochruros*   L 13–14 cm
Regular winter migrant and seasonal visitor (all islands except Go). Prefers cultivated rural areas on coastal sites, also hotel gardens, abandoned pasture areas. **ID** Sexes differ. Often shivers tail (which is rusty-red in all plumages). Adult male is greyish-black overall, and has orange vent, white wing patch and dark legs. Adult female/first-summer male is mouse-grey overall with no white wing-patch. First-year in autumn similar to adult female. Less colourful plumage than Common Redstart. **Voice** Song unlikely to be given in the region, but may utter a *tic-tic-tic* and a monosyllabic *tac* and a sharp *tsip*. **Tax.** Ssp. *gibraltariensis* occurs in the Canary Islands.

Common Redstart *Phoenicurus phoenicurus*   L 13–14 cm
Seasonal visitor (all islands except H). Could be found anywhere with trees or shrubs. **ID** Sexes differ. Adult male has black face and throat, slate-grey crown and upperparts, deep orange breast fading towards belly, white forehead and rusty tail, differing from adult male Black Redstart by its three-coloured pattern. Adult female similar to female Black Redstart, but with orange tinge to the underside and paler overall. First-winter male similar to adult female, but with hint of white forehead and dark cheeks. **Voice** Song unlikely to be heard in the archipelago. A *hooeet* not unlike Willow Warbler and a sharp *tek* are sometimes given. **Tax.** The nominate subspecies occurs in the Canary Islands.

Whinchat *Saxicola rubetra*   L 12–14 cm
Seasonal visitor (all islands except H). Favours open country with scattered bushes. **ID** Sexes differ. Summer adult male has white supercilium, black face, orange throat and breast, brown upperparts with dark streaks and one or two white wing-patches. Female is duller overall, as female European Stonechat, but with a heavily spotted rump, a prominent buff supercilium and orange throat. First-winter female similar to adult female, but finely spotted on breast and with white spots on back. In all plumages shows a diagnostic white patch at base of outer tail feathers, broad pale supercilium and heavy dark spots on rump. **Voice** Song unlikely to be heard in the Canary Islands. Most typical call is a *tek-tek* or *whu-tek-tek*.

European Stonechat *Saxicola rubicola*   L 11.5–13 cm
Irregular winter migrant (all islands except H). Favours unforested rural cultivated areas and often near freshwater ponds. **ID** Sexes differ. Summer male has a conspicuous thick white half-collar on neck, black head and throat, a small white wing patch, orange breast extending down the underside, dark streaked upperparts and spotted rump (when bleached can look white). Summer female as male, but inconspicuous white neck collar, browner and duller overall with brown head, throat and upperparts, small white wing patch and orange breast and underside. First-winter as female, but throat white and more buff overall. Confusion likely with first-year Canary Islands Stonechat, which is more buff and with the orange patch restricted to upper breast. **Voice** May give a strident *chak* or a soft *wheet*. Song unlikely to be heard. **Tax.** Nominate ssp. occurs on Canary Islands.

Canary Islands Stonechat *Saxicola dacotiae*   L 11–12.5 cm
Endemic. Resident breeder (F). Tends to avoid stony and sandy semi-desert plains, but prefers hillsides with rocky ground and scattered low bushes and gullies, both with and without running water. **ID** Sexes differ. Adult male has black head with thin white supercilium, white half collar and throat, dark brown mantle, small white wing-patch and buff-whitish underside with diagnostic orange upper breast-patch. Adult female paler brown overall, with a white throat and an indistinct supercilium. Juvenile weakly spotted on the head and upperparts. First-winter male is slightly duller than adult and shows no white wing-patch, but does have a pale panel on secondaries and pale-tipped greater coverts creating a faint wing-bar. **Voice** Song similar to European Stonechat and most characteristic call is a single *chut*, often repeated. **Tax.** Nominate ssp. occurs on Fuerteventura. Ssp. *murielae* extinct from Alegranza.

ad ♂

gibraltariensis

ad ♀

Black Redstart

ad ♂

nominate

ad ♂

ad ♀

Common Redstart

ad ♂

ad ♀

Whinchat

ad ♂

ad ♀

nominate

European Stonechat

ad ♂

nominate

ad ♀

Canary Islands Stonechat

PLATE 65: WHEATEARS

Northern Wheatear *Oenanthe oenanthe*   L 15–16.5 cm
Seasonal visitor (all islands). Open areas such as cultivated fields, airfields and golf courses. **ID** Sexes differ. Summer male has grey crown and upperparts, white supercilium and forehead, yellowish throat and breast, and white underside. Autumn adult male similar, but with brown crown and upperparts, some black on ear-coverts, and pale fringes to wing-coverts and tertials. Summer female similar to adult male, but brown-grey crown and upperparts, yellowish-buff ear-coverts, throat and breast, diagnostic buff-white supercilium (white behind the eye) and white underside. Female in autumn/first-winter similar to adult female in summer, but paler overall with same white-buff supercilium and black centre to median coverts similar in colour to black alula. In flight all plumages rather dark on axillaries and underwing-coverts. Male and female of ssp. *leucorhoa* are larger and more colourful. Confusion likely with vagrant Isabelline Wheatear. **Voice** Most typical call is a *chack* and a whistling *wheet* often given singly or combined.

Black-eared Wheatear *Oenanthe hispanica*   L 13.5–15.5 cm
Vagrant. Found in both cultivated and uncultivated open areas with bushes. **ID** Sexes differ. Summer male has yellow-ochre crown, mantle and upper breast, black mask and black or pale throat, white underside, black wings and diagnostic black tail with a lot of white. Summer female resembles adult male, but duller overall with browner wings and variable amount of black on the throat; sometimes throat is pale. Female in autumn is yellowish-brown on head and upperparts, and has pale throat and yellowish-orange breast. Likely to be confused with vagrant Desert Wheatear and autumn plumages of Northern Wheatear, but never shows grey on crown or mantle, therefore only separated from both in all plumages by diagnostic black tail with much white. **Voice** May give a *zack-zack* or *chep-chep* unlike Northern. Song unlikely to be heard in the region.

Desert Wheatear *Oenanthe deserti*   L 14.5–15.5 cm
Vagrant. Prefers semi-desert, stony and sandy plains and wadis. **ID** Sexes differ. All plumages show a diagnostic almost all-black tail contrasting with white rump. Summer male similar to adult male Black-eared Wheatear, but black mask reaches the shoulder and white scapulars form a white line near the shoulder. First-winter male similar to adult male, but pale fringes to all-black areas, except tail and also noticeable on lesser coverts. Adult female similar to first-winter male, but head generally rufous and throat greyish. **Voice** May give a low *tchuk* or a low *peeeoo* and a rolling *trrr*. Song unlikely to be heard in the region.

ad ♂ sum

ad ♀ sum
nominate

Northern Wheatear

ad ♂
leucorhoa

ad ♀

ad ♂ sum
dark-throated
morph

ad ♂ sum
pale-throated
morph

Black-eared Wheatear

ad ♀ sum
dark-throated
morph

Northern Wheatear

Black-eared Wheater

Desert Wheatear

ad ♂

ad ♀

Desert Wheatear

PLATE 66: WAXBILL AND SPARROWS

Common Waxbill *Estrilda astrild* — L 9 cm
Introduced (GC). Prefers gullies with running water and with stands of giant reeds or tamarisks. **ID** Adult male has diagnostic deep red mask, bill and belly patch, grey-brown upperparts, buff ear-coverts, throat and flanks and black vent and legs. The body is finely vermiculated all over, but this is only visible at close range. Adult female difficult to differentiate, but duller overall with brownish vent and less bright reddish belly and mask. Juvenile similar to adult female and easily told by dusky bill and duller mask. **Voice** Most typical contact call is a soft *tchip*. Song a monotonous *titichir-tititchir....* **Tax.** The subspecies *jagoensis* occurs in the Canary Islands.

House Sparrow *Passer domesticus* — L 14–16 cm
Introduced (GC). Favours urbanised areas. **ID** Sexes differ. Summer male has chestnut supercilium behind the eye extending towards the nape and sides of neck, diagnostic grey crown and dusky cheeks, black lores, chin, breast patch and bill, dark grey underside, brown mantle with black streaks, and brownish wings with white wing-bar on median coverts. Adult female has light brownish upperparts, greyish underside with a pale buff supercilium behind the eye, pale wing-bar on median coverts and a dusky-coloured bill with yellowish base. Winter adult male as adult male in summer, but duller overall and black breast patch restricted to chin. Confusion likely with Eurasian Tree Sparrow and Spanish Sparrow (which see). **Voice** Song is a combination of chirp calls including *chissick* notes. Most typical call is a rattle *churr-r-r-it-it-it* and *chee-ep*, *chissick* or *chip* calls.

Spanish Sparrow *Passer hispaniolensis* — L 14–16 cm
Resident breeder (all islands). Prefers rural areas near towns and villages from coast to mid-altitude, but also found in parks and gardens in big cities. **ID** Sexes differ. Summer male differs from similar House Sparrow by diagnostic chestnut crown, white cheeks and heavy pattern of black marks on breast. Confusion also possible with Eurasian Tree Sparrow, which (in both sexes) has a uniform greyish breast and a conspicuous black spot on the cheeks. Winter male as summer, but duller on the crown and mantle and finely streaked on the underside. Female is brownish above with dark streaks on the mantle, greyish below with inconspicuous grey streaks, pale buff supercilium behind the eye, dusky bill with yellow at base, and pale wing-bar on median coverts. Female Spanish difficult to separate from female House in the field. **Voice** Most typical call is a House Sparrow-like *chirp* and *chirrup*. Song is a series of monotonous *chilli* notes. **Tax.** The nominate ssp. *hispaniolensis* occurs in the region.

Eurasian Tree Sparrow *Passer montanus* — L 12.5–14 cm
Resident breeder (GC). Prefers towns and tourist resorts with gardens and parks. **ID** Sexes similar. Adult has conspicuous black spot on white cheek and dusky grey underside, chestnut crown, black bill with yellow base during breeding, black bib, dark-streaked brown mantle and rufous wings with two white wing-bars on median and greater coverts. Separated from Spanish Sparrow by the dark spot on the white cheek; also by lack of streaks on underside, white supercilium and white neck collar. Juvenile similar to adult, but with hint of dark spot on greyish cheek. **Voice** Song similar to House Sparrow, but some notes higher in pitch. Most typical call is a *chep* or *check*, often given in flight. **Tax.** The nominate ssp. *montanus* occurs in the Canary Islands.

Rock Sparrow *Petronia petronia* — L 15–17 cm
Resident breeder (H, Go, T, GC), extinct from one island (P). **ID** Sexes similar. Adult has diagnostic pale median crown-stripe on brown crown, pale creamy supercilium, strong bill with pale lower mandible, often a yellow spot visible on chest, dark-streaked brownish-buff mantle, thick streaks on white underside, and white tips to outer tail feathers, visible at long range in flight. Best told from the other sparrows on the Canary Islands by pale median crown-stripe, white tips to tail and diagnostic contact call. Juvenile similar to adult, but lacks the yellow spot. **Voice** Most characteristic call is a nasal high-pitched *pee-ip*. Song is a combination of calls. **Tax.** Formerly ssp. *madeirensis* in the Canaries but today nominate *petronia* recognised for the archipelago.

Common Waxbill

ad ♂
juv
ad ♀

House Sparrow

ad ♂ breeding
ad ♀

Spanish Sparrow

ad ♂ breeding
ad ♀

Eurasian Tree Sparrow

ad breeding

Rock Sparrow

ad

PLATE 67: WAGTAILS

Western Yellow Wagtail *Motacilla flava* — L 15–16 cm

Seasonal visitor (all islands) and vagrant (ssp. *feldegg*). Favours grassy areas while visiting the archipelago and often near freshwater ponds and golf courses. **ID** Sexes differ. Five subspecies. Summer adult male of ssp. *flava* is olive-brown above and yellow below, has grey head and white supercilium. Female and winter male have grey head with white supercilium, throat and upper breast, and are olive-brown above, dull yellow below. First-winter has pale lower mandible, pale yellow vent, is olive brown overall with dark lores, dark legs and variable black collar on throat. Summer adult male of ssp. *iberiae* as summer adult male *flava*, but with white throat and darker ear-coverts. Summer adult male of ssp. *flavissima* has deep yellow face and underside, green-olive upperparts; adult female duller with pale underside. Summer adult male of ssp. *thunbergi* has grey crown and nape, and blackish ear-coverts – a thin white supercilium behind the eye occurs on some individuals. Summer adult male of vagrant ssp. *feldegg* has black head and ear-coverts, olive back and deep yellow underside. **Voice** A *pseet* flight call and a disyllabic *swee-eep* is often heard.

Citrine Wagtail *Motacilla citreola* — L 15.5–17 cm

Vagrant. Prefers moist open areas with pools or freshwater reservoirs. **ID** Sexes differ. Summer female and winter adult have greyish on crown and cheeks, no black on nape, yellow throat, breast and cheek-surround, white wing-bars and dark legs. First-winter in autumn as first-winter White Wagtail, but no black collar and a diagnostic pale cheek-surround. First-winter from December to January has yellowish cheek-surround. Summer adult male, also possible in the archipelago, has grey upperparts, yellow head extending to the underside, white vent, black on nape, white fringes to wing-coverts and tertials, and dark legs. **Voice** Most typical call is a *tzreep*, not unlike Yellow Wagtail.

White Wagtail *Motacilla alba* — L 16.5–19 cm

Regular winter migrant and seasonal visitor (all islands), also vagrant (ssp. *yarrellii*). Prefers the lowlands of the archipelago in rural areas often associated with farms, but also near freshwater reservoirs and ponds. **ID** Sexes similar in winter. Winter adult similar to summer adult, but black is restricted to a neat breast-band. Summer adult has black on rear crown, nape, chin and breast, white forehead and ear-coverts; grey upperparts contrast with white underside, black legs and tail with white outer tail feathers. Summer adult female as adult male, but browner on upperparts and with grey nape patch. First-winter similar to adult female, but face tinged yellowish and upperparts olive-grey. Confusion likely with first-winter Citrine Wagtail (which see). Male of ssp. *yarrellii* in winter has black mantle and white throat, but in spring throat also black. Adult female ssp. *yarrellii* in summer has dark grey, often blotchy, mantle and blackish rump. **Voice** Most often heard in flight is a harsh *chizzick*, and a repetitive *tslee-wee*.

Grey Wagtail *Motacilla cinerea* — L 17–20 cm

Resident breeder (P, Go, T, GC) and regular winter migrant (F, L, g, a), recorded elsewhere (H). Favours riparian areas in gullies with either fresh or brackish water, but also reservoirs. **ID** Sexes differ. Summer male is grey above with conspicuous white supercilium and malar stripe, black bib, white fringes to tertials, lemon-yellow underside becoming brighter on vent, and white outer tail feathers visible in flight. Summer female and first-summer male show variable amount of black on throat, but similar to adult male in summer in every other character. First-winter similar to adult summer female, but with white throat and underside, deep yellow vent, yellow-green rump, buff supercilium and breast patch. In flight all plumages show a wide white wing-bar on the secondaries. **Voice** Most typical call in undulating flight is a *tzip*, usually repeated. When alarmed gives a *ziss-sis-sis-sis-sis*. Song a series of trills and melodious phrases. **Tax.** Formerly, Canarian birds considered as ssp. *canariensis* but today accepted as nominate *cinerea*.

Western Yellow Wagtail

Citrine Wagtail

White Wagtail

Grey Wagtail

PLATE 68: PIPITS I

Richard's Pipit *Anthus richardi*   L 17–20 cm
Vagrant. Favours moist grassland and often near golf courses. **ID** Sexes similar. A large pipit that tends to stand upright with neck extended. Adult has a stout bill, pale lores that can appear dusky, long legs and tail, buff breast and flanks, white belly, heavy streaking on upper breast, and often shows a black wedge on the sides of the throat. Confusion likely with juvenile (but less so adult) Tawny Pipit. The fringes of the median and greater coverts and tertials are rusty on adult Richard's, although first-winter birds tend to show white and rusty feather fringes as in juvenile Tawny. The longer hind-claw is diagnostic in separating juvenile Richard's from juvenile Tawny. **Voice** A harsh sparrow-like *schree* is often heard when flushed.

Tawny Pipit *Anthus campestris*   L 15–18 cm
Seasonal visitor (all islands except P and H). Prefers semi-deserts and dry grasslands. **ID** Sexes similar. Adult has pale supercilium, dark moustachial stripe and pinkish legs, uniform unstreaked buff-white underside and plain greyish upperparts, although there may be a few fine streaks on sides of upper breast. Juvenile resembles adult, but clearly spotted on breast and darker on crown and upperparts. Confusion possible with juvenile Yellow Wagtail, which has dark legs visible even at long range. Neat dark centres to white fringed median coverts, black lores and short hind-claw is diagnostic in separating Tawny from vagrant Richard's Pipit. **Voice** A single mellow *tchilp* or *chup* in flight.

Berthelot's Pipit *Anthus berthelotii*   L 13–14.5 cm
Resident breeder (all islands). Prefers semi-desert stony plains with scattered *Euphorbia* bushes at low and mid-altitude, but also occurs in high alpine areas, open, dry pine forests, pastures and grasslands. **ID** Sexes alike. Adult is dirty-white below with conspicuous thick dark streaks on upper breast extending to flanks, greyish above, pale tips to median coverts and greater coverts form two obvious wing-bars, legs are pinkish and hind-claw fairly long, Juvenile similar to adult, but browner on crown and upperparts and more boldly marked in fresh plumage, with diagnostic rufous fringes to median and greater coverts. Confusion likely with Tawny Pipit, but separated from adult Tawny by streaks on breast and from juvenile Tawny by lack of buff coloration on breast and flight feathers. **Voice** Song is a monotonous series of variations on the most common call *tsilee*, given in a circling flight display or from a bush or stone. **Tax.** Now treated as monotypic.

Olive-backed Pipit *Anthus hodgsoni*   L 14.5 cm
Vagrant. Prefers semi-desert scrub. **ID** Sexes similar. Adult has faintly streaked back, tinged olive, heavily streaked buff chest and more lightly streaked flanks, short hind-claw, bold whitish supercilium is rusty-buff in front of eye, black border at side of crown. Confusion likely with similar Tree Pipit (Plate 69) but head pattern is diagnostic with crown bordered by a dark stripe and supercilium broad and creamy with an orange-buff patch in front of the eye. Ear-coverts also diagnostic with a black and a white spot not present in Tree Pipit. **Voice** Similar to Tree Pipit but a shorter, softer *tsiit* diagnostic.

Richard's Pipit ad
juv

Tawny Pipit ad
juv

Berthelot's Pipit ad

Olive-backed Pipit ad

PLATE 69: PIPITS II

Tree Pipit *Anthus trivialis* L 14–16 cm

Seasonal visitor (all islands). Prefers areas of open woodland of several types and while visiting the archipelago mainly associated with areas with trees. **ID** Sexes similar. Adult shows pinkish bill, unmarked rump, tertials rather narrowly edged pale, greenish mantle and buff chest heavily streaked (less so the flanks with fine streaks). Confusion likely with Meadow Pipit but different call, heavier build, supercilium less diffuse, lack of clear olive-tinge to upperparts, bill stronger with a pink lower mandible, also diagnostic underside showing a conspicuous contrast between buff breast and flanks and the white belly, streaks bold on chest but fine on flanks. Tends to perch on trees and at very close range the short and curved hind-claw can be observed. **Voice** A high-pitched single call note *teeez*, not unlike Red-throated Pipit.

Meadow Pipit *Anthus pratensis* L 14–15.5 cm

Regular winter migrant and seasonal visitor (all islands except H). Prefers cultivated areas, abandoned pastures, grassy patches near freshwater ponds and reservoirs, golf courses and stubble fields in winter. **ID** Sexes similar. Adult is greenish-tinged on mantle and crown, buff chest with bold streaks on chest and flanks, faint supercilium and slender bill. Juvenile lacks flank streaks. Confusion likely with Tree Pipit, but different voice diagnostic, also less heavy build, slender bill often looking all dark, more diffuse supercilium and dirty eye-ring, longer hind-claw, and uniform thickness of breast and flank streaks. **Voice** Most often heard call is a repetitive *jip jip jip jip…* given when flushed and in the air.

Red-throated Pipit *Anthus cervinus* L 14–15 cm

Seasonal visitor (all islands except H). Favours grasslands, both natural and artificial, such as golf courses. **ID** Sexes differ. Adult male type has conspicuous rusty patch on throat that varies in intensity and extent. Female is typically heavily streaked on upper breast and rust colour is restricted to throat. First-winter similar to adult, but has white throat and pale tips to tertials, less olive and more grey-brown overall coloration, pale lores and thicker streaks on upperparts. Similar in size and shape to Tree Pipit and Meadow Pipit, but separated from both by the whitish stripes on mantle and the obvious black streaks on rump. **Voice** Most typical call when flushed is a single high-pitched short note *pseeee*, similar to Tree Pipit.

Water Pipit *Anthus spinoletta* L 15.5–17 cm

Vagrant. Favours freshwater habitats, artificial reservoirs and ponds. **ID** Sexes similar. Confusion likely with extreme vagrant but sturdier and darker Rock Pipit. Winter adult differs from Rock by yellow lower mandible, browner upperparts (no olive tinge), bold streaking on cleaner breast and flanks, white wing-bars and outer tail feathers. Leg colour as in Rock Pipit, varying from black to reddish-brown. Summer adult unlikely in region, but pink unstreaked chest diagnostic. Juvenile similar to adult in winter, but has more and darker streaks on upperparts. In flight white rectrices (greyish in Rock Pipit) and two prominent white wing-bars. **Voice** A monosyllabic oft-repeated *west*.

Tree Pipit — ad

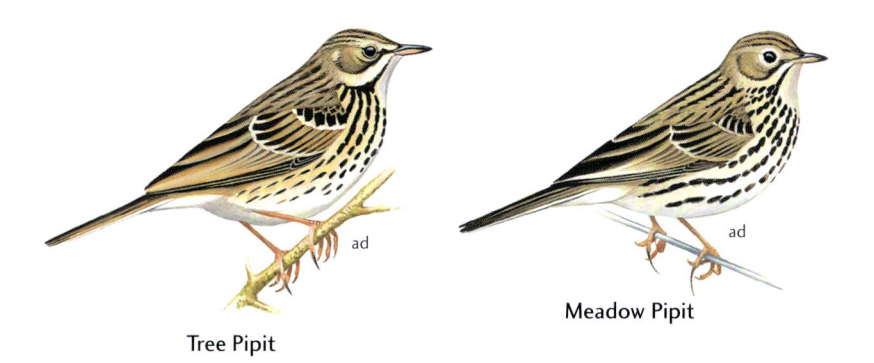

Meadow Pipit — ad

Red-throated Pipit — ad sum / 1st-win

Water Pipit — ad sum / ad win

PLATE 70: FINCHES I

European Serin *Serinus serinus*   L 11–12 cm
Resident breeder (T, GC) and occasional winter visitor (F, L). Favours gardens and parks and non-native Australian Pine for overwintering when also near cultivated areas and golf courses. **ID** Sexes differ. Shorter tail and bill than similar Atlantic Canary. Adult male separated from Atlantic Canary by bold streaking on mantle and flanks, bright lemon-yellow supercilium bordering the darker ear-coverts, off-white belly, bright yellow rump and greyish bill. Adult female as female Atlantic Canary, but shows no grey on head or chest and generally has bold streaking on chest and flanks, with diagnostic light yellow rump. Juvenile best separated from juvenile Atlantic Canary by call but also by bill shape and shorter tail. **Voice** Most typical flight-call is a *triirlilit* trill. Song consists of a very rapid series of unmusical wheezy notes *chirrizchirriz...* given perched or in display flight, unlike melodious song of Atlantic Canary.

Atlantic Canary *Serinus canaria*   L 12.5–13.5 cm
Resident breeder (all islands). A wide array of habitats from cultivated rural areas, both pasture and arable, to endemic laurel and pine forest, but also in alpine areas. **ID** Adult male has stout bill, bright yellow head, throat and underside, streaked greyish mantle and fine streaking on flanks, and pinkish-white vent. Yellow-green fringes to median and greater coverts diagnostic. Adult female similar to adult male, but finely streaked on chest, flanks, mantle and rump, duller overall with grey crown, ear-coverts, nape and sides of neck contrasting with yellowish supercilium and chin. Juvenile as adult female, but brownish overall with buff fringes to median and greater coverts. Confusion likely with European Serin (which see). **Voice** Most typical call is a whinny and rising *juuuit*. Song is a familiar melodious series of warbling trills *chur-r-r-r...chewchewchew...juitjuitjuitjuit*.

European Greenfinch *Chloris chloris*   L 14–16 cm
Resident breeder (P, H, Go, T, GC); rarely overwinters (F, L, g, a). Prefers rural areas, parks and gardens. **ID** Sexes differ. Adult male has greyish sides to head, is grey-green on upperparts and yellow-green on underside, grey wings with diagnostic yellow edges to primaries and ivory-coloured bill. In flight shows a lot of yellow at base of outer tail feathers, unlike any of the *Serinus* species, but as Eurasian Siskin (Plate 71). Adult female as adult male, but brownish overall with inconspicuous streaks on mantle, dull yellow edges to primaries, less yellow at base of tail feathers and greyish-green underside. Juvenile as adult female, but with greyer upperparts and grey-white streaking on underside. **Voice** Song is a series of twittering phrases ending in a nasal *dzweeeed* that rises. **Tax.** The ssp. *aurantiiventris* occurs in the Canary Islands but ssp. *vanmarli* from north Africa should not be ruled out in winter.

European Goldfinch *Carduelis carduelis*   L 12–13.5 cm
Resident breeder (all islands). In the archipelago favours farmland areas with trees, also cultivated areas, woodland edges, tamarisk woodland, parks and gardens. **ID** Adult shows red face, black-and-white head, black wings with yellow wing-bar, white dots to tertials, off-white underside, brown upperparts and flanks, white rump and black tail with white mirrors. All birds have long, pointed ivory-coloured bills. Juvenile similar to adult, but easily told by plain light brown face. **Voice** Song is a combination of twittering phrases with *tickelit* calls in between. Most typical call given when perched and in flight is a liquid *tickelit*. **Tax.** The ssp. *parva* occurs in the archipelago.

European Serin

ad ♂ ad ♀ juv

Atlantic Canary

ad ♂ ad ♀ juv

European Greenfinch

ad ♂ juv

European Goldfinch

ad juv

PLATE 71: FINCHES II

Eurasian Siskin *Spinus spinus*   L 11–12.5 cm
Irregular winter migrant (all islands except H and Go). Prefers areas with trees for wintering. **ID** Sexes differ. Winter adult male has lemon-yellow wing-bar on greater coverts, yellow rump and base of tail feathers, black crown and bib, grey-green dark-streaked mantle, yellow face and chest and white belly with fine streaking on flanks. Adult female as adult male, but lacking black crown and bib, duller and with grey-green crown. Juvenile similar to adult female, but greyer overall, with a tinge of yellow restricted to wing-coverts and base of tail feathers, heavily streaked above and below. **Voice** Most typical flight-call is a thin *dlu-ee*. Song unlikely to be heard in the region.

Common Linnet *Linaria cannabina*   L 12.5–14 cm
Resident breeder (all islands). Prefers farmland, both pasture and arable land, but also in semi-desert scrub near cultivated areas. **ID** Sexes differ. Adult male has greyish bill, grey head with red-pink forecrown and breast (duller and less extensive outside breeding season), brown mantle, white ventral region, black wings with white fringes to primaries and black tail with white outer tail feathers. Adult female/juvenile has grey bill but lacks any red-pink on plumage, and greyish head contrasts less with brownish dark-streaked mantle and brownish-buff finely streaked chest. Confusion likely with the two *Serinus* species in the region, but these lack the white wing patch created by white fringes to primaries. **Voice** Most characteristic flight-call is a *tow-tow*, often repeated. Song is a series of twittering phrases mixed with trills and *tsooeet* notes. **Tax.** Two subspecies in the Canaries (under review by SOC): *meadewaldoi* (P, H, Go, T, GC) and *harterti* (F, L, g).

Hawfinch *Coccothraustes coccothraustes*   L 16.5–18 cm
Vagrant. Prefers gullies with trees. **ID** Sexes differ. Adult male can be separated from female by the dark purple-bluish secondaries and inner primaries, which are greyer on the female. Adult has massive bluish-grey bill (yellowish in winter adult), orange head, grey nape, black lores and bib, dark brown mantle, orange rump and tail with white outer tips. White median and outer greater coverts (orange inner coverts), bluish edges to secondaries (males) or greyish edges (females), and white vent. In flight shows heavy front end and short tail with pale terminal band, broad wings with conspicuous white band at base of primaries. **Voice** May give a *tzik* in flight and a thin *seep*. Song unlikely to be heard in the archipelago.

Trumpeter Finch *Bucanetes githagineus*   L 11.5–13 cm
Resident breeder (Go, GC, F, L, g) and officially extinct from Tenerife since 2005, despite the fact that some individuals have been released recently. **ID** Sexes differ. Summer adult male has red bill, greyish head, brownish mantle, and pinkish breast, rump, edges to greater coverts and tertials. Adult female/male in winter duller and browner, lacking greyish and pinkish coloration and with yellowish bill. Juvenile resembles adult female, but ivory-coloured bill, uniform sandy on the upperparts and slightly paler on the underside. **Voice** Most often heard call is a nasal *eeez*. Song is a characteristic, repeated, nasal bleat, similar to a toy trumpet. **Tax.** The ssp. *amantum* occurs in the Canary Islands.

Eurasian Siskin

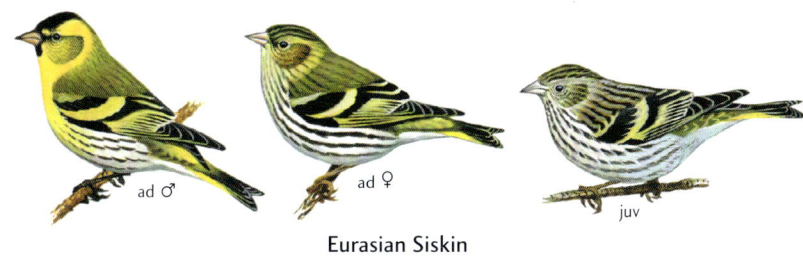

ad ♂ ad ♀ juv

Common Linnet

meadewaldoi harterti
ad ♂ ad ♂
ad ♀ ad ♀

Hawfinch

ad ♂ ad ♀

Trumpeter Finch

ad ♂ ad ♀

PLATE 72: FINCHES III

Common Chaffinch *Fringilla coelebs* — L 14–16 cm
Resident breeder (P, H, Go, T, GC); also nominate subspecies occurs as a vagrant. Prefers primary and secondary laurel forest, but also pine forests and cultivated areas. **ID** Sexes differ. Adult male ssp. *canariensis* (Go, T) shows ochre face and underside, blue-grey above, with white vent, two white wing-bars, variable greenish rump and white outer tail feathers. Adult male ssp. *palmae* (P) similar to ssp. *canariensis*, but ochre on underside restricted to chest, thus much white on lower breast, no greenish rump but this is difficult to see in the field. Adult male ssp. *ombriosa* (H) similar to *palmae* but ochre breast coloration not restricted to chest. Young males of all subspecies easily told from adult males by brownish mantle. Adult female in all subspecies is brown above, buff below, with two whitish wing-bars and white outer tail feathers. Winter adult male ssp. *coelebs* is brown on upperparts with rusty-red cheeks and underside, with blue-grey nape and crown. **Voice** Song varies slightly between subspecies, but generally is a loud series of notes on a descending scale and ending in a flourish *chew-chew-chew...*. Most typical call is a *chivi-chivi*, but also a *chowp* given in flight and a thin *tsee* when alarmed. **Tax.** Three subspecies are resident in the archipelago.

Tenerife Blue Chaffinch *Fringilla teydea* — L 16 cm
Endemic. Resident breeder (T). Prefers areas of endemic Canary Pine forest; more abundant in mature areas. **ID** Sexes differ. Adult male is deep bluish above, paler below, with two bluish wing-bars on median and greater coverts, a broken white eye-ring and a whitish vent. Young male is overall brownish-tinged to bluish, greater coverts mainly brown but depending in extent of moult will show some bluish feathers. Adult female is brownish-olive above, paler below and with two silvery-grey wing-bars. Juvenile has shorter all-black bill, buff fringes to greater coverts and pale and discontinuous median coverts wing-bar. Males can be sexed when some bluish feathers appear. **Voice** A loud rising series of monosyllabic *che* notes finishing in a flourish, transcribed as *che-che-che-che-CHE-CHE-CHE-CHE-freeebeeer*. Most typical call is a double chirp *tchweep, tchwew* (first rising, second falling), but also a thin *tsee* when alarmed, a *pit* in flight and a *tsrrrre-ah* given by juveniles.

Gran Canaria Blue Chaffinch *Fringilla polatzeki* — L 15 cm
Endemic. Resident breeder (GC). Restricted to some fragments of Canary Pine forests. **ID** Sexes differ. Adult male is similar to Tenerife Blue Chaffinch, but has two clear white wing-bars on median and greater coverts, and is whiter on the belly giving the overall impression of a slate-blue finch. Young male is browner overall with some variable bluish tinges on body and greater coverts, wing-bar is not all white due to some unmoulted brownish feathers. Adult female similar to adult female Tenerife Blue Chaffinch but slightly paler on the belly and with broad double white wing-bars. Juvenile is similar to female but bill is shorter, median coverts bar is broken and has buff fringes to greater coverts. **Voice** Song with disyllabic *che-e* notes and finishing in a descending *freber* note. The call is a Chiffchaff-like *hooet*. **Tax.** Elevated to species rank by Lifjeld *et al* (2016).

Brambling *Fringilla montifringilla* — L 14–16 cm
Vagrant. Prefers open parts of woodlands. **ID** Sexes differ. Summer male has orange throat, lesser coverts and chest, black head and mantle, black spots on flanks and black bill. Winter male as summer male, but black on head less uniform and has yellow bill. Adult female as adult male, but browner-grey on crown, mantle and sides of head, rusty greater coverts and yellow bill. First-winter male similar to adult male in winter, but often with black spots on lesser coverts. **Voice** May give a nasal *tsweek* while in the air and a *slitt* call when alarmed. Song unlikely to be heard in the region.

Common Chaffinch

ad ♂ ombriosa

ad ♂ palmae

ad ♂ nominate

ad ♂ canariensis

ad ♀ canariensis

Tenerife Blue Chaffinch

ad ♂

ad ♀

Gran Canaria Blue Chaffinch

ad ♂

Brambling

ad ♂ win

ad ♀ win

PLATE 73: BUNTINGS AND BOBOLINK

Snow Bunting *Plectrophenax nivalis* L 15.5–18 cm
Vagrant. Found in the alpine zone but also in lower areas such as golf courses or semi-desert. **ID** Sexes differ. Summer male has black bill and legs, white head and underside contrasting with black mantle and black-and-white wings. Summer female as male, but brownish crown, ear-coverts, sides of chest and mantle. In autumn/winter plumage has brownish streaked mantle, yellow bill with dark tip, rusty-brown on crown, ear-coverts, sides of chest and flanks. During autumn or winter males differ from females by conspicuous white wing patch on primaries and primary coverts. **Voice** A soft *pirrr-rit* or a ringing *peeu* may be given in the region. Song unlikely to be heard in the archipelago.

Bobolink *Doluchonyx oryzivorus* L 16–18 cm
Vagrant. Prefers low crops and stubble fields in native area, has only been found on golf courses in the Canary Islands. **ID** Sexes similar. Adult male in summer unmistakable but this plumage is unlikely to be seen in the region. Female similar to female Spanish Sparrow but yellower overall, with prominent crown-stripes (dark lateral crown-stripe, buff median crown-stripe), pinkish bill, buff supercilium, pale lores and diagnostic pointed tips to the tail. Often stands upright on ground and extends neck. **Voice** Most likely call is a sharp *pink*.

Corn Bunting *Emberiza calandra* L 16–19 cm
Resident breeder (all islands), but very rare on Lanzarote and extinct from La Palma. Favours arable land of different cereal crops, but also abandoned pastures on semi-desert scrub. **ID** Sexes similar. Adult has dark malar stripe, stout grey bill with pink lower mandible, often a dark spot on ear-coverts, finely dark-streaked grey-brown upperparts, buff-white underside with streaks near the throat and extending towards the flanks and pinkish legs. Flight action diagnostic with quick flapping and dangling legs. Confusion in the archipelago likely with smaller Rock Sparrow, which has conspicuously pale-tipped tail, boldly striped crown and different flight-call. **Voice** Song is a rapid and monotonous series of chipping notes followed by a jangling rattle that could be transcribed as *teuk-teuk-teuk zik-zee-zrrississ*, similar to a bunch of keys being shaken. **Tax.** Nominate ssp. *calandra* occurs in the Canary Islands.

Ortolan Bunting *Emberiza hortulana* L 15–16.5 cm
Vagrant. Prefers stubble fields and dry cultivated areas, but also attracted to golf courses. **ID** Sexually dimorphic and in all plumages the yellowish eye-ring is diagnostic. Summer male has a prominently black-streaked mantle, grey-green head, moustachial stripe and breast collar contrasting with yellow throat and orange-brown underside, two white wing-bars on median and greater coverts and chestnut edges to wing feathers. Summer female/first-winter male similar to adult male in summer, but duller overall. **Voice** May utter a short *plit* or a metallic *ts-leuu*. Song unlikely to be heard in the region.

Little Bunting *Emberiza pusilla* L 13–14 cm
Vagrant. Attracted to golf courses. **ID** Sexes similar. Summer adult has distinct red-brown median crown-stripe, ear-coverts and throat, finely streaked on chest and flanks, brownish upperparts with dark streaks and pinkish legs. Similar to female Common Reed Bunting but smaller and with a bolder eye-ring. The pale eye-ring, chestnut ear-coverts and straight culmen are diagnostic, as are the prominent lateral crown-stripes with dark border to ear-coverts, which does not reach the bill. On some occasions shows a cream spot on rear ear-coverts. **Voice** A soft *tsik* may be heard.

Common Reed Bunting *Emberiza schoeniclus* L 13.5–15.5 cm
Vagrant. Prefers coastal grasslands, stubble fields and cultivated areas. **ID** Sexes differ. Summer male has dark mantle with yellowish stripes, conspicuous black head, bill and throat contrasting with white collar and underside, chestnut wing-coverts and darkish legs. Summer female as male, but head pattern different with grey supercilium, pale throat and bold streaking on chest and underside. First-winter shows pale median crown-stripe and buff supercilium. **Voice** May utter a *tseeu* or a *chup* call while in the air. Song unlikely to be heard in the region.

Snow Bunting
ad ♂ win
ad ♀ win

Bobolink
ad win

Corn Bunting
ad

Ortolan Bunting
ad ♀
ad ♂

Little Bunting
juv
ad

Common Reed Bunting
ad ♀ sum
ad ♂ sum

SYSTEMATIC LIST OF THE BIRDS OF THE CANARY ISLANDS

This list is an updated version, as at 1 July 2017, of the official list of the Sociedad Ornitologica Canaria (SOC) as published in Garcia-del-Rey (2017). Taxonomy mostly follows the *IOC World Bird List* (Gill & Donsker 2017) with minor deviations. Trinomials are given for breeding species and for those species that are represented by more than one subspecies in the Canary Islands.

Key to islands and islets
P = La Palma
H = El Hierro
Go = La Gomera
T = Tenerife
GC = Gran Canaria
F = Fuerteventura
L = Lanzarote
g = La Graciosa
mc = Montaña Clara
a = Alegranza
c = Conception Bank

Key to status in the Canary Islands
RB = Present year-round with breeding confirmed
R = Present year-round but breeding not confirmed
OB = Occasional breeder
FB = Former breeder
I = Introduced with a self-sustaining population
MB = Migrant breeder, present in winter (W) or summer (S)
SV = Seasonal visitor, non-breeding
PM = True passage migrant with a known migration route
WM = Winter migrant (r = regular; i = irregular)
V = Vagrant
EX = Presumed indigenous species extinct within historical times

Key to presence on individual islands
x = present or recorded
(x) = formerly present (now extinct)
b = breeds (For those species that do not breed on all the islands where they occur, the symbol 'b' is used to specify breeding as opposed to presence 'x')
numbers = number of accepted records for each island
? = record(s) under review by SOC

English name	Scientific name	Status	P	H	Go	T	GC	F	L	g	mc	a	c	Total
ANATIDAE Ducks and geese														
Brent Goose	Branta bernicla	V				2	2	1						5
Greylag Goose	Anser anser	V				3		1						4
Greater White-fronted Goose	Anser albifrons	V				1	1		1					3
Common Shelduck	Tadorna tadorna	V	1				6	3	4					14
Ruddy Shelduck	Tadorna ferruginea	RB			x	b	b	b	b					
Wood Duck	Aix sponsa	V				3								3
Gadwall	Anas strepera	iWM	x			x	x	x	x					
Eurasian Wigeon	Anas penelope	rWM	x	x	x	x	x	x	x					
American Wigeon	Anas americana	V				9	7	2						18
American Black Duck	Anas rubripes	V				1								1
Mallard	Anas platyrhynchos	V				2	3	3	1					9
Blue-winged Teal	Anas discors	V	2	1		10	4	9	1					27
Northern Shoveler	Anas clypeata	rWM	x	x		x	x	x	x					
Northern Pintail	Anas acuta	rWM	x	x		x	x	x	x	x				
Garganey	Anas querquedula	SV	x	x		x	x	x	x					
Eurasian Teal	Anas crecca	rWM	x	x	x	x	x	x	x					
Green-winged Teal	Anas carolinensis	V				10	1	1	1					13
Marbled Duck	Marmaronetta angustirostris	OB				x	b	b	x					
Common Pochard	Aythya ferina	iWM	x		x	x	x	x	x					
Ferruginous Duck	Aythya nyroca	V				•	1		1					2
Ring-necked Duck	Aythya collaris	V	7	3	3	28	4	20						65
Tufted Duck	Aythya fuligula	rWM	x	x	x	x	x	x						
Greater Scaup	Aythya marila	V				4	4	4	2					14
Lesser Scaup	Aythya affinis	V		3		13	5	4	1					26
Common Scoter	Melanitta nigra	V	1			1			1					4
Long-tailed Duck	Clangula hyemalis	V							1					1
Hooded Merganser	Lophodytes cucullatus	V				1								1
Red-breasted Merganser	Mergus serrator	V				1								1
PHASIANIDAE Partridges and quails														
Barbary Partridge	Alectoris barbara koenigi	I	x	x	x	x		x	x	x				
Red-legged Partridge	Alectoris rufa intercedens	I					x							
Common Quail	Coturnix coturnix coturnix	RB/MBS	x	x	x	x	x	x	x					
GAVIIDAE Divers														
Black-throated Diver	Gavia arctica	V				1	1							2
Great Northern Diver	Gavia immer	V			1	3			1					5
OCEANITIDAE Austral Storm-petrels														
Wilson's Storm-petrel	Oceanites oceanicus	V											4	4
White-faced Storm-petrel	Pelagodroma marina hypoleuca	MBS									x	x		
Black-bellied Storm-petrel	Fregetta tropica	V											3	3

English name	Scientific name	Status	Islands and islets											Total
			P	H	Go	T	GC	F	L	g	mc	a	c	
HYDROBATIDAE Northern Storm-petrels														
European Storm-petrel	Hydrobates pelagicus	MBS	x	x	x		x			x	x	x		
Madeiran Storm-petrel	Oceanodroma castro	MBW	x		x				x		x	x		
Swinhoe's Storm-petrel	Oceanodroma monorhis	V							2				2	4
Leach's Storm-petrel	Oceanodroma leucorhoa	SV	x	x	x	x	x	x	x					
PROCELLARIIDAE Petrels and shearwaters														
Northern Fulmar	Fulmarus glacialis	V				1	1	4	1					7
Zino's/Fea's/Desertas Petrel	Pterodroma madeira/feae/deserta	V	1			1		1				4		7
Scopoli´s Shearwater	Calonectris diomedea	V									2			2
Cory's Shearwater	Calonectris borealis	MBS	x	x	x	x	x	x	x	x	x	x		
Cape Verde Shearwater	Calonectris edwardsii	V					1			3				4
Sooty Shearwater	Ardenna grisea	V			1	3			2				1	7
Great Shearwater	Ardenna gravis	SV	x	x	x	x	x	x				x		
Manx Shearwater	Puffinus puffinus	MBS	x			x								
Balearic Shearwater	Puffinus mauretanicus	V										1		1
Barolo Shearwater	Puffinus baroli	RB		x	x			x	x	x	x			
Boyd´s Shearwater	Puffinus boydi	V				1								1
Bulwer's Petrel	Bulweria bulwerii	MBS	x	x	x	x	x	x	x	x	x			
PODICIPEDIDAE Grebes														
Little Grebe	Tachybaptus ruficollis	V				1		1	1					3
Pied-billed Grebe	Podilymbus podiceps	V				1	2							3
Black-necked Grebe	Podiceps nigricollis	rWM	x	x		x	x	x	x					
PHOENICOPTERIDAE Flamingos														
Greater Flamingo	Phoenicopterus roseus	V	4			2	3	3	5	1				18
Lesser Flamingo	Phoeniconaias minor	V				3		1						4
PHAETHONTIDAE Tropicbirds														
Red-billed Tropicbird	Phaethon aethereus mesonauta	OB	x	b	x	x	x	b	b	x		x		
CICONIIDAE Storks														
Black Stork	Ciconia nigra	V				6	13	1						20
White Stork	Ciconia ciconia	SV	x	x	x	x	x	x	x	x		x		
THRESKIORNITHIDAE Ibises														
African Sacred Ibis	Threskiornis aethiopicus	FB				7		1	3					11
Glossy Ibis	Plegadis falcinellus	SV	x	x	x	x	x	x	x					
Eurasian Spoonbill	Platalea leucorodia	rWM/SV	x	x	x	x	x	x	x		x			
ARDEIDAE Herons and bitterns														
Eurasian Bittern	Botaurus stellaris	V				4		3	2					9
American Bittern	Botaurus lentiginosus	V				1								1
Little Bittern	Ixobrychus minutus minutus	OB/SV	x	x	x	b	x	x	x					
	Ixobrychus minutus payesii	V	1?											

English name	Scientific name	Status	P	H	Go	T	GC	F	L	g	mc	a	c	Total
Dwarf Bittern	*Ixobrychus sturmii*	V				2	1							3
Black-crowned Night Heron	*Nycticorax nycticorax nycticorax*	RB/SV	x	x	x	x	x	x	x					
Green Heron	*Butorides virescens*	V				1								1
Squacco Heron	*Ardeola ralloides*	SV	x		x	x	x	x	x					
Western Cattle Egret	*Bubulcus ibis ibis*	RB/rWM	x	x	x	x	x	x	b					
Grey Heron	*Ardea cinerea cinerea*	rWM/SV/R	x	x	x	x	x	x	x		x			
Great Blue Heron	*Ardea herodias*	V				1								1
Purple Heron	*Ardea purpurea*	SV	x	x	x	x	x	x			x			
Great Egret	*Ardea alba*	V				5	2							7
Tricolored Heron	*Egretta tricolor*	V				1								1
Little Egret	*Egretta garzetta garzetta*	rWM/OB	x	x	x	b	x	x	b					
Western Reef Heron	*Egretta gularis*	V				3	8							11
FREGATIDAE Frigatebirds														
Frigatebird sp.	*Fregata sp.*	V	2	1										3
SULIDAE Gannets and boobies														
Northern Gannet	*Morus bassanus*	SV/PM	x	x	x	x	x	x	x	x	x	x		
Red-footed Booby	*Sula sula*	V		1		2								3
Brown Booby	*Sula leucogaster*	V		1					1					2
PHALACROCORACIDAE Cormorants														
Double-crested Cormorant	*Phalacrocorax auritus*	V		1										1
Great Cormorant	*Phalacrocorax carbo*	iWM	x	x	x	x	x	x	x					
PANDIONIDAE Osprey														
Osprey	*Pandion haliaetus haliaetus*	RB	x	b	b	b	x	x	b	x	b	b		
ACCIPITRIDAE Kites, hawks and eagles														
Egyptian Vulture	*Neophron percnopterus majorensis*	RB						x	x		x			
European Honey Buzzard	*Pernis apivorus*	V				2	2	1						5
Swallow-tailed Kite	*Elanoides forficatus*	V						1						1
Short-toed Snake Eagle	*Circaetus gallicus*	V				6	3		2					11
Booted Eagle	*Hieraaetus pennatus*	SV	x	x	x	x	x	x			x			
Bonelli's Eagle	*Aquila fasciata*	V		2										2
Eurasian Sparrowhawk	*Accipiter nisus nisus*	iWM						x	x		x			
	Accipiter nisus granti	RB	x	x	x	x								
Northern Goshawk	*Accipiter gentilis*	V				2								2
Western Marsh Harrier	*Circus aeruginosus*	SV		x	x	x	x	x	x		x			
Hen Harrier	*Circus cyaneus*	SV	x	x	x	x	x	x	x		x			
Pallid Harrier	*Circus macrourus*	V				1		1	1					3
Montagu's Harrier	*Circus pygargus*	SV	x			x	x	x	x		x			
Red Kite	*Milvus milvus*	EX		(x)	(x)	(x)	(x)							
Black Kite	*Milvus migrans*	SV	x	x	x	x	x	x	x		x			

English name	Scientific name	Status	Islands and islets											Total
			P	H	Go	T	GC	F	L	g	mc	a	c	
Common Buzzard	Buteo buteo insularum	RB	x	x	x	x	x	x						
Long-legged Buzzard	Buteo rufinus	V						4?						
OTIDIDAE Bustards														
Houbara Bustard	Chlamydotis undulata fuertaventurae	RB						x	x	x				
RALLIDAE Rails, crakes and coots														
Water Rail	Rallus aquaticus	V				1								1
African Crake	Crex egregia	V				4	2							6
Corn Crake	Crex crex	V	2	1	1	1	1	3	2					11
Little Crake	Porzana parva	V				5		3						8
Baillon's Crake	Porzana pusilla	V	1			5		3	3					12
Spotted Crake	Porzana porzana	SV	x	x	x	x	x	x	x					
Allen's Gallinule	Porphyrio alleni	V		2		7	4	2	1					16
Purple Gallinule	Porphyrio martinica	V				1	1							2
Common Moorhen	Gallinula chloropus chloropus	RB	x		x	x	x	x						
Eurasian Coot	Fulica atra atra	RB/rWM	x		x	x	x	x						
GRUIDAE Cranes														
Common Crane	Grus grus	V						1		1				2
BURHINIDAE Stone-curlews														
Eurasian Stone-curlew	Burhinus oedicnemus distinctus	RB	x	x	x	x	x							
	Burhinus oedicnemus insularum	RB						x	x	x		x		
HAEMATOPODIDAE Oystercatchers														
Canary Islands Oystercatcher	Haematopus meadewaldoi	EX						(x)	(x)	(x)		(x)		
Eurasian Oystercatcher	Haematopus ostralegus	SV/iWM	x	x	x	x	x	x				x		
RECURVIROSTRIDAE Stilts and avocets														
Black-winged Stilt	Himantopus himantopus	RB				x	x	b	b					
Pied Avocet	Recurvirostra avosetta	SV	x	x		x	x	x						
CHARADRIIDAE Plovers														
Northern Lapwing	Vanellus vanellus	iWM	x	x		x	x	x	x		x	x		
Sociable Lapwing	Vanellus gregarius	V		1										1
White-tailed Lapwing	Vanellus leucurus	V				1								1
European Golden Plover	Pluvialis apricaria	iWM	x			x	x	x	x					
American Golden Plover	Pluvialis dominica	V	5			15	2	4	6					32
Grey Plover	Pluvialis squatarola	rWM/SV	x	x	x	x	x	x	x		x			
Common Ringed Plover	Charadrius hiaticula	rWM/SV	x	x	x	x	x	x	x					
Semipalmated Plover	Charadrius semipalmatus	V	1											1
Little Ringed Plover	Charadrius dubius curonicus	RB/SV	x	x		x	x	x	x					
Kentish Plover	Charadrius alexandrinus alexandrinus	RB				x	x	x	x					
Lesser Sand Plover	Charadrius mongolus	V	1					1						2
Eurasian Dotterel	Charadrius morinellus	iWM	x		x	x	x	x			x			

English name	Scientific name	Status	P	H	Go	T	GC	F	L	g	mc	a	c	Total
SCOLOPACIDAE Sandpipers														
Eurasian Woodcock	*Scolopax rusticola*	RB	b	b	b	b	b	x	x			x		
Jack Snipe	*Lymnocryptes minimus*	iWM	x	x	x	x	x	x						
Common Snipe	*Gallinago gallinago*	rWM	x	x	x	x	x	x						
Wilson's Snipe	*Gallinago delicata*	V				1								1
Long-billed Dowitcher	*Limnodromus scolopaceus*	V	1			1			1					3
Black-tailed Godwit	*Limosa limosa*	rWM/SV	x	x	x	x	x	x	x					
Bar-tailed Godwit	*Limosa lapponica*	SV	x	x	x	x	x	x	x	x				
Whimbrel	*Numenius phaeopus*	rWM/SV	x	x	x	x	x	x	x	x	x			
Eurasian Curlew	*Numenius arquata*	SV	x	x	x	x	x	x	x	x				
Spotted Redshank	*Tringa erythropus*	iWM/SV	x			x	x	x	x					
Common Redshank	*Tringa totanus*	rWM/SV	x	x	x	x	x	x						
Marsh Sandpiper	*Tringa stagnatilis*	V				1	2	1						4
Common Greenshank	*Tringa nebularia*	rWM/SV	x	x	x	x	x	x	x		x			
Greater Yellowlegs	*Tringa melanoleuca*	V							1					1
Lesser Yellowlegs	*Tringa flavipes*	V	3			5	4	3	2					17
Green Sandpiper	*Tringa ochropus*	rWM/SV	x	x	x	x	x	x	x					
Wood Sandpiper	*Tringa glareola*	SV	x	x	x	x	x	x						
Common Sandpiper	*Actitis hypoleucos*	rWM/SV	x	x	x	x	x	x	x		x			
Spotted Sandpiper	*Actitis macularius*	V			2	2	10	3		3				20
Ruddy Turnstone	*Arenaria interpres*	rWM/SV	x	x	x	x	x	x	x	x		x		
Red Knot	*Calidris canutus*	SV/iWM	x	x		x	x	x	x					
Ruff	*Calidris pugnax*	SV	x	x	x	x	x	x	x					
Curlew Sandpiper	*Calidris ferruginea*	SV	x	x	x	x	x	x	x	x		x		
Temminck's Stint	*Calidris temminckii*	V				1	5		5					11
Sanderling	*Calidris alba*	rWM/SV	x	x	x	x	x	x	x					
Dunlin	*Calidris alpina*	rWM/SV	x	x	x	x	x	x	x					
Purple Sandpiper	*Calidris maritima*	V	1			2	1		1					5
Baird's Sandpiper	*Calidris bairdii*	V			1		3		2					6
Little Stint	*Calidris minuta*	SV/rWM	x	x		x	x	x	x					
Least Sandpiper	*Calidris minutilla*	V							1					1
White-rumped Sandpiper	*Calidris fuscicollis*	V	10	3	2	13	9	6	11					54
Buff-breasted Sandpiper	*Calidris subruficollis*	V	2			6	3	5	2					18
Pectoral Sandpiper	*Calidris melanotos*	V	8	2	2	26	5	11	11					65
Semipalmated Sandpiper	*Calidris pusilla*	V	2	1		2			1					6
Wilson's Phalarope	*Phalaropus tricolor*	V	1			3		1	1					6
Red-necked Phalarope	*Phalaropus lobatus*	V					1							1
Grey Phalarope	*Phalaropus fulicarius*	SV/iWM			x	x	x	x				x		
GLAREOLIDAE Coursers and pratincoles														
Cream-coloured Courser	*Cursorius cursor cursor*	RB			x	x	x	b	b	x				

English name	Scientific name	Status	Islands and islets											Total
			P	H	Go	T	GC	F	L	g	mc	a	c	
Collared Pratincole	Glareola pratincola	SV	x	x	x	x	x	x	x					
LARIDAE Gulls and terns														
Black-legged Kittiwake	Rissa tridactyla	SV/iWM	x	x	x	x	x	x	x	x				
Sabine's Gull	Xema sabini	PM		x	x	x		x				x		
Slender-billed Gull	Chroicocephalus genei	V				2	1	3	4					10
Bonaparte's Gull	Chroicocephalus philadelphia	V	1											1
Black-headed Gull	Chroicocephalus ridibundus	rWM/SV	x	x	x	x	x	x	x	x				
Grey-headed Gull	Chroicocephalus cirrocephalus	V					1							1
Little Gull	Hydrocoloeus minutus	V				4	1		2					7
Laughing Gull	Leucophaeus atricilla	V	2			3	4	3						12
Franklin's Gull	Leucophaeus pipixcan	V				1			1					2
Audouin's Gull	Ichthyaetus audouinii	iWM/SV				x	x	x	x	x				
Mediterranean Gull	Ichthyaetus melanocephalus	iWM/SV	x	x	x	x	x	x	x					
Common Gull	Larus canus	V				1		3	2					6
Ring-billed Gull	Larus delawarensis	V	2	2		12	5	1	6					28
Great Black-backed Gull	Larus marinus	iWM/SV				x	x	x	x					
Kelp Gull	Larus dominicanus	V				1								1
Glacous-winged Gull	Larus glaucescens	V		1										1
Glaucous Gull	Larus hyperboreus	V	2				3	1	2	1				9
Iceland Gull	Larus glaucoides	V	1			3		1						5
Yellow-legged Gull	Larus michahellis atlantis	RB	x	x	x	x	x	x	x	x	x			
Lesser Black-backed Gull	Larus fuscus fuscus/graellsii	rWM/SV/OB	x	x	x	x	x	x	x	x	x			
Gull-billed Tern	Gelochelidon nilotica	SV	x	x	x	x	x	x						
Caspian Tern	Hydroprogne caspia	V				1		1						2
Lesser Crested Tern	Thalasseus bengalensis	V				1								1
Sandwich Tern	Thalasseus sandvicensis	rWM/SV	x	x	x	x	x	x	x		x			
Little Tern	Sternula albifrons	V				3		4						7
Sooty Tern	Onychoprion fuscatus	V				1		1						2
Roseate Tern	Sterna dougallii dougallii	OB/V	2				1	2	3					8
Common Tern	Sterna hirundo hirundo	MBS/SV	x	x	x	x	x	x						
Arctic Tern	Sterna paradisaea	PM				x	x	x			x			
Whiskered Tern	Chlidonias hybrida	SV	x			x	x	x		x				
White-winged Tern	Chlidonias leucopterus	V					2							2
Black Tern	Chlidonias niger	V	1	1	1	2	3		2			2		12
STERCORARIIDAE Skuas														
South Polar Skua	Stercorarius maccormicki	V	1					1				1		3
Great Skua	Stercorarius skua	SV	x	x	x	x	x	x	x	x	x	x		
Pomarine Skua	Stercorarius pomarinus	SV	x	x	x	x	x	x	x	x	x	x		
Arctic Skua	Stercorarius parasiticus	SV		x	x	x	x	x	x		x			
Long-tailed Skua	Stercorarius longicaudus	PM				x	x		x			x		

English name	Scientific name	Status	Islands and islets										Total
			P	H	Go	T	GC	F	L	g	mc	a	c	
ALCIDAE Auks														
Little Auk	Alle alle	V				1								1
Common Guillemot	Uria aalge	V							1					1
Atlantic Puffin	Fratercula arctica	V				1		2						3
PTEROCLIDAE Sandgrouse														
Black-bellied Sandgrouse	Pterocles orientalis orientalis	RB						b	x	x				
COLUMBIDAE Pigeons and doves														
Rock Dove	Columba livia livia	RB	x	x	x	x	x	x	x	x	x	x		
Common Wood Pigeon	Columba palumbus	SV	x			x	x	x	x					
Bolle's Pigeon	Columba bollii	RB	x	x	x	x								
Laurel Pigeon	Columba junoniae	RB	x	x	x	x	1							
European Turtle Dove	Streptopelia turtur turtur	MBS	x	x	x	x	x	x	x					
Eurasian Collared Dove	Streptopelia decaocto decaocto	RB	x	x	x	x	x	x						
African Collared Dove	Streptopelia roseogrisea roseogrisea	I	x		x	x	x	x						
Laughing Dove	Streptopelia senegalensis phoenicophila	RB	x	x	x	x	x	x						
CUCULIDAE Cuckoos														
Great Spotted Cuckoo	Clamator glandarius	SV	x	x		x	x	x	x		x			
Common Cuckoo	Cuculus canorus	SV	x		x	x	x	x			x			
TYTONIDAE Barn Owls														
Western Barn Owl	Tyto alba alba	RB	x	x	x	x	x							
	Tyto alba gracilirostris	RB						x	x	x	x	x		
STRIGIDAE Owls														
Eurasian Scops Owl	Otus scops	V				2	1	2	2		1	1		9
Long-eared Owl	Asio otus canariensis	RB	b	b	b	b	b	x	x					
Short-eared Owl	Asio flammeus	iWM/SV	x		x	x	x	x	x		x	x		
CAPRIMULGIDAE Nightjars														
Common Nighthawk	Chordeiles minor	V				1								1
Red-necked Nightjar	Caprimulgus ruficollis	V					1	2						3
European Nightjar	Caprimulgus europaeus	V				2		1						3
Egyptian Nightjar	Caprimulgus aegyptius	V					1							1
APODIDAE Swifts														
Chimney Swift	Chaetura pelagica	V				2	1	1						4
Alpine Swift	Tachymarptis melba	SV	x	x	x	x	x	x	x					
Common Swift	Apus apus apus	SV	x	x	x	x	x	x						
Plain Swift	Apus unicolor	MBS	x	x	x	x	x							
Pallid Swift	Apus pallidus brehmorum	MBS				x		x	x					
Little Swift	Apus affinis	V	1			7	4	1						13
White-rumped Swift	Apus caffer	V				1								1

English name	Scientific name	Status	Islands and islets											Total
			P	H	Go	T	GC	F	L	g	mc	a	c	
CORACIIDAE Rollers														
Abyssinian Roller	*Coracias abyssinicus*	V						1						1
European Roller	*Coracias garrulus*	SV	x	x	x	x	x	x	x	x				
ALCEDINIDAE Kingfishers														
Common Kingfisher	*Alcedo atthis*	V				1	3				1			5
MEROPIDAE Bee-eaters														
Blue-cheeked Bee-eater	*Merops persicus*	V				1	1							2
European Bee-eater	*Merops apiaster*	SV	x	x	x	x	x	x	x	x				
UPUPIDAE Hoopoes														
Eurasian Hoopoe	*Upupa epops epops*	RB	x	x	x	x	x	x	x	x				
PICIDAE Woodpeckers														
Eurasian Wryneck	*Jynx torquilla*	SV	x			x			x	x	x			
Great Spotted Woodpecker	*Dendrocopos major canariensis*	RB				x								
	Dendrocopos major thanneri	RB					x							
FALCONIDAE Falcons														
Lesser Kestrel	*Falco naumanni*	SV				x	x	x	x	x				
Common Kestrel	*Falco tinnunculus canariensis*	RB	x	x	x	x								
	Falco tinnunculus dacotiae	RB						x	x	x	x			
Red-footed Falcon	*Falco vespertinus*	V	1	2		8	1		4			1		17
Eleonora's Falcon	*Falco eleonorae*	MBS		x		x	x	x	x	x	b	b		
Merlin	*Falco columbarius*	iWM/SV		x		x	x	x	x	x				
Eurasian Hobby	*Falco subbuteo*	SV	x		x	x	x	x	x					
Peregrine Falcon	*Falco peregrinus*	V				7	1							8
Barbary Falcon	*Falco pelegrinoides pelegrinoides*	RB	b	b	b	b	b	b	b	x	b	b		
PSITTACIDAE Parrots														
Monk Parakeet	*Myiopsitta monachus* (ssp. unknown)	I	x			b	b	b						
Nanday Parakeet	*Aratinga nenday*	I				x								
Rose-ringed Parakeet	*Psittacula krameri* (ssp. unknown)	I	x			b	b	b	b					
LANIIDAE Shrikes														
Red-backed Shrike	*Lanius collurio*	V				1			1					2
Great Grey Shrike	*Lanius excubitor koenigi*	RB				x	x	x	x	x	mc	x		
Woodchat Shrike	*Lanius senator*	SV	x	x	x	x	x	x	x		x			
ORIOLIDAE Orioles														
Eurasian Golden Oriole	*Oriolus oriolus*	SV	x	x	x	x	x	x	x		x			
CORVIDAE Crows														
Red-billed Chough	*Pyrrhocorax pyrrhocorax barbarus*	RB	x											
Western Jackdaw	*Corvus monedula*	V				1								1

English name	Scientific name	Status	Islands and islets											Total
			P	H	Go	T	GC	F	L	g	mc	a	c	
Carrion Crow	Corvus corone	V				1	1							2
Northern Raven	Corvus corax canariensis	RB	x	x	x	x	x	x	x	x	x	x		
PARIDAE Tits														
African Blue Tit	Cyanistes teneriffae palmensis	RB	x											
	Cyanistes teneriffae ombriosus	RB		x										
	Cyanistes teneriffae teneriffae	RB				x	x							
	Cyanistes teneriffae hedwigae	RB						x						
	Cyanistes teneriffae ultramarinus	RB							x	x				
ALAUDIDAE Larks														
Greater Hoopoe-Lark	Alaemon alaudipes	V							3	1				4
Bar-tailed Lark	Ammomanes cinctura	V				1	2							3
Eurasian Skylark	Alauda arvensis	rWM/SV		x	x	x	x	x	x	x	x	x		
Greater Short-toed Lark	Calandrella brachydactyla	SV	x			x		x	x	x				
Calandra Lark	Melanocorypha calandra	V				6	1	3						10
Lesser Short-toed Lark	Alaudala rufescens rufescens	EX				(x)								
	Alaudala rufescens polatzeki	RB					x	x	x					
HIRUNDINIDAE Swallows														
Sand Martin	Riparia riparia	SV	x	x	x	x	x	x	x	x	x	x		
Barn Swallow	Hirundo rustica rustica	SV/OB	x	x	x	x	x	x	x	x	x			
Eurasian Crag Martin	Ptyonoprogne rupestris	V							2					2
Common House Martin	Delichon urbicum	SV	x	x	x	x	x	x	x	x	x	x		
Red-rumped Swallow	Cecropis daurica	SV	x	x	x	x	x	x	x					
PHYLLOSCOPIDAE Old world leaf warblers														
Willow Warbler	Phylloscopus trochilus	SV	x	x	x	x	x	x	x					
Common Chiffchaff	Phylloscopus collybita	rWM						x	x					
Canary Islands Chiffchaff	Phylloscopus canariensis	RB	x	x	x	x								
Western Bonelli's Warbler	Phylloscopus bonelli	SV		x		x	x	x	x		x			
Wood Warbler	Phylloscopus sibilatrix	SV	x		x	x	x	x	x		x			
Yellow-browed Warbler	Phylloscopus inornatus	V				11	3	26	38	4				82
ACROCEPHALIADE Reed warblers and allies														
Great Reed Warbler	Acrocephalus arundinaceus	V				1	1	1	3					6
Sedge Warbler	Acrocephalus shoenobaenus	SV			x	x	x	x	x		x	x		
Eurasian Reed Warbler	Acrocephalus scirpaceus	SV	x	x	x	x	x	x	x					
Western Olivaceous Warbler	Iduna opaca	V				2	1	1	3					7
Melodious Warbler	Hippolais polyglotta	SV				x	x	x	x	x				
Icterine Warbler	Hippolais icterina	V				1	1		2	1				5
LOCUSTELLIDAE Bush warblers														
Common Grasshopper Warbler	Locustella naevia	SV				x	x	x	x			x		

English name	Scientific name	Status	Islands and islets											Total
			P	H	Go	T	GC	F	L	g	mc	a	c	
SYLVIIDAE Sylvia warblers													
Eurasian Blackcap	*Sylvia atricapilla atricapilla*	rWM						x	x					
	Sylvia atricapilla heineken	RB	b	b	b	b	b							
Garden Warbler	*Sylvia borin*	SV			x	x	x	x	x	x		x			
Lesser Whitethroat	*Sylvia curruca*	V						3						3
Western Orphean Warbler	*Sylvia hortensis*	V				2	1	4	1		1			9
African Desert Warbler	*Sylvia deserti*	V				1	1	3	1	1				7
Common Whitethroat	*Sylvia communis*	SV			x	x	x	x	x	x		x			
Tristram's Warbler	*Sylvia deserticola*	V						1						1
Spectacled Warbler	*Sylvia conspicillata*	RB	x	x	x	x	x	x	x		x			
Subalpine Warbler	*Sylvia cantillans inornata*	SV	x		x	x	x	x	x	x	x			
Sardinian Warbler	*Sylvia melanocephala melanocephala*	RB	x	x	x	x	x	x						
REGULIDAE Goldcrests													
Goldcrest	*Regulus regulus teneriffae*	RB				x	x							
	Regulus regulus ellenthalerae	RB	x	x										
STURNIDAE Starlings													
Common Starling	*Sturnus vulgaris vulgaris*	RB/rWM	x	x	x	b	b	x	x	x				
TURDIDAE Thrushes													
Ring Ouzel	*Turdus torquatus*	iWM	x	x	x	x		x	x		x	x		
Common Blackbird	*Turdus merula cabrerae*	RB	b	b	b	b	b	x	x					
Fieldfare	*Turdus pilaris*	V				2		2	4					8
Redwing	*Turdus iliacus*	iWM				x		x	x	x		x		
Song Thrush	*Turdus philomelos*	rWM	x	x	x	x	x	x	x	x				
Mistle Thrush	*Turdus viscivorus*	V				5		3						8
MUSCICAPIDAE Chats & flycatchers													
Rufous-tailed Scrub Robin	*Cercotrichas galactotes*	V						5						5
Spotted Flycatcher	*Muscicapa striata*	SV	x	x	x	x	x	x	x	x				
European Robin	*Erithacus rubecula rubecula*	RB/rWM	b	b	b			x	x					
	Erithacus rubecula superbus	RB				b								
	Erithacus rubecula marionae	RB					b							
Bluethroat	*Luscinia svecica svecica/cyanecula*	V				2		8	1		1			12
Common Nightingale	*Luscinia megarhynchos*	SV				x	x	x	x		x			
European Pied Flycatcher	*Ficedula hypoleuca*	SV	x	x	x	x	x	x	x		x			
Collared Flycatcher	*Ficedula albicollis*	V						2	2					4
Red-breasted Flycatcher	*Ficedula parva*	V				5		2	1					8
Black Redstart	*Phoenicurus ochruros*	rWM/SV	x	x		x	x	x	x	x	x			
Common Redstart	*Phoenicurus phoenicurus*	SV	x			x	x	x	x	x	x			
Common Rock Thrush	*Monticola saxatilis*	V	1			1								2

English name	Scientific name	Status	Islands and islets											Total
			P	H	Go	T	GC	F	L	g	mc	a	c	
Blue Rock Thrush	Monticola solitarius	V				1		1						2
Whinchat	Saxicola rubetra	SV	x		x	x	x	x	x	x				
Canary Islands Stonechat	Saxicola dacotiae dacotiae	RB						x						
	Saxicola dacotiae murielae	EX										(x)		
European Stonechat	Saxicola rubicola	iWM	x		x	x	x	x	x	x		x		
Northern Wheatear	Oenanthe oenanthe oenanthe/leucorhoa	SV	x	x	x	x	x	x	x	x		x		
	Oenanthe oenanthe seebohmi	V				1								1
Isabelline Wheatear	Oenanthe isabellina	V						1						1
Desert Wheatear	Oenanthe deserti	V				6		6						12
Black-eared Wheatear	Oenanthe hispanica	V	1			1	1		2					5
White-crowned Wheatear	Oenanthe leucopyga	V	1											1

PASSERIDAE Sparrows

English name	Scientific name	Status	P	H	Go	T	GC	F	L	g	mc	a	c	Total
House Sparrow	Passer domesticus (ssp. unknown)	I					x							
Spanish Sparrow	Passer hispaniolensis hispaniolensis	RB	b	b	b	b	b	b	x					
Eurasian Tree Sparrow	Passer montanus montanus	RB					x							
Rock Sparrow	Petronia petronia petronia	RB	(x)	x	x	x	x							

ESTRILDIDAE Waxbills

English name	Scientific name	Status	P	H	Go	T	GC	F	L	g	mc	a	c	Total
Common Waxbill	Estrilda astrild jagoensis	I					x							

MOTACILLIDAE Wagtails and pipits

English name	Scientific name	Status	P	H	Go	T	GC	F	L	g	mc	a	c	Total
Western Yellow Wagtail	Motacilla flava (4 ssp.)	SV	x	x	x	x	x	x	x	x		x		
	Motacilla flava feldegg	V						1	1					2
Citrine Wagtail	Motacilla citreola	V	1	1	1	3		1	6					13
Grey Wagtail	Motacilla cinerea cinerea	RB/rWM	x		x	x	x	x	x	x		x		
White Wagtail	Motacilla alba alba	rWM/SV	x	x	x	x	x	x	x	x		x		
	Motacilla alba yarrellii	V				1			1					2
Richard's Pipit	Anthus richardi	V				3		1	1					5
Tawny Pipit	Anthus campestris	SV			x	x	x	x	x	x		x		
Meadow Pipit	Anthus pratensis	rWM/SV	x		x	x	x	x	x	x		x		
Tree Pipit	Anthus trivialis	SV	x	x	x	x	x	x	x	x	x	x		
Olive-backed Pipit	Anthus hodgsoni	V					2	1						3
Red-throated Pipit	Anthus cervinus	SV	x		x	x	x	x	x			x		
Water Pipit	Anthus spinoletta	V	1				2	1						4
Eurasian Rock Pipit	Anthus petrosus	V						1						1
Berthelot's Pipit	Anthus berthelotii	RB	x	x	x	x	x	x	x	x	x	x		

FRINGILLIDAE Finches

English name	Scientific name	Status	P	H	Go	T	GC	F	L	g	mc	a	c	Total
Common Chaffinch	Fringilla coelebs palmae	RB	x											
	Fringilla coelebs ombriosa	RB		x										
	Fringilla coelebs canariensis	RB			x	x	x							

English name	Scientific name	Status	Islands and islets											Total
			P	H	Go	T	GC	F	L	g	mc	a	c	
	Fringilla coelebs coelebs	V				1	1	3	2			1		8
Tenerife Blue Chaffinch	Fringilla teydea	RB				x								
Gran Canaria Blue Chaffinch	Fringilla polatzeki	RB					x							
Brambling	Fringilla montifringilla	V				1		6	1					8
Hawfinch	Coccothraustes coccothraustes	V				1	1	1	2					5
Trumpeter Finch	Bucanetes githagineus amantum	RB			x	(x)	x	x	x					
Common Rosefinch	Carpodacus erythrinus	V										1		1
European Greenfinch	Chloris chloris aurantiiventris	RB	x	x	x	x	x							
Common Linnet	Linaria cannabina meadewaldoi	RB	x	x	x	x	x							
	Linaria cannabina harterti	RB						x	x	x				
Red Crossbill	Loxia curvirostra	V				1								1
European Goldfinch	Carduelis carduelis parva	RB	x	x	x	x	x	x						
European Serin	Serinus serinus	RB				x	x							
Atlantic Canary	Serinus canaria	RB	x	x	x	x	x	x						
Eurasian Siskin	Spinus spinus	iWM	x			x	x	x	x					
PARULIDAE New World warblers														
Northern Waterthrush	Parkesia noveboracensis	V	1											1
Black-and-white Warbler	Mniotilta varia	V					1							1
ICTERIDAE New World blackbirds														
Bobolink	Dolichonyx oryzivorus	V						2						2
EMBERIZIDAE Buntings														
Corn Bunting	Emberiza calandra calandra	RB	(x)	x	x	x	x	x	x					
Ortolan Bunting	Emberiza hortulana	V				2		2	12	1		3		20
Little Bunting	Emberiza pusilla	V						1	2	1				4
Common Reed Bunting	Emberiza schoeniclus	V				1		1	1					3
CALCARIIDAE Longspurs														
Lapland Longspur	Calcarius lapponicus	V				1								1
Snow Bunting	Plectrophenax nivalis	V			1	4			3					8

BIBLIOGRAPHY

Bannerman, D. A. 1963. *Birds of the Atlantic Islands. Volume I: A History of the Birds of the Canary Islands and of the Salvages.* Edinburgh and London: Oliver & Boyd.

Beaman, M. & Madge, S. 1998. *The Handbook of Bird Identification for Europe and the Western Palearctic,* London: Christopher Helm.

Clarke T. 2006. *Birds of the Atlantic Islands.* London: Christopher Helm.

del Hoyo, J., Elliott, A., Sargatal, J. & Christie D. A. (eds) 1992–2011. *Handbook of the Birds of the World. Vols. 1–16.* Barcelona: Lynx Edicions.

Dietzen, C., Garcia-del-Rey, E., Castro, G. D. & Wink, M. 2008. Phylogenetic differentiation of *Sylvia* species in Macaronesia based on mitochondrial DNA sequence data and morphometrics. *Biological Journal of the Linnean Society* 95: 157–174.

Dietzen, C., Garcia-del-Rey, E., Delgado Castro, G., Witt, H. -H. & Wink, M. 2006. Molecular phylogeography of passerine bird species on the Atlantic islands. *Journal of Ornithology* 147 (5) Suppl. 1: 157.

Fernandez-Palacios, J. M. 2011. The islands of Macaronesia. In: Serrano, A. R. M., Borges, P. A. V., Boieiro, M. & Oromi, P. (eds). *Terrestrial Arthropods of Macaronesia: Biodiversity, ecology and evolution.* Sociedad Portuguesa de Entomología, pp. 1–30.

Garcia-del-Rey, E. 2000. *Where to Watch Birds on Tenerife.* Santa Cruz de Tenerife: Publicaciones Turquesa S. L.

Garcia-del-Rey, E. 2001. *Checklist of the Birds of the Canary Islands.* Santa Cruz de Tenerife: Publicaciones Turquesa S. L.

Garcia-del-Rey, E. 2004. Foraging behaviour by the Fuerteventura Blue Tit (*Parus caeruleus degener*) during the pre-breeding period and its implications in long-term habitat management. *Vieraea* 32: 177–182.

Garcia-del-Rey, E. 2011. *Field Guide to the Birds of Macaronesia. Azores, Madeira, Canary Islands, Cape Vede.* Bellaterra, Barcelona: Lynx Edicions.

Garcia-del-Rey, E. 2015. *Birds of the Canary Islands.* Barcelona: Sociedad Ornitologica Canaria.

Garcia-del-Rey, E. 2017. *Checklist of the Birds of the Canary Islands/Lista de las Aves de las Islas Canarias.* Tenerife, Canary Islands: Sociedad Ornitologica Canaria.

Garcia-del-Rey, E. 2017. *Birds of Arona: A photographic guide/Aves de Arona: guía fotografica.* Canary Islands: Sociedad Ornitologica Canaria.

Garcia-del-Rey, E. & Garcia, F. J. 2013. *Rare Birds of the Canary Islands/Aves Raras de las islas Canarias.* Sociedad Ornitologica Canaria. Barcelona, Spain: Lynx Edicions.

Garcia-del-Rey, E. y Rodríguez Lorenzo, J. M. 2010. Breeding status of the Ruddy Shelduck Tadorna ferruginea at Fuerteventura Canary Islands: natural colonization of two habitat types on an oceanic island. *Ostrich* 81(2): 93–96.

Gill, F. & Donsker, D. (eds) 2017. *IOC World Bird List* (v.7.2). doi: 10.14344/IOC.ML.7.2.

Gohli, J., Leder, E. H., Garcia-del-Rey, E., Johannenssen, L. E., Johnsen, A., Laskemoen, T., Popp, M. & Lifjeld, J. 2015. The evolutionary history of Afrocanarian blue tits inferred from genome-wide SNPs. *Molecular Ecology* 24(1): 180–191.

Lifjeld, J. T., Anmarkrud, J. A., Calabuig, P., Cooper, J., Johannenssen, L. E., Johnsen, A., Kearns, A. M., Lachlan, R., Laskemoen, T., Marthinsen, G., Stensrud, E., Garcia-del-Rey, E. 2016. Species-level divergences in multiple functional traits between the two endemic subspecies of Blue Chaffinches *Fringilla teydea* in Canary Islands. *BMC Zoology.* 1:4. DOI 10. 1186/s40850-016-0008-4

Sjogren, E. 2000. Aspects on the biogeography of Macronesia from a botanical point of view. *Arquipe'lago. Life and Marine Sciences.* Supplement 2 (Part A): 1–9. Ponta Delgada. ISSN 0873-4704.

INDEX

Accipiter gentilis 62
  nisus 62
Acrocephalus arundinaceus 140
  schoenobaenus 140
  scirpaceus 140
Actitis hypoleucos 88
  macularia 88
Aix sponsa 34
Alaemon alaudipes 134
Alauda arvensis 134
Alaudala rufescens 134
Alcedo atthis 124
Alectoris barbara 40
  rufa 40
Alle alle 98
Ammomanes cinctura 134
Anas acuta 38
  americana 36
  carolinensis 38
  clypeata 34
  crecca 38
  discors 34
  penelope 36
  platyrhynchos 36
  querquedula 38
  strepera 36
Anser albifrons 28
  anser 28
Anthus berthelotii 162
  campestris 162
  cervinus 164
  hodgsoni 162
  pratensis 164
  richardi 162
  spinoletta 164
  trivialis 164
Apus affinis 122
  apus 122
  pallidus 122
  unicolor 122
Aquila fasciata 68
Aratinga nenday 130
Ardea alba 54
  cinerea 54
  purpurea 54
Ardenna gravis 48
  grisea 48
Ardeola ralloides 52
Arenaria interpres 96
Asio flammeus 120
  otus 120

Auk, Little 98
Avocet, Pied 76
Aythya affinis 32
  collaris 32
  ferina 30
  fuligula 32
  marila 32
  nyroca 34

Bee-eater, Blue-cheeked 124
  European 124
Bittern, Dwarf 50
  Eurasian 50
  Little 50
Blackbird, Common 148
Blackcap, Eurasian 142
Bluethroat 150
Bobolink 172
Booby, Brown 58
  Red-footed 58
Botaurus stellaris 50
Brambling 170
Branta bernicla 28
Bubulcus ibis 52
Bucanetes githagineus 168
Bulweria bulwerii 48
Bunting, Common Reed 172
  Corn 172
  Little 172
  Ortolan 172
  Snow 172
Burhinus oedicnemus 76
Bustard, Houbara 70
Buteo buteo 66
  rufinus 66
Buzzard, Common 66
  European Honey 66
  Long-legged 66

Calandrella brachydactyla 134
Calidris alba 90
  alpina 94
  bairdii 92
  canutus 90
  ferruginea 92
  fuscicollis 92
  maritima 94
  melanotos 92
  minuta 90
  pugnax 94
  pusilla 90

  subruficollis 94
  temminckii 90
Calonectris borealis 46
  diomedea 46
  edwardsii 48
Canary, Atlantic 166
Caprimulgus europaeus 118
  ruficollis 118
Carduelis carduelis 166
Cecropis daurica 136
Cercotrichas galactotes 150
Chaetura pelagica 122
Chaffinch, Common 170
  Gran Canaria Blue 170
  Tenerife Blue 170
Charadrius alexandrinus 80
  dubius 80
  hiaticula 80
  mongolus 80
  morinellus 78
Chiffchaff, Canary Island 138
  Common 138
Chlamydotis undulata 70
Chlidonias hybrida 110
  leucopterus 110
  niger 110
Chloris chloris 166
Chough, Red-billed 132
Chroicocephalus genei 102
  ridibundus 102
Ciconia ciconia 50
  nigra 50
Circaetus gallicus 68
Circus aeruginosus 64
  cyaneus 64
  macrourus 64
  pygargus 64
Clamator glandarius 118
Coccothraustes coccothraustes 168
Columba bollii 116
  junoniae 116
  livia 116
  palumbus 116
Coot, Common 74
  Eurasian 74
Coracias garrulus 124
Cormorant, Great 58
Corvus corax 132
  corone 132
Coturnix coturnix 40
Courser, Cream-coloured 98

Crake, African 72
   Baillon's 72
   Corn 72
   Little 72
   Spotted 72
Crane, Common 70
Crex crex 72
   egregia 72
Crow, Carrion 132
Cuckoo, Common 118
   Great Spotted 118
Cuculus canorus 118
Curlew, Eurasian 84
Cursorius cursor 98
Cyanistes teneriffae 130

Delichon urbicum 136
Dendrocopos major 124
Diver, Black-throated 42
   Great Northern 42
Doluchonyx oryzivorus 172
Dotterel 78
Dove, African Collared 114
   Eurasian Collared 114
   European Turtle 114
   Laughing 114
   Rock 116
Dovekie 98
Dowitcher, Long-billed 82
Duck, Ferruginous 34
   Marbled 30
   Ring-necked 32
   Tufted 32
   Wood 34
Dunlin 94

Eagle, Bonelli's 68
   Booted 68
   Short-toed 68
   Short-toed Snake 68
Egret, Great White 54
   Little 54
   Western Cattle 52
   Western Reef 52
Egretta garzetta 54
   gularis 52
Emberiza calandra 172
   hortulana 172
   pusilla 172
   schoeniclus 172
Erithacus rubecula 150
Estrilda astrild 158

Falco columbarius 126
   eleonorae 128
   naumanni 126
   pelegrinoides 128
   peregrinus 128
   subbuteo 128
   tinnunculus 126
   vespertinus 126
Falcon, Barbary 128
   Eleonora's 128
   Peregrine 128
   Red-footed 126
Ficedula albicollis 152
   hypoleuca 152
   parva 152
Fieldfare 148
Finch, Trumpeter 168
Flamingo, Greater 40
   Lesser 40
Flycatcher, Collared 152
   European Pied 152
   Red-breasted 152
   Spotted 152
Fratercula arctica 98
Fregata magnificens 56
Fregetta tropica 44
Frigatebird, Magnificent 56
Fringilla coelebs 170
   montifringilla 170
   palatzeki 170
   teydea 170
Fulica atra 74
Fulmar, Northern 46
Fulmarus glacialis 46

Gadwall 36
Gallinago gallinago 82
Gallinula chloropus 74
Gallinule, Allen's 74
   American Purple 74
   Purple 74
Gannet, Northern 58
Garganey 38
Gavia arctica 42
   immer 42
Gelochelidon nilotica 108
Glareola pratincola 98
Godwit, Bar-tailed 84
   Black-tailed 84
Goldcrest 146
Goldfinch, European 166
Goose, Brant 28
   Brent 28
   Greater White-fronted 28
   Greylag 28

Goshawk, Northern 62
Grebe, Black-necked 42
   Little 42
   Pied-billed 42
Greenfinch, European 166
Greenshank, Common 86
Grus grus 70
Guillemot, Common 98
Gull, Audouin's 102
   Black-headed 102
   Common 104
   Franklin's 100
   Glaucous 106
   Great Black-backed 106
   Iceland 106
   Laughing 100
   Lesser Black-backed 104
   Little 102
   Mediterranean 100
   Mew 104
   Ring-billed 104
   Sabine's 100
   Slender-billed 102
   Yellow-legged 104

Haematopus ostralegus 76
Harrier, Hen 64
   Montagu's 64
   Pallid 64
   Western Marsh 64
Hawfinch 168
Heron, Black-crowned Night 52
   Grey 54
   Purple 54
   Squacco 52
   Western Reef 52
Hieraaetus pennatus 68
Himantopus himantopus 76
Hippolais icterina 140
   polyglotta 140
Hirundo rustica 136
Hobby, Eurasian 128
Hoopoe, Eurasian 124
Hoopoe-lark, Greater 134
Hydrobates pelagicus 44
Hydrocoloeus minutus 102
Hydroprogne caspia 108

Ibis, African Sacred 56
   Glossy 56
Ichthyaetus audouinii 102
   melanocephalus 100
Iduna opaca 140
Ixobrychus minutus 50

sturmii 50

Jaeger, Long-tailed 112
    Parasitic 112
    Pomarine 112
Jynx torquilla 124

Kestrel, Common 126
    Lesser 126
Kingfisher, Common 124
Kite, Black 60
    Red 60
Kittiwake, Black-legged 106
Knot, Red 90

Lanius collurio 132
    excubitor 132
    senator 132
Lapwing, Northern 78
Lark, Bar-tailed 134
    Calandra 134
    Greater Short-toed 134
    Lesser Short-toed 134
Larus canus 104
    delawarensis 104
    fuscus 104
    glaucoides 106
    hyperboreus 106
    marinus 106
    michahellis 104
Leucophaeus atricilla 100
    pipixcan 100
Limnodromus scolopaceus 82
Limosa lapponica 84
    limosa 84
Linaria cannabina 168
Linnet, Common 168
Locustella naevia 140
Loon, Black-throated 42
    Common 42
Luscinia megarhynchos 150
    svecica 150
Lymnocryptes minimus 82

Mallard 36
Marmaronetta angustirostris 30
Martin, Common House 136
    Eurasian Crag 136
    Sand 136
Melanitta nigra 28
Melanocorypha calandra 134
Merlin 126
Merops apiaster 124
    persicus 124
Milvus migrans 60

milvus 60
Monticola saxatilis 146
    solitarius 146
Moorhen, Common 74
Morus bassanus 58
Motacilla alba 160
    cinerea 160
    citreola 160
    flava 160
Murre, Common 98
Muscicapa striata 152
Myiopsitta monachus 130

Neophron percnopterus 62
Nightingale, Common 150
Nightjar, European 118
    Red-necked 118
Numenius arquata 84
    phaeopus 84
Nycticorax nycticorax 52

Oceanites oceanicus 44
Oceanodroma castro 44
    leucorhoa 44
    monorhis 44
Oenanthe deserti 156
    hispanica 156
    oenanthe 156
Onychoprion fuscatus 108
Oriole, Eurasian Golden 130
Oriolus oriolus 130
Osprey 60
    Western 60
Otus scops 120
Ouzel, Ring 148
Owl, Barn 120
    Eurasian Scops 120
    Long-eared 120
    Northern Long-eared 120
    Short-eared 120
Oystercatcher, Eurasian 76

Pandion haliaetus 60
Parakeet, Monk 130
    Nanday 130
    Rose-ringed 130
Partridge, Barbary 40
    Red-legged 40
Passer domesticus 158
    hispaniolensis 158
    montanus 158
Pelagodroma marina 44
Pernis apivorus 66
Petrel, Bugio 46

Bulwer's 48
Cape Verde 46
Desertas 46
Fea's 46
Madeira 46
Zino's 46
Petronia petronia 158
Phaethon aethereus 58
Phalacrocorax carbo 58
Phalarope, Grey 96
    Red 96
    Wilson's 96
Phalaropus fulicarius 96
    tricolor 96
Phoeniconaias minor 40
Phoenicopterus roseus 40
Phoenicurus ochruros 154
    phoenicurus 154
Phylloscopus bonelli 138
    canariensis 138
    collybita 138
    inornata 138
    sibilatrix 138
    trochilus 138
Pigeon, Bolle's 116
    Common Wood 116
    Laurel 116
    Thermophile 116
Pintail, Northern 38
Pipit, Berthelot's 162
    Meadow 164
    Olive-backed 162
    Red-throated 164
    Richard's 162
    Tawny 162
    Tree 164
    Water 164
Platalea leucorodia 56
Plectrophenax nivalis 172
Plegadis falcinellus 56
Plover, American Golden 78
    Black-bellied 78
    Common Ringed 80
    European Golden 78
    Grey 78
    Kentish 80
    Lesser Sand 80
    Little Ringed 80
Pluvialis apricaria 78
    dominica 78
    squatarola 78
Pochard, Common 30
Podiceps nigricollis 42
Podilymbus podiceps 42

Porphyrio martinica 74
Porphyrula alleni 74
Porzana parva 72
   porzana 72
   pusilla 72
Pratincole, Collared 98
Psittacula krameri 130
Pterocles orientalis 70
Pterodroma deserta 46
   feae 46
   madeira 46
Ptyonoprogne rupestris 136
Puffin, Atlantic 98
Puffinus baroli 48
   puffinus 48
Pyrrhocorax pyrrhocorax 132

Quail, Common 40

Raven, Northern 132
Recurvirostra avosetta 76
Redshank, Common 86
   Spotted 86
Redstart, Black 154
   Common 154
Redwing 148
Regulus regulus 146
Riparia riparia 136
Rissa tridactyla 106
Robin, European 150
   Rufous Scrub 150
   Rufous-tailed Scrub 150
Roller, European 124
Ruff 94

Sanderling 90
Sandgrouse, Black-bellied 70
Sandpiper, Baird's 92
   Buff-breasted 94
   Common 88
   Curlew 92
   Green 88
   Marsh 86
   Pectoral 92
   Purple 94
   Semipalmated 90
   Spotted 88
   White-rumped 92
   Wood 88
Saxicola dacotiae 154
   rubetra 154
   torquata 154
Scaup, Greater 32
   Lesser 32

Scolopax rusticola 82
Scoter, Common 28
Serin, European 166
Serinus canaria 166
   serinus 166
Shearwater, Barolo 48
   Cape Verde 48
   Cory's 46
   Great 48
   Macaronesian 48
   Manx 48
   Scopoli's 46
   Sooty 48
Shelduck, Common 30
   Ruddy 30
Shoveler, Northern 34
Shrike, Great Grey 132
   Red-backed 132
   Woodchat 132
Siskin, Eurasian 168
Skua, Arctic 112
   Great 112
   Long-tailed 112
   Pomarine 112
   South Polar 112
Skylark, Eurasian 134
Snipe, Common 82
   Jack 82
Sparrow, Eurasian Tree 158
   House 158
   Rock 158
   Spanish 158
Sparrowhawk, Eurasian 62
Spinus spinus 168
Spoonbill, Eurasian 56
Starling, Common 146
Stercorarius longicaudus 112
   maccormicki 112
   parasiticus 112
   pomarinus 112
   skua 112
Sterna dougallii 110
   hirundo 110
   paradisaea 110
Sternula albifrons 108
Stilt, Black-winged 76
Stint, Little 90
   Temminck's 90
Stone-curlew, Eurasian 76
Stonechat, Canary Islands 154
   European 154
Stork, Black 50
   White 50
Storm-petrel, Band-rumped 44

   Black-bellied 44
   European 44
   Leach's 44
   Madeiran 44
   Swinhoe's 44
   White-faced 44
   Wilson's 44
Streptopelia decaocto 114
   roseogrisea 114
   senegalensis 114
   turtur 114
Sturnus vulgaris 146
Sula leucogaster 58
   sula 58
Swallow, Barn 136
   Red-rumped 136
Swift, Alpine 122
   Chimney 122
   Common 122
   Little 122
   Pallid 122
   Plain 122
Sylvia atricapilla 142
   borin 142
   cantillans 142
   communis 144
   conspicillata 142
   curruca 144
   deserti 144
   hortensis 144
   melanocephala 144

Tachybaptus ruficollis 42
Tachymarptis melba 122
Tadorna ferruginea 30
   tadorna 30
Teal, Blue-winged 34
   Common 38
   Eurasian 38
   Green-winged 38
   Marbled 30
Tern, Arctic 110
   Black 110
   Caspian 108
   Common 110
   Gull-billed 108
   Little 108
   Roseate 110
   Sandwich 108
   Sooty 108
   Whiskered 110
   White-winged 110
   White-winged Black 110
Thalasseus sandvicensis 108

Threskiornis aethiopicus 56
Thrush, Blue Rock 146
    Common Rock 146
    Mistle 148
    Rufous-tailed Rock 146
    Song 148
Tit, African Blue 130
Tringa erythropus 86
    flavipes 86
    glareola 88
    nebularia 86
    ochropus 88
    stagnatilis 86
    totanus 86
Tropicbird, Red-billed 58
Turdus iliacus 148
    merula 148
    philomelos 148
    pilaris 148
    torquatus 148
    viscivorus 148
Turnstone, Ruddy 96
Tyto alba 120

Upupa epops 124
Uria aalge 98

Vanellus vanellus 78
Vulture, Egyptian 62

Wagtail, Citrine 160
    Grey 160
    Western Yellow 160
    White 160
Warbler, African Desert 144
    Common Grasshopper 140
    Eurasian Reed 140
    Garden 142
    Great Reed 140
    Icterine 140
    Isabelline 140
    Melodious 140
    Sardinian 144
    Sedge 140
    Spectacled 142
    Subalpine 142
    Western Bonelli's 138

Western Olivaceous 140
Western Orphean 144
Willow 138
Wood 138
Yellow-browed 138
Waxbill, Common 158
Wheatear, Black-eared 156
    Desert 156
    Northern 156
Whimbrel 84
Whinchat 154
Whitethroat, Common 144
    Lesser 144
Wigeon, American 36
    Eurasian 36
Woodcock, Eurasian 82
Woodpecker, Great Spotted 124
Wryneck, Northern 124

Xema sabini 100

Yellowlegs, Lesser 86